The commonweal and American Catholicism

The Magazine
The Movement
The Meaning

Rodger Van Allen

WITHDRAWN

FORTRESS PRESS   Philadelphia

In grateful thanks
for my wife Judy,
and our children,
Rodger, Katie, Tom, Paul, and Peter.

Library of Congress Catalog Card Number 73-89063

ISBN 0-8006-1076-8

4055K73   Printed in U.S.A.   1-1076

CONTENTS

iii

ACKNOWLEDGMENTS

I am grateful to Dr. Leonard Swidler who suggested the topic of this book to me and under whom the original dissertation on which it is based was prepared, to Dr. Dennis Clark and Dr. Gerard Sloyan who were members of the dissertation committee; to Mrs. JoAnne Zanin who typed the manuscript, to Mr. Stanley Jaxa-Diebicki and the Reverend John Shellem of the library of St. Charles Borromeo Seminary, to the staffs of the Villanova University library, the Library of Congress, the Catholic University library, and the archivist, the Reverend Christopher Bayer, OSB, St. John's University, Collegeville, Minnesota. This book would not have been possible without the kind assistance of *Commonweal* editors past and present, and their willingness to share recollections and existing documents with me. Unfortunately, due to limited office space, all but the most recent five years of correspondence files of the magazine have been disposed of. George N. Shuster, Edward Skillin, John Cogley, Daniel Callahan, and James O'Gara, however, gave generously of their time for taped interviews and follow-up correspondence. Philip Burnham and Ross Hoffman corresponded with the writer. Many others contributed to this project: scholars on whose work I drew, colleagues with whom I discussed various ideas, others in the process of preparing works in related areas, such as Robert Clements of Notre Dame, who shared some source material with me. To these and others whom I may have forgotten to mention, my thanks. Neither teachers nor acquaintances, of course, should be held responsible for errors of fact or interpretation that may be detected in this essay.

Finally, my thanks to my wife Judy and our children, Rodger, Katie, Tom, Paul, and Peter, who were a great source of inspiration and good humor throughout this project.

COMMONWEAL STAFF—1924-1974

MICHAEL WILLIAMS *Editor, 1924-1938; Special Editor, 1938-1945*

THOMAS WALSH *Assistant Editor, 1928*

HELEN WALKER *Assistant Editor, 1924-1927*

HENRY LONGAN STUART *Assistant Editor, 1925-1928*

GEORGE N. SHUSTER *Assistant Editor, 1926-1928; Managing Editor, 1928-1937*

MARY KOLARS *Assistant Editor, 1927-1938*

FREDERIC THOMPSON *Assistant Editor, 1930-1936*

PHILIP BURNHAM *Editorial Staff, 1934-1938; Co-Editor, 1938-1942, 1946-1947; (United States Army, 1942-1946); Executive Editor, 1947-1949; Contributing Editor, 1949-1956*

EDWARD S. SKILLIN *Editorial Staff, 1934-1938; Co-Editor, 1938-1947; Editor, 1947-; Publisher, 1967-*

JOHN J. O'CONNOR *Acting Managing Editor, 1937-1938*

HARRY LORIN BINSSE *Managing Editor, 1938-1947; National Affairs Editor, 1947; Corresponding Editor, 1947-1948*

C. G. PAULDING *Associate Editor, 1940; Literary Editor, 1940-1947; Managing Editor, 1947-1948*

JOHN C. CORT *Associate Editor, 1943-1954; Contributing Editor, 1954-1959*

JOHN BRODERICK *Assistant Managing Editor, 1947*

GREGORY SMITH *Associate Editor, 1947-1950*

ANNE FREMANTLE *Associate Editor, 1947-1952; Contributing Editor, 1952-1958*

EDWARD F. MEAGHER *Assistant Editor, 1948-1949; Managing Editor, 1949-1952*

WILLIAM PFAFF *Assistant Editor, 1949-1952, 1953-1954, (U.S. Army, 1952-1953); Associate Editor, 1954-1955*

JOHN COGLEY *Executive Editor, 1949-1952; Feature Editor, 1952-1954*

FRANCIS DOWNING *Associate Editor, 1950-*

JAMES O'GARA *Managing Editor, 1952-; Editor, 1967-*

WILLIAM CLANCY *Assistant Editor, 1952-1954; Associate Editor, 1954-1955*

JAMES FINN *Associate Editor, 1955-1961*

PHILIP SCHARPER *Associate Editor, 1955-*

RICHARD HORCHLER *Associate Editor, 1957-1962*

DANIEL CALLAHAN *Associate Editor, 1961-1967; Executive Editor, 1967-1968*

WALTER ARNOLD, JR. *Assistant Editor, 1962-1963*

JOHN LEO *Associate Editor, 1963-1967*

JOHN FANDEL *Poetry Editor, 1964-*

PETER STEINFELS *Editorial Assistant, 1964-1965; Assistant Editor, 1965-1967; Associate Editor, 1967-1972*

PAUL VELDE *Assistant Editor, 1965-1966*

ANNE ROBERTSON *Editorial Assistant, 1965-*

WILFRID SHEED *Literary Editor, 1967-1969*

JOHN DEEDY *Managing Editor, 1967-*

MICHAEL NOVAK *Associate Editor (at large), 1967-1971*

OONA SULLIVAN *Associate Editor, 1967-1968*

JONATHAN EISEN *Editorial Assistant, 1967-1969*

PHILIP NOBILE *Assistant Editor, 1968-1970*

RAYMOND A. SCHROTH *Assistant Editor, 1972-1973; Associate Editor, 1973-*

CRITICS

RICHARD DANA SKINNER *The Stage, 1924-1934*

GRENVILLE VERNON *The Stage, 1934-1941*

JAMES P. CUNNINGHAM *Movies, 1935-1938*

PHILIP T. HARTUNG *Movies, 1938-1973*

DAVID BURNHAM *The Stage, 1941-1942*

JAMES N. VAUGHAN *The Stage, 1942-1943*

KAPPO PHELAN *The Stage, 1943-1950*

WALTER KERR *The Stage, 1950-1952*

RICHARD HAYES *The Stage, 1952-1961*

RICHARD GILMAN *The Stage, 1961-1964*

WILFRID SHEED *The Stage, 1964-1967*

JOHN SIMON *The Stage, 1967-1968*

GERALD WEALES *The Stage, 1968-1971*

COLIN L. WESTERBECK, JR. *Movies, 1971-*

BUSINESS MANAGERS

JOHN F. McCORMICK *Business Manager, 1924-1938*

JOHN BRUBAKER *Advertising Manager, 1938, 1940-*

JAMES F. FALLON *Advertising Manager, 1938-1940*

I. FROM PATRICIAN ORIGINS: THE COMMONWEAL, 1924–38

The Background

The Commonweal, a weekly review of literature, the arts, and politics, edited by Catholic laymen, was born in 1924. The story of its inception and its life through its first fifteen years is in great measure the story of Michael Williams, as colorful and controversial a character as American Catholicism has produced. We will maintain that the magazine that he launched, and to whose founding and first years he was indispensable, developed into perhaps the most significant lay enterprise and achievement in the history of American Catholicism. The history books, however, barely mention him or the magazine and, rather typically, chronicle an institutional history and a succession of bishops. Indeed, American Catholic historiography in general has until quite recently concentrated almost exclusively on the lives of leading bishops, and hence a story such as ours, of lay people, and of an independent movement within Catholicism, has gone unrecorded.

Nineteen twenty-four was a rather quiet time in American history. In that year, Calvin Coolidge was elected to a full term as president, having just fulfilled the term of Warren Harding who had died in office in 1923. Wilsonian idealism and involvement had been rejected, notably in the decision not to join the League of Nations, and a period of isolation had begun in which the full meaning of World War I was being assimilated. Harding had been elected on the promise of a "return to normalcy." Coolidge had risen to national political prominence through the Boston police strike, in the course of which the then governor of Massachusetts declared that there was "no right to strike against the public safety by anybody, anywhere, anytime." This statement found great approval with a public that was nervous about the "Red menace."

Nationalism, encouraged during the war years, had taken a virulent form and a period of intolerance and shaky civil liberties prevailed. The Ku Klux Klan, organized in Atlanta, Georgia, in 1915, anti-Negro, anti-Catholic, anti-Jew, flourished in the postwar years to a membership of six million. Attorney General A. Mitchell Palmer sought to make political hay by a series of lawless raids on allegedly radical immigrants.

Silent Cal Coolidge is recalled for his comment that "the business of the United States is business," and this was perhaps never truer than at that time. It was a period of conservatism and economic expansion both here and abroad. The novels of Sinclair Lewis, such as *Main Street* (1920) and *Babbitt* (1922), satirized an emerging smug and intolerant middle class, while Ernest Hemingway in his first novel, *The Sun Also Rises*, portrayed another dimension of the atmosphere of the times. Hemingway's book carried a quotation from Gertrude Stein on the title page, "You are all a lost generation."

In Europe, as in America, however, things were becoming quiet. In Germany, a major crisis with the inflation of 1923 had been faced as the government had stabilized the mark. The German middle class had been virtually wiped out by the stabilization, but for the time were content to nurse their grievances quietly and bitterly. In Russia, Joseph Stalin was consolidating his authority following Lenin's death in January, 1924. In Italy, Mussolini, who had recently obtained a massive political victory in the rigged elections of 1924, was experiencing difficulty over the officially ordered murder of Socialist Giacomo Matteotti, but was shortly to consolidate his power and produce an imposed period of calm. In Ireland, Eamon de Valera and those struggling for Irish independence had been finally overwhelmed in the spring of 1923, and here too a certain variety of stability was effected.

The years 1924–29 were years of stability both on the national and international scene, and so were they also with regard to Catholicism. Pius XI, who had become pope in 1922, inherited a reasonably friendly attitude toward the Church, was able to resume diplomatic relations with France and to exchange some quietly friendly gestures with the Italian government. In American Catholicism there was also a period of consolidation. Immigration legislation in 1917, 1921, and especially 1924, greatly restricted the influx of Catholics to this country, as it was at least in part designed to do. As Martin Marty has commented, not only Klansmen but many Protestant moderates throughout the nation feared that America would go Catholic by immigration.[1] Another consolidating and unifying influence which had created an impact in American Catholicism was World War I which necessarily forced many Catholic immigrants to forge a new identity, especially German immigrants.

During the late nineteenth century some lively battles had been fought by leading bishops over Americanization, that is, over the degree of social and cultural assimilation and cooperation which was appropriate for their largely immigrant communities. The rather acrimonious debate became indirectly involved in some developments in France, and in 1899 the papal letter *Testem Benevolentiae* condemned "Americanism." This was not a condemnation of the American political system, but rather a condemnation of certain more activistic trends in spirituality, deemed heretical. It had acquired the name "Americanism," though prelates such as Cardinal Gibbons denied that any of the condemned doctrines or practices was found here. While it may have been a phantom heresy, the effect of the condemnation was real enough, for it seriously undercut the confidence and intellectual energy which had been rather remarkably present in a youthful American Catholicism that was officially considered a missionary operation until 1908. The condemnation of "modernism" in 1907, in conjunction with the earlier condemnation of "Americanism" completed the loss of confidence. Creative theological scholarship was discouraged. In 1917, a new Code of Canon Law promulgated throughout Roman Catholicism had a strongly centralizing influence which reduced local incentives to Catholic activity. All of this tended to produce a period of quietness and consolidation on the American Catholic scene.

In 1917, Catholics were a large minority of seventeen million in a nation of one hundred five million, and with the coming of American participation in the War, became numerous in the armed forces. To meet the necessity of rendering pastoral care to these men, the Catholic War Council was formed. This was the beginning of a real ongoing national organizational framework for Catholicism, which had been limited before to periodic meetings of bishops. While the wartime organization had been on an ad hoc basis, the experience proved so favorable that it was reorganized on a permanent basis and called the National Catholic Welfare Council.

Though initiated by laymen, especially the Knights of Columbus, in their concern to meet the problems of Catholics in the armed forces, the organization rapidly became essentially the bishops' organization and this was even more clearly so when it became the National Catholic Welfare Council. It was a nonbishop, however, who greatly shaped the organization. Father John J. Burke, CSP, who had been the editor of the *Catholic World* magazine, was elected by the bishops to the position of general secretary of the council, and personal representative of the chairman of the Administrative Committee, Archbishop Edward J. Hanna. It was Burke who named Justin McGrath and Michael Williams to begin the direction of the Press and Publicity Department of the council, and it is the latter who is the protagonist in the early story of *The Commonweal*.

Michael Williams had a remarkable range of talents and emotions. He was a publicist and a pragmatist, a romantic and an idealist. He was a mystic. "Mankind," he said, "is progressing constantly toward a condition of life-in-love, and art must be made the ruling influence in all things. Then man in general shall know a life wider and deeper and more glorious than any men save a few prophetic artists now dream of. My idea, then, is to help advance the race on its journey to its destined end."[2] He knew the strength of a recovery from TB; he knew the weakness of alcoholism. Edward Skillin has stated that Michael Williams was a manic-depressive, living life in a cyclical fashion. "When he was at the peak of his cycle, he could walk into the White House and ask to see the president, and they would usher him right in; and when he was at the bottom, he was just so sunk."[3]

Life had not been easy for Michael. Born in Halifax, Canada, in 1877, he was one of six children. He studied at St. Joseph's College, New Brunswick, until his father's death, when he found work in a warehouse. He ceased the practice of his Catholic religion at about this time. Self-study and writing occupied most of his free time, but he met with no success until Philip Hale of the Boston *Journal* bought one of his stories. Things were beginning to improve when he became ill, a problem which plagued him through much of his life. A husky man, he would often joke of his "iron constitution" which was "heavily beset with rust."[4] With a sojourn in a depressing "health" town in North Carolina, he recovered from the TB attack and resumed a journalism career which led him from Boston to New York to San Francisco, where he was named city editor of the *Examiner*, the day before the earthquake of 1906. He was next attracted to join the colony of "advanced thinkers" that Upton Sinclair had founded at Helicon Hall, Englewood, New Jersey. In this atmosphere, he wrote one book and most of a second, but misfortune struck again as Helicon Hall burned down, and he lost his manuscripts, books, and personal property, though he, his wife, and their two children escaped unharmed. They next settled in Carmel, California, where in 1912 he experienced a religious conversion reported in his spiritual autobiography, *The Book of the High Romance*, and was united again at age thirty-five with the faith of his youth. From this, the next step was to the position as assistant director of the Press Department of the National Catholic War Council. Father John Burke had been much impressed with the *High Romance* and with Michael's credentials as a journalist. Among the services Michael performed in his new position were his going to Rome to write about the conclave which resulted in the election of Pope Pius XI, and producing a book, *American Catholics in the War*, which was a vigorously-written history of the National Catholic War Council, 1917–21. By 1922, Michael Williams left Washington, however, for New York, with an idea of founding an intellectual Catholic weekly like the then highly influential *New Republic* and *Nation*.

The Idea

"The idea, broadly stated, was this: How can Catholic thought, the Catholic outlook on life and the Catholic philosophy of living, as distinct from what might be called the Catholic inlook and individual religious experience, be conveyed to the mind of the whole American people?"[1] With this question and desire the Calvert Associates and *The Commonweal* were born. It would be two full years, however, before the attempt to answer this question would be expressed in magazine typescript in 1924.

The first meeting of what was later to be known as the Calvert Associates was held at the Hotel Belmont in New York on the evening of October 19, 1922. The group of four priests and nine laymen included one non-Catholic, the distinguished architect Ralph Adams Cram of Boston. Among the clerics were Francis C. Kelly of Chicago who would later become bishop of Oklahoma, and Lawrason Riggs of the Washington banking family, who would serve as Catholic chaplain at Yale until 1943. Carlton J. H. Hayes of Columbia and Summerfield Baldwin of Harvard were perhaps the most notable of the laymen, all of whom, save Baldwin, were from New York or Philadelphia. The meeting was informal, but Michael Williams was clearly the leader of the group.

They rather quickly reached general agreement that they wanted a review which would be "expressive of the Catholic note" in literature, the arts, and the discussion of economic and social topics. This simplified matters and allowed an early discussion of ways and means. A special committee was set up for the launching of a financial campaign, and when the group met a month later it was announced that more than $6,000 had been subscribed to a preliminary fund. From the very first, it was recognized that this was not a commercial venture and that substantial financial support would be necessary.

It was decided that the magazine should be lay edited and that it should not be a Church organ. It was logical, therefore, to look to laymen for financial support. As the name for the group which was banding together, they took that of the Calvert Associates, after George Calvert, Lord Baltimore, the founder of Maryland. Further, they set as their goal something more than publishing a review. They decided to found branches of Associates with gatherings to perpetuate Calvert ideals, especially religious understanding and liberty. These groups of Associates in various places throughout the country would also work together for a fitting celebration of the third centennial of the arrival of the *Ark* and the *Dove* and the founding of Maryland in 1634, "as the land of sanctuary for the oppressed of all creeds." There is no written evidence of a conscious imitation of the *Mayflower* cult in these plans, but it is not improbable that some of these arrangements proceeded from a quite conscious desire to show WASP America that Catholics had a similar tradition, and that furthermore it stood for religious freedom for all.

The group elected Thomas F. Woodlock their first president; John F. McCormick, treasurer and business manager; and Michael Williams, secretary. Williams spent nearly two years in promotional activities: addressing meetings in many of the larger cities, interviewing prominent members of various communities, and forming committees for the carrying on of the work. He met with general encouragement. From one patron, however, he heard indirectly that he should not be editor of the new magazine because he lacked a college degree. He decided, however, to continue his work on behalf of the project no matter how the question of his own participation might be settled. Also, money problems were inevitable. The preliminary fund had been raised to pay for an office and to keep a skeleton staff together until there were enough pledges of support to start publication. The pledges came slowly. Weeks ran into months, and the preliminary funds ran out. Some at this point felt the idea should be abandoned. Thomas Woodlock, however, exerted leadership, stating that the project was "an adventure, not a business enterprise" and that it should and must go on as it had begun. Woodlock's influential words saved *The Commonweal* and more emergency funds were made available. Finally, three-year pledges totaling more than $250,000 came to the rescue.[2]

The name for the projected journal was not a serious problem. *The Criterion* was the name Michael Williams favored. Standards were needed in a muddled world, criteria for sound judgments in art, literature, drama, economics, and our whole way of life. That name, however, was preempted. At least fifty other names were proposed, but *The Commonweal* as Michael Williams's second choice won out, as being most indicative of the purposes of the proposed magazine.

Dana Skinner, the magazine's first drama critic, has reported that at the time of the financing of the project there was some discussion of editorial freedom and policy. How hospitable would the new paper be to Catholic opinion of all shades, "from ultra conservatism to the radicalism of Leo XIII?" He has stated, however, that "no pledge of financial support was ever accepted save on the clear understanding that both the conservative and the liberal or radical Catholic viewpoints would find a real forum in *The Commonweal*." This point delayed many pledges, but Skinner has recorded his surprise at the final number of large pledges from men of a highly conservative background.

John F. McCormick, the first business manager of *The Commonweal*, has stated that "at no time did any one person, no matter how large his contribution try to control or influence the editorial policy of the paper."[3] Who were some of the large contributors? One who was described by McCormick as "the backbone of *The Commonweal*'s financial struggle" was William V. Griffin.

> From the beginning ours was an informal organization and he was the informal Chairman of the Board. No man ever gave so unstintingly of his time and thought to our problems than he. At times he was an ogre to the force, especially to Michael Williams and myself, but we knew deep down in our hearts that he was always thinking of the ultimate end and that to him the success of *The Commonweal* and its original ideals were the burning passion of his life. He knew no compromise. Personal reactions meant nothing to him. Yet I know how much he suffered in making certain decisions which meant life to *The Commonweal*. To him more than anyone else behind the scenes, in time, money and thought, *The Commonweal* owes an impossible-to-pay debt.

Another person who was singled out for special praise by John McCormick was Robert J. Cuddihy who was experienced in the publishing business through his work with Funk and Wagnalls. He gave both money and thought to every *Commonweal* emergency. John McCormick has described him as an outstanding Catholic, who "knew the problems of the Church and saw in *The Commonweal* at least a partial remedy." McCormick continued:

> I remember one night he addressed a dinner meeting arranged by John Raskob and pleaded with a group of wealthy Catholics to come to our rescue. Michael Williams had spoken of our needs, of the work we wanted to do for the Church and had spoken brilliantly and effectively as he has always done from a heart and mind full of undying love for his great ideal. He was followed by Mr. Cuddihy, a practical business man and publisher. He didn't pretend to be an orator. He, too, spoke from his heart. He aimed his remarks at successful Catholic business men and he climaxed his short, effective talk by indicating his belief in *The Commonweal* by pledging $10,000 for its support.

McCormick has stated that one after another, those at the meeting made pledges to *The Commonweal*, and that John Raskob, not wanting to pressure or embarrass his guests, made his own generous pledge later in the evening.

Others whom McCormick has mentioned as early supporters of *The Commonweal* were Father T. Lawrason Riggs, "one of our most generous contributors from the very beginning of the project," Professor Carlton J. H. Hayes of Columbia, Monsignor John A. Ryan, and Thomas F. Woodlock—all of whom gave generously of their money, time, and thought. John S. Burke, a New York businessman, has been credited with finding the funds on two occasions in the Depression, which kept *The Commonweal* alive. A similar rescue has been acknowledged to patriarch Joseph P. Kennedy and his associate, John J. Burns.[4]

The Commonweal, then, was born in 1924, and had a rather affluent birth. Dana Skinner has recalled the magazine as being about $250,000 in the black; George Shuster has maintained it as being more like a backlog of $300,000, which he hastens to add "was a whale of a lot of money then."[5]

The editor was Michael Williams. "The stature of Michael Williams as the only possible and appropriate editor, grew with every speech he gave and every new friend he made," said Skinner, and "what his native talent had won in the university of journalism and experience was so obvious that by 1924, the worst skeptic was convinced."[6]

The assistant editors were Thomas Walsh and Helen Walker. The former was a poet, critic, and authority on Spanish literature; the latter was stolen from the *New Republic*. George Shuster, who joined the magazine very shortly after its inception, has stated that the fact that the editors insisted on being as "highbrow" as the *New Republic* cost a good deal in terms of subscribers and in terms of good will. "Very few people objected to *The Commonweal* in those days in terms of doctrine or even in terms of being a lay organ, but they detested the notion that we were going to be highbrow."[7] Much of the early criticism of *The Commonweal* was on the basis that it was not aimed at the average Catholic.

The editorial council consisted of Henry Jones Ford, former newspaper editor and professor of politics at Princeton; Carlton J. H. Hayes, historian at Columbia; Bertram C. A. Windle, English writer on religion and science; James J. Walsh, author of *The Thirteenth, the Greatest of Centuries*; Henry Longan Stuart, the novelist, critic, and newspaperman who along with George Shuster, the critic and professor from Notre Dame, would shortly become assistant editor; T. Lawrason Riggs, the Catholic chaplain at Yale; and Frederick J. Kinsman, the professor and author of *Catholicism and Americanism*. R. Dana Skinner, the drama critic and Washington correspondent of the *Boston Herald*, completed the group and served as regular dramatic critic for *The Commonweal*.

The First Issue and an Early Platform

The organization and preparations were complete, and on Wednesday, November 12, 1924, the first issue of *The Commonweal* appeared with a lead editorial on Calvin Coolidge, the newly elected president of the United States. An editorial introducing the journal explained that the editors felt that they would occupy a place hitherto left vacant in the field of weekly literary reviews. They would be different from the reviews designed for general circulation in that they would be expressly Christian in their presentation of religious principles and their application of these to various subjects. As a "sure background," *The Commonweal* would have "the continuous, unbroken tradition and teachings of the historic Mother Church," but in no sense would it or could it assert itself to be an authoritative or authorized mouthpiece of the Catholic church. "It will be the independent, personal product of its editors and contributors, who, for the most part, will be laymen."[1] *The Commonweal* declared its independence and would shortly be known as being a "liberal" Catholic weekly, but the liberal tag would probably not be apt by the standards of the 1970s. It was rather defensively and triumphalistically Catholic. In this first number, it spoke of the Petrine Rock as that force which would resist the full seduction of pagan hedonism, and declared that "upon that Rock *The Commonweal* stands." As opposed to the "conflicting complex of private opinions and personal impressionism mirrored in many influential journals," the editors of *The Commonweal* expressed their belief "that nothing can do so much for the betterment, the happiness, and the peace of the American people as the influence of the enduring and tested principles of Catholic Christianity," and they concluded their observation by stating that to that high task *The Commonweal* was dedicated.

It was by no means a narrow or introverted Catholicism which *The Commonweal* represented, however. It was, especially for its day, particularly open, ecumenical, and outward-turning. Not all of the Calvert Associates were Catholics. Some non-Catholics were attracted by the idea of helping to move Catholics to turn outward toward a more creative contribution to American society. The magazine's first editorial pointed out that:

> those members of our association who are not Catholics believe equally firmly that it is unquestionably a clear social duty for Catholics to contribute to the efforts now being made by all men and women of good will, to bring peace upon earth, brotherhood among men, happiness to all peoples, and prosperity, good order, and the fruits of civilization—art, beauty, culture—to our own nation.

The pages of *The Commonweal* were declared to be open to writers holding different forms of Christian belief, and also to those who professed no form of Christian faith. Where the opinion of its editors, readers, and contributors differed, it would serve as an open forum for the discussion of such differences in a spirit of good temper.[2]

The first article published in *The Commonweal* was by Hoffman Nickerson, a non-Catholic author of a book on the Inquisition. Nickerson wrote in his article "On Alliance with Rome" an appeal to those outside the community of the Roman Catholic church that in general social action it was wise for them to cooperate with Roman Catholics. Catholics were the most numerous and most widely distributed of Christian bodies, and while one might reject the claims of the Catholic church and its manner of stating them, its existence was a fact, and Christian witness would be strengthened by recognizing this.

Among the other contributors to the first issue were G. K. Chesterton with an article on religion and sex, Theodore Maynard with an article on Junipero Serra, Bertram Windle with an essay, "Science Sees the Light," and Henry Longan Stuart, who wrote in praise of Louis Veuillot, the nineteenth-century conservative Catholic Frenchman and editor of *L'Universe*. Drama critic Dana Skinner described *What Price Glory* as a very fine though not a great play. A section of report and commentary entitled "Week by Week" lamented Ku Klux Klan violence in Niles, Ohio, but was encouraged by signs indicating the Klan wave as receding. By a vote of two-to-one the voters of Michigan had defeated a Klan effort to outlaw private and parochial schools. In other matters, a *Herald-Tribune* report on religious conditions in South America brought a vigorous response. The article claimed religious conditions in South America were similar to those of the Middle Ages. *The Commonweal* responded that this was "glorious news, if true, though we suspect the writer implies something entirely different." The editors seemed quite ready to contest any charge of widespread religious unbelief or indifference in the land of our southern neighbors.

The magazine was very well received. An editorial in the *New York Times*, under the title "A Defender Who Doesn't Attack" said:

> Judging from the issue now at hand . . . its purposes are to be carried out with a moderation of language and a command of facts that usually are lacking from the journalistic and other outgivings of contemporaneous enemies of the old Church, and most notably absent from the "literature" of the Ku Klux Klan. Suavity not ferocity marks The Commonweal style of exposition and argument, and it refrains sedulously from insult or denunciation of those disagreeing with its ideas. The usual bitterness of theological controversy is missing from this new comer in the weekly field. . . .

The Jesuit weekly, *America*, extended a welcome, and commented on the "impressive launching" of the magazine, and so did a wide range of denominational publications.[3]

This first issue of *The Commonweal* was in many respects typical. It was literate, well-written, and attractively laid out in a type which the editors shortly informed us was a Roman style type used by the Stamperia Vaticana. While a bit conservative and defensive by today's standards, and surely we should be careful of anachronistic evaluations in this, it was chiefly distinguished by the fact that it was quite consciously aware of itself as speaking to informed Catholics and to those who were not Catholics. It was concerned, as Michael Williams had expressed it, with the Catholic outlook as opposed to what might be called the Catholic inlook.[4]

This concern continued to express itself in various ways. One of the most important and indicative series of articles in the early days of *The Commonweal* carried this theme forward as in January, 1925, Carlton J. H. Hayes published a three-part treatment on Catholics and their relationship to America. Its chief thrust was an emphasis on the civic duties of Catholics. Among these, Hayes put first the Catholic obligation to American culture and civilization, because though basic, it was frequently overlooked and almost always minimized. Catholics should be well-informed and furnish the nation more than their numerical quota of first-rate artists, scientists, and critics. They should raise the standards of Catholic schools and cooperate with others in raising the standards of public schools. They should support worthwhile publications and learned societies, should better their Catholic colleges and universities, and work with rather than against the efforts of nondenominational universities to enlarge the boundaries of knowledge. The next obligation, that of being good and loyal citizens, Hayes maintained, had always been well-heeded by Catholics as far as military service was concerned, but he also called for taking a conscientious and enlightened part in the operation of our political democracy. "The welfare of the whole community should be the aim of Catholic Americans, and they should be particularly on their guard against using political machinery for purely group designs." Surely they should guard against preferring for public office a candidate whose sole distinction lies in external profession of the Catholic faith. "They who resent the current un-American attempts to make public office safe only for white, Gentile Protestants should keep themselves spotlessly innocent of any counteroffense." Among the other obligations listed was the respect for individual liberties and support for the separation of church and state. On these, Hayes found little to apologize for in the Catholic record.

In addition to these concerns, Hayes outlined three kinds of general problems which were particularly deserving of the attention of Catholic Americans. The first was the problem or set of problems created during the past century by the industrial revolution and the rise of large-scale capitalistic production, and now affecting not only the relationships of capital and labor, but virtually all social relationships. Catholics were greatly uninformed in defining these problems and offering approaches to them. The least that they should do, Hayes observed, was to study the famous encyclical letter of Pope Leo XIII, *Rerum Novarum*, and seek the best means of translating its general precepts into specific legislation and social action.

The second problem area indicated was that of "the contemporary confusion of proper and ennobling patriotism with intolerant blatant nationalism." A genuine patriotism called for a humble and truthful fidelity of service which was capable of combining a love for one's country with an active concern to improve and perfect it. Humility was essential to this love and service, and between this pure patriotism and Christianity there was no conflict. Nationalism, however, differed from this. It was "a vainglorious assumption that one's own nation is superior to all other nations and entitled to pursue its selfish ends without any regard to others' welfare. Its roots are selfishness and pride, and its whole spirit is antithetical to that of Christianity."

The third area of problems, said Hayes, consisted of those on the international scene, particularly the problem of warfare. For centuries, the Catholic church had preached the cessation of war, and a long line of popes had labored to bring peace on earth. In the midst of "the latest and greatest war in human annals," Pope Benedict XV pleaded for the adoption of covenants which would provide for the settlement of differences by peaceful arbitration. Hayes left open the question of whether the League of Nations was the best or surest

agency for this, but called on Catholics to recognize their clear obligation to study the subject carefully and to champion whatever
agency was most likely in their matured judgment to promote dur-
able world peace, whether it was the League of Nations or something
else.

What the time presented, Hayes suggested, was nothing less than a
turning point in American history to which he hoped Catholics would
be equal. To meet this challenge, he felt that it was necessary that
Catholics cease their past tendency of shutting themselves off from
the life and thought of their fellow countrymen. They must not insu-
late themselves from the intellectual and social currents in their own
nation. "Whatever may have been the justification for such a tendency and for such resulting clannishness in the past—and I am well
aware of the urgent need of assuring the Faith to our children and of
preserving it among immigrants and other adults—there is now I
submit, another side to the question." The other side which Hayes
referred to was the possibility of the eventual failure of the Catholic
church to exercise any appreciable influence on the major destinies of
the American republic. "Before it is too late it behooves Catholic
Americans to sublimate their inferiority complex, . . . to practice
their religion publicly as well as privately, and to cooperate on a
basis of equality with their fellow Americans."

Reproduced in pamphlet form and widely circulated at cost by the
editors, it seems safe to conclude that this statement was not simply a
position paper of Carlton Hayes, but a kind of platform upon which
The Commonweal stood. Indeed, its very coming to life as a publication with the ends it sought to achieve was an embodiment of these
principles and attitudes.

Early Controversies

Situated as it was then, atop the walls of the Catholic ghetto and in
ready dialogue with those on both sides, it was inevitable that *The
Commonweal* was drawn into questions of controversy both with
those who were not Catholics and those who were. The first concerned *The Commonweal*'s response to some non-Catholics who
were opposed to the election of a Catholic as a fellow of Harvard
University. It was indicative of an issue close to home for the rather
aristocratic and Ivy League Catholics closely associated with *The
Commonweal* in this period of the magazine's history. The second

was an exchange with the *Christian Century* about church taxation and whether Catholics were Christians or not. The third was a vigorous controversy among Catholics on the lack of intellectual Catholic leadership. The debate was almost completely engineered by the remarkable George Shuster, and some may find that the discussion has a contemporary sound belying its fifty-year age.

Shortly after publication of the magazine had begun, John Jay Chapman, a rather well-known writer of the day, sent an open letter to Bishop Lawrence, the Anglican bishop of Massachusetts and a member of the Harvard Board of Overseers, objecting to the election of a Catholic as a fellow of Harvard University. He regarded the election of a Catholic, the first and only one among the seven fellows who in Chapman's words "control Harvard's destinies," as a dangerous development since "the outspoken purpose of the Roman Church is to control American education." *The Commonweal* asked when, where, and through whom did the Church announce its "outspoken purpose to control American education"? Four of the Harvard University Board of Overseers announced themselves in entire disagreement with Chapman, but one member, Owen Wister, the novelist, announced his approval of Chapman's action, saying that he welcomed discussion on a topic so vital as "the strategic control of education in the United States by an organized power alien to American ideals." As the discussion heated, *The Commonweal* with some reluctance and an expressed preference for more positive themes, became a forum for it. Ralph Adams Cram published an open letter to Chapman in *The Commonweal* in which he called the Chapman charge absurd and unfounded and urged him to investigate more closely the facts in regard to Catholic education and honorably withdraw from an untenable position. In the next issue Chapman replied to Cram by charging that the Catholic church in every branch of its discipline was "openly drilling its adherents into contempt for American institutions, and especially proclaiming its intention to control our education." He called on Protestant intellectuals to speak up and "give articulate warning of the danger that confronts the republic." *Commonweal*, for its part, expressed the view that if patriotic Americans saw danger to the republic they should certainly take action, and if they regarded the Catholic church as such a danger they should by all means be articulate in their warnings, but let them also be definite and present facts. Mr. Chapman, the editors observed, had made a particular charge—that the Catholic church had the "outspoken purpose to control American education"—and he had not produced proofs for his charge.[1] The real root of the Chapman charge, however, was church-state doctrine, a question which would annoy and haunt American Catholicism until the patient scholarship of John Courtney Murray would put it effectively to rest in Vatican II in 1965.

It was basically the same problem which occasioned a battle with the *Christian Century* in 1925. At issue was an editorial in the *Century* which outlined a plan for eliminating or at least greatly diminishing the Roman "menace" in America.[2] The plan in brief was to accept the imposition of taxation on all religious institutions. The Roman church "would be most profoundly affected by this." The plan would not be a panacea for the Roman menace but it would offer great hope.

> It [the Roman church] would still hold in allegiance the minds of many who do not wish to think for themselves, those who wish to commit their spiritual interests to the arbitrament of a self-constituted authority. All of which would be sad, and would still incite all thoughtful citizens to seek rational means of removing that menace to democratic civilization. But as intelligence increases, and the normal means of cultivating it becomes more efficient, hierarchic perils would less and less alarm.

The article observed that "reading history from the beginning and on all its pages, it is doubtless correct to say that no other one cause has been so prolific of decay and wreck among civilizations as the ensconcing of priesthoods in the arbitrary or irresponsible control of property."

Commonweal challenged the article on the basis of the *Christian Century*'s statement of purpose as a free interpreter of essential Christianity, published for all Christians, not any single denomination, with an effort to occupy a catholic point of view for its readers in all communions. *The Commonweal*'s editorial entitled "Are Catholics Christians?" asked if they considered Catholics to be among those for whom their journal was intended. They also asked if such views as those contained in the article were representative of the views of the Protestant bodies represented on its editorial board. "Do Protestants as a class really believe that Catholics are more alien to the spirit of America than the followers of other creeds? Is it a work of 'essential Christianity' to describe Catholic Americans as a menace to their country, their church a ravening monster that will destroy civilization if unchecked?"[3]

This controversy eventually subsided, but a good many others followed, although the general tone of *The Commonweal* was irenic. At times *The Commonweal* was quite defensive, even ludicrously so. An example of this was occasioned by a discussion of the possible significance of the 1925 decision of Pope Pius XI not to sanction the use of the electric light for illuminating St. Peter's Basilica. This was not conservativeness for its own sake, *The Commonweal* observed. Rather, there was a special kind of strength "in this very ignoring of the fashions which the world put on and off. . . ."[4]

The Commonweal did, however, have the ability to be critical of certain facets of Catholic life, and especially was willing to serve as an open forum for constructive Catholic criticism and exchange. An early example of such a discussion was a critical exchange on the health of Catholic colleges and universities. The issue was cleverly exposed by George N. Shuster, the man who along with Michael Williams virtually was *The Commonweal* for its first thirteen years. Shuster began writing for the magazine with its third issue and rather quickly became its managing editor. He was a person of remarkable intellect, scope of interest, and energy. He was equally at home in the fields of literature, politics, and theology. He had graduated from Notre Dame in 1912 and returned there to teach English after his service in a bilingual intelligence unit in World War I. He became chairman of the English department, and in 1922 published *The Catholic Spirit in Modern English Literature*. He also became an associate editor of *Ave Maria* magazine. In 1924, however, he took a leave of absence to begin his work for his doctorate at Columbia University. It was thus that he came to New York and made contact with *The Commonweal*. Returning to Notre Dame for the summer session of 1925, he had several lengthy talks with Father James Burns, CSC, the president of the university and the one to whom much credit should go for his model of greatness for its future. Together, Burns and Shuster plotted two broadsides for opening a critical discussion of Catholic higher learning.[5] The first was an article entitled "Have We Any Scholars?" which Shuster published in *America*. The "We" referred to American Catholics, and the answer was negative. The *America* editors published it with a note saying they did not completely agree with the article, but that they felt it would rouse keen discussion. Their estimate was correct. The second broadside was a lengthy editorial entitled "Insulated Catholics," that Shuster wrote for *The Commonweal*, which was published the same week as the *America* article.[6] The first part of it was a critique of the pastoral methods employed by Father John O'Hara, the chaplain at Notre Dame, who in later years became the cardinal archbishop of Philadelphia.

> It is quite in harmony with the modern mood that the spiritual adventures of university students should be carefully investigated, tabulated and disseminated. The Rev. John O'Hara, C.S.C., religious director at Notre Dame University, has for several years published an interesting annual bulletin based on intimate spiritual information supplied, anonymously, by the students themselves. This bulletin has been widely discussed; it has met with well-deserved praise. Recently, however, a distinguished Canadian Archbishop subjected it to scrutiny and criticism. "To what extent does the religious training of these students prepare them to be leaders in their various spheres of activity after they leave college?" he asked. It seemed to him they were not being prepared at all. "Remarks of seventy-five students of their experience with frequent Communion fill eight pages of the bulletin," he noted. "The charity effects are stated by three students— covering greater thought for parents and prayer for others. All the rest are individualistic." In other words, these young men apparently looked at life without giving any thought whatever to public-spirited service or to their neighbors.

The second part of the editorial presented Father Burns himself. It read in part: "Indeed the situation is so obvious, so many-sided and pernicious that it rises upon a mound of supporting testimony. But what can be done? The Rev. James Burns, CSC, a distinguished and far-sighted educator, introduced a resolution at the last meeting of the Catholic Educational Association which read as follows:

> Graduates of Catholic schools are rightly expected to have an interest in the welfare of their fellow men, for this is the natural and obvious expression of Christian charity. At a time when philanthropic effort is so active and widespread, it is the duty of Catholic teachers to explain the meaning of Christian brotherhood and to show the opportunities for its exercise in modern social organization. In colleges and universities this may well be regarded as a necessary element in the training of men."

Notre Dame was in an uproar over the editorial, but none of it was directed at Father Burns, who was in fact elected provincial of the religious order. It was all directed at Shuster. The Honorable Dudley Wooten, at the time a member of the Notre Dame Faculty of Law, penned a long letter to the editor of *The Commonweal*, accusing Shuster of being a "liberal Catholic," bent on undermining the Church as well as the nation. Wooten made no reference to Father Burns, who was the accomplice to Shuster in the plot. "Later on,"

Shuster has recalled, "Father Burns visited the Shuster household and proved to be a very congenial and let me add 'liberal' guest."[7]

Meanwhile, a free-swinging discussion of Catholic education ensued, much of it revolving around a particularly critical letter sent *The Commonweal* by C. Molanphy of New York, who endorsed the idea of the investigation of the "state of health of our Catholic colleges and the reason for their failure to function as the producers of leaders in the fields of intellectual activity."[8] The root of the problem, he felt, was that there were too many Catholic colleges, especially in certain areas. He pointed out that there were eight Catholic men's colleges within his own general area, and the question of Catholic women's colleges brought up "absurdities." "It seems to be the aim of every religious community of women to establish a college without considering resources, equipment, or its own ability to understand the problem." On the whole, he found a "complacency in the production of mediocrity." As a solution, he suggested a restriction of any further proliferation and a consolidation of existing institutions. "If the existing Catholic colleges are not willing to submerge their identity for the general good, there will be left only the question of strengthening of the Newman Clubs at the non-sectarian colleges, and extending their activities to include courses in Catholic philosophy and moral theology. Catholic colleges at the present time are not providing opportunities for scholarship, culture, and self-development."

Beneath the letter the editors pointed out that they did not necessarily subscribe to the ideas expressed, but felt that the subject was of such interest and importance as to warrant its publication. They expressed the hope that a general discussion of the subject would follow.

They didn't have to wait long. Of Mr. Molanphy, one correspondent observed that "evidently the glamor of worldliness and the dust of materialism has blinded him to the work of the Catholic college." While there is no doubt more to be gained in material aspects of life, Catholic students in nonsectarian institutions "are apt to lose that most precious and cultured asset—their Catholic faith." Besides, many Catholic institutions, though still in their youth, are on a par with most nonsectarian colleges. The women's colleges have achieved a great deal in the short span of time since the first was founded in 1899. While the Newman Clubs should be strengthened, their possible courses in philosophy and moral theology "would be a drop of bichloride in a bucket of contaminated water."

Father Ignatius W. Cox, SJ, challenged Molanphy by asking him about the fifty percent or more Catholics who attended nonsectarian institutions. These were not, he observed, notably more conspicuous than their Catholic college confreres for their scholarship, culture, and self-development.

James J. Walsh, of *The Commonweal*'s editorial council, wrote to defend Catholic colleges and said that he had heard these same charges of proliferation fifty years before. John J. Wynne, SJ, the editor of the Catholic encyclopedia, wrote that in his experience the Catholic school graduates who worked on the encyclopedia had been superior workers to those from nonsectarian schools.

Some correspondents lined up with Mr. Molanphy, observing that the needless multiplication of Catholic colleges, especially for women, was regrettable. "Duplication of activities is costly; and convent colleges in particular are, by their unwillingness to combine their forces, prepared to increase their expenses to a degree that would not be tolerated by reputable business concerns." Others observed that the development of numerous Catholic colleges had perhaps been pastorally sound, but that now good opportunities presented themselves for cooperative arrangements which would see members of various religious communities teaching together.

William Franklin Sands, a distinguished Catholic observer of foreign affairs, assessed the debate when he observed:

> It is quite natural that graduates should fly to the defense of alma mater under what they take to be an attack; quite natural too that members of our harassed teaching orders should resent what, hastily read and without further elucidation, might seem to indicate a lack of appreciation of their burdens. Still, Mr. Molanphy is not answered by drawing into discussion Dante and Copernicus as products of Catholic education, nor, I submit, by the statement that graduates of Catholic schools were found to be more satisfactory than those of other schools in the compilation of the Catholic Encyclopedia. That seems fairly obvious. The point is not, either, that on the whole morality is better safeguarded in Catholic schools than in some others. It seems to me that the gist of Mr. Molanphy's remarks is contained in the question—Are Catholic American schools today as good as they should be, giving fullest credit for their achievement in solving particular problems in the last fifty years?

Sands concluded with the observation that he for one should like to read a sober answer to the query of Mr. Molanphy.

The debate went on, with Molanphy writing again to underscore the problem of the "dissipation of forces which interested Catholics must view with regret." The discussion closed some weeks later with a female correspondent expressing gratitude to the magazine for initiating the discussion of Catholic lethargy and commenting that it was refreshing to see such energy in the expression of opinion. "Everyone ought to be glad to witness such signs of vitality, not to say pugnacity. Of course, scholastic people would like to observe a controversy conducted in a more restrained and academic way; but I for one am delighted to see a good hot fight."

These were battles that would emerge again. Thirty years later, the dean of American Catholic historians would express the view that only the danger of insolvency would put an end to the "senseless duplication of effort and wasteful proliferation" in Catholic higher education.[9] Finally, in 1965, after a peak of three hundred nine colleges and universities was reached, a period of some significant cooperation and consolidation emerged, largely because of financial pressures.

Through the 1925 discussion reported above, *The Commonweal* had shown its ability and openness to serve as a medium for the vigorous exchange of Catholic thinking. It was a quality it would demonstrate again and again.

Evolution and Theology, Protestants and Catholics

The editors predicted that the major world problems of 1925 would concern the tangled economic conditions of Europe, the attempt to reduce armaments, the friction and strain between the Western nations and the peoples of Africa and Asia, and the menace of Russian Bolshevism.[1] Their prediction was largely correct, but none of these world problems really commanded much attention in 1925 as Americans found a strange fascination with the trial of a Tennessee high school teacher, John Scopes, on grounds that he had violated a state law by his teaching of evolution. The trial proved to be an event that revealed a good deal about religion and culture in the United States. It was also the occasion of some of the finest reporting in the career of Michael Williams.

The Commonweal had taken up the question of the teaching of evolution a few months before the Scopes trial, and had held that the subject "not only should not be banned, but that it should be definitely laid before the higher grades of students—it is no subject of the kindergarten as some foolish persons seem to think."[2] They felt, however, that it was at least as wrong to teach the evolutionary theory without dwelling reasonably on the doubts which were and had been entertained about it, as it would be to keep students in entire ignorance of it. "What is far worse than either, however, is to teach it with a sneer at religion as a worn out toothless dog which has long stood in the way of progress, especially of scientific progress, but is now worsted and forever—more than worsted—thoroughly discredited." They found the evolutionary view compatible with the Christian doctrine of creation, but went to some trouble to show that it was hypothesis and not fact.

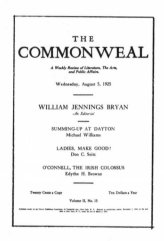

As the trial in Dayton, Tennessee, approached, *The Commonweal* expressed its reservations about it, saying that it was hardly likely to advance genuine knowledge of a highly complex and technical matter, but would likely confuse the real issues involved through "the stirring up of a raucous and heated debate between such emotional extremists as Mr. W. J. Bryan and Mr. Clarence Darrow, to the accompaniment of the jazz-band to be installed in Dayton's baseball field among the batteries of radio machines and newspaper cameras."[3] In the same issue, they had a praising review by Bertram Windle of *The Case Against Evolution* by Father George Barry O'Toole.

When the trial opened in Dayton, editor Michael Williams was there to cover it for *The Commonweal*. He explained, however, that twenty-five years of newspaper experience had not in the least prepared him for the bewilderment of the carnival atmosphere of Dayton. A report of "a typical night all through the trial" included descriptions of competing barkers selling corn plasters or atheism, a store featuring the presence of a caged live gorilla, and the breaking up of a Holy Rollers' meeting by a jeering crowd of photographers and sensation seekers.[4]

There were also a variety of religious personalities present whom the reporters found to lend color to the proceedings. There was Deck Carter, the Bible Champion of the World, the only person to whom God has talked since Joan of Arc; Lewis Levi Johnson Marshall, Absolute Ruler of the Entire World, without Military, Naval or Other Physical Force; Elmer Chubb, fundamentalist and miracle worker, who announced that miracles would be performed on the public square during the trial of "the infidel Scopes." Michael Williams, however, pointed out that the religion of most of the Dayton people themselves was restrained, sober, puritanical, devout, and fully convinced. No Catholic, he observed, "can help but admiring their constancy and their earnestness, and their open profession of their faith, even while he deplores their eccentricities and their loss of the authority and guidance which only one Church can give to humanity."[5]

While Williams expressed a certain admiration for these people and a distaste for the professional antireligionists who formed part of their opposition, he in no way minimized the danger which he felt they represented to the country. The real issue, he reported, could be expressed in eleven words: Were church and state to remain separate in the United States? The Tennessee fundamentalist looking over a state in which the simple Bible faith prevailed, overwhelmingly felt he had the right to protect his children against scepticism in the schools provided by the state, said Williams. But the person who believed in the tradition of separation of church and state and regarded the guarantees for minorities embodied in the Constitution as real expressions of vital principles, had to remain steadfast.[6]

The judge instructed the jury to confine itself to the aspect of the trial which was the reason why there was a trial and a judge and a jury to try it—the fact that Mr. Scopes had broken a law of the state of Tennessee. Scopes was found guilty. It proved to be a fundamentalist victory, however, only in the technical sense—no one much doubted Scopes would be found guilty—as the notoriety of the case over a period of years gradually erased the antievolution legislation from the several Southern states that had enacted it. An even greater loss to their cause, however, was the death of William Jennings Bryan which came shortly after the end of the trial.

About this time, T. Lawrason Riggs contributed an essay on the strife between conservative and liberal Protestants which, as he expressed it, had "attained a more energetic boil in the Scopes trial."[7] The Catholic viewpoint in the opposing tendencies which divided "the Reformation's spiritual children" was one of "sincerest sympathy with the fundamentalist's devotion to supernatural Christianity, above all to the Incarnation with its attendant miracles, as beliefs which cannot be abandoned without the surrender of the historic faith." Conservative protagonist J. Gresham Machen was praised by Riggs for his analysis of liberalism "in a manner often suggestive of Pius X's condemnation of modernism." The fundamentalists' defense of supernatural Christianity was, however, destined to be a losing struggle, said Riggs, for they lacked a living authority in matters of religion, and had a heritage of antiintellectualism which regarded reason as radically corrupt and faith as totally unrelated to reason. It was a fault of the reformers that they failed to see that their principles were incompatible with the maintenance of any deposit of faith,

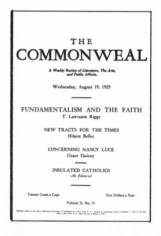

THE
COMMONWEAL

A Weekly Review of Literature, The Arts, and Public Affairs.

Wednesday, August 19, 1925

FUNDAMENTALISM AND THE FAITH
T. Lawrason Riggs

NEW TRACTS FOR THE TIMES
Hilaire Belloc

CONCERNING NANCY LUCE
Grace Guiney

INSULATED CATHOLICS
An Editorial

Twenty Cents a Copy   Ten Dollars a Year

Volume II, No. 15

and this fault is the misfortune of their spiritual descendants. "Professor Machen objects to being called a fundamentalist on the ground that it sounds like the name of some 'strange new sect.' But, alas the difficulties of his school lie precisely in the fact that they are members of a 'strange new sect' called Presbyterianism." This observation, however, was relatively irenic compared with Riggs's abrupt dismissal of Protestant liberalism: "It is evident that private judgment and intellectual agnosticism are carrying the left wing of Protestantism to a position further and further away from anything more than a nominal resemblance to historic Christianity, and constantly closer to a vaguely pantheistic humanitarianism."

Such statements as this when published in *The Commonweal* were not simply statements about Protestants but statements to Protestants, who as we have mentioned, were constantly kept in mind as being part of the readership. Father Riggs was the Catholic chaplain at Yale, a member of the editorial council of *The Commonweal*, and an active worker and supporter of the Calvert Associates. He was an early ecumenist who toured the country with a Protestant minister and a Jewish rabbi, holding discussions under the auspices of the National Conference of Christians and Jews. George Shuster has described him as "a very fine and distinguished person" and has added that "we treated him quite as if he were a layman."[8] While Riggs's remarks seem harsh today, they were rather typical of the way in which even relatively informed Protestants and Catholics spoke to one another (in what few exchanges there were) in 1925 in the United States.

It might be observed at this point that the early editors of *The Commonweal* did not think of it as an exclusively lay organ and in fact there has never been a rigid attitude on this. Father Riggs and Father John A. Ryan were quite active with *The Commonweal* and there were also certain ties with the Dominicans in New York upon which Shuster has reported that he relied quite a bit. Later years saw connections with Fathers Virgil Michel, H. A. Reinhold, Gregory Baum, and others. Monsignor Paul Hanley Furfey has contributed to *The Commonweal* almost since its inception.

The early editors tended to tread lightly in matters theological, where the later editors would walk somewhat more confidently. George Shuster has recalled:

> For my part I had an almost scrupulous respect for orthodoxy in the theological sense; and my concern was that in the light of the then current European thought, American Catholicism often seemed not orthodox at all but only backward. We introduced a great deal from abroad—Von Huegel, Guardini and the Jesuits of the *Nouvelle Révue Théologique* for example. It pained me to think of the possibility that we, who after all were not theologians except in an amateur way, might unwittingly be espousing heterodox positions. And so I actually favored getting continuing professional advice. Indeed, I wanted to enter into a pact with some of our Dominican friends to supply that advice.[9]

This was never done. Shuster has explained that the problem was not a great concern to Michael Williams. "He thought that if we did make a serious mistake we would hear about it and then take refuge in the fact that we were after all laymen." Shuster has added, "I wasn't sure that some of those from whom we were likely to hear would know more about the matter than did we. But Michael would have bowed to the Chancery Office without expostulating seriously."

During the early years of the magazine there were no attempts to move against it on grounds of departure from orthodoxy. Shuster reports that while there were undoubtedly people who would have liked to, "one of the things that they seemed to find very strange was that we had a protector in a place where you would never have expected to find one. It was in Boston in the person of Cardinal O'Connell. He was all in favor of the magazine. "Among the things the cardinal did was to give financial help with great generosity." He also sent the editors some pleasant and friendly personal correspondence. Shuster states: "If you got into any serious difficulty, you could always depend on him, not to get up in a pulpit and say you were Simon-pure, but enough so that people knew they would have to take him on."

Early in 1925, Thomas F. Woodlock, the president of the Calvert Associates and one of the principal supporters of its work, was appointed a member of the Interstate Commerce Commission by President Coolidge, and gave his full energies to that work. He would, in later years, join the staff of the *Wall Street Journal* and contribute occasional reviews and articles to *The Commonweal*. The work of the Calvert Associates advanced, however. In cooperation with the Paulist Fathers' radio station WLWL of New York City, they broadcast talks on Friday evenings by *Commonweal* editors and contributors. At the suggestion of Hilaire Belloc and under his editorship, Macmillan published The Calvert Series, a group of books eventually numbering ten which were to be an "apologetics suited to our time." They included works by Belloc himself, G. K. Chesterton, Leo Ward, and Vincent McNabb. Other Calvert Associates' activities included meetings and interreligious discussions sponsored by Calvert Associates' groups in various cities.

While these matters were progressing, death struck the *Commonweal* editorial council as Henry Jones Ford who was then also serving as president of the Catholic Historical Association died in August, 1925. The next few years brought death to assistant editor Henry Longan Stuart and associate editor Thomas Walsh. Sir Bertram Windle of the editorial council followed not long after them. Assistant editor Helen Walker left her post for marriage and was replaced by Mary Kolars. For the period 1927–37, the personnel remained stable with Mary Kolars as assistant editor, George Shuster, managing editor, and Michael Williams. The editorial council consisted of Carlton Hayes, Lawrason Riggs, Dana Skinner, and James Walsh.

The beginning circulation of *The Commonweal,* as the result of two years of hard promotional work, had been about three thousand copies. The cost of a subscription was rather high—ten dollars. From the first, it was praised for its moderate tone, openness, and literary qualities. It was, before long, speaking of itself as "the voice of the Catholic layman."[10] When in 1928 a papal encyclical on ecumenism was published, *The Congregationalist* magazine in an editorial stated that they "should like to know what such excellent and intelligent Roman Catholic laymen as, for instance, those who conduct *The Commonweal,* really think of this business [the pope's encyclical]." Editorials and articles from *The Commonweal* were widely quoted and discussed in the press, both secular and religious.[11] Circulation of the magazine, however, was not increasing as quickly as the founders and editors had hoped, and in February, 1927, the subscription price was cut to five dollars. A year later, a special introductory subscription price of one dollar for fifteen issues was presented. Promotional material on the special offer included a list of *Commonweal* endorsers among whom were Walter Lippmann, Agnes Repplier, G. K. Chesterton, and Cardinals O'Connell, Dougherty, and Hayes. Michael Williams was not one to think in small terms, and hence he expressed the following vision of the possible scope of influence for *The Commonweal:*

> By now, when this magazine, The Commonweal, has been published for almost three years and a half, it may be asked whether the time has not come for a greater harvest. It would appear, for example, that the program of the Calvert Associates might be adopted to advantage by every one of the 60,000 students in Catholic colleges, not to speak of the 185,000 pupils in Catholic high schools. . . . There are about 250,000 living graduates of Catholic colleges for men, and roughly, 350,000 living alumnae of Catholic colleges for women; Catholic graduates from other colleges must surely number around 400,000. For the great bulk of these The Commonweal should have a very special appeal; it talks in their terms, it discusses the subjects to which they gave years of preparatory study. . . .[12]

Williams made these remarks to an assembly of Catholic laymen. It may be questioned whether he really thought of *The Commonweal* in those terms, which amount virtually to a mass-appeal publication.

George Shuster has pointed out opposition which *The Commonweal* met because it was "highbrow." It must therefore be doubted that the publication really talked in the terms of the "great bulk" of the more than one million potential readers cited by Michael Williams. Surely he was at least partially aware of this, but it is also possible that he sustained what some recall as his periodic tremendous outpourings of energy and enthusiasm with just such visions.

The Candidacy of Al Smith

A modest but significant jump in circulation did take place at this time, however, principally because of the attitudes and exchanges which came with the presidential candidacy of Alfred E. Smith, a matter in which *The Commonweal* was officially nonpartisan, but obviously at least quite interested. The experience of the Smith campaign was something that would leave its mark both on American Catholicism and on *The Commonweal*.

In 1924, an effort to nominate Smith as the Democratic candidate for president was lost in a drawn out struggle in the Democratic National Convention in Madison Square Garden. In 1925, as early speculation on 1928 candidates began, the Board of Temperance, Prohibition, and Morals of the Methodist Episcopal Church issued a statement expressing the view that Smith was not an acceptable candidate. The statement brought a strong reply by *The Commonweal* in a lead editorial.

> Governor Smith may not run for office, it [the Methodist Board] declares, because he does not support and further a particular statute, the subject and matter of which has now become part and parcel of the creed and dogma of a group of churches. He is un-American say the spokesmen of this group, because he does not support the Constitution, which means, in plain language, that he may wish to change the Constitution, from what it is now to what it once was. When those same reverend board members actually changed the same Constitution from what it once was to what it now is, none would have more heatedly resented the implication that, in seeking that change and pleading for it, they too might be considered un-American.[1]

The specific complaint against Smith was that he did not further a state enforcement act, that is, an act to enforce the provisions of the Eighteenth Amendment. To this the editors retorted:

> One might plausibly inquire when, in its most ardent accesses of social indignation the same board has complained of lack of an "act"

to assist federal authority in the suppression of counterfeiting, or against the restriction of Negro voting in the South, or to help carry out the purposes of so moral a measure as the Mann Act. . . . It would really seem that all measures do not require the same cooperation. . . .

The editorial went on to observe that the prohibition amendment seemed to be the result of an unwise intrusion of a particular church concern into the domain of the state.

The prohibition question was destined to be entwined with the candidacy of Smith. The question had attracted the attention of the editors of *The Commonweal* in one of their first numbers as they editorialized on the "zeal gone mad" of the governor of Colorado who proposed in his first message to the state legislature the passage of an amendment to the prohibition enforcement laws of the state forbidding the use of wine for sacramental purposes. Later, they commended a commencement speech by Nicholas Murray Butler, president of Columbia, who lamented the lack of integrity of public officials who "talk, act, and vote one way, and daily drink another." Cardinal O'Connell stated that "it has been made clear a thousand times that we will work with our separated brethren as temperance men, but not as tools of those whose confessed policy is world-wide prohibition by installments." *The Commonweal* pointed out that there was no single Catholic position on the Volstead Act. Prohibition was most properly a question of national policy, rather than church controversy. "It is simply a matter of getting at the social facts in the case and of determining whether prohibition is the best way of meeting them."[2]

The controversy surrounding the Smith candidacy and the 1928 election, however, concerned more than prohibition. In April, 1927, Charles C. Marshall of the *Atlantic Monthly* published in its pages an open letter to Smith, then the governor of New York, questioning whether his religious beliefs were reconcilable with the Constitution and with the principles of civil and religious liberty, and whether if elected to the presidency he could conscientiously support and defend these principles. Smith immediately announced that he would answer the letter in the May number of the *Atlantic. The Commonweal* itself published a response to the Marshall letter, however, pointing out that the question raised involved more people than Governor Smith. "If a President cannot or should not be trusted to uphold the Constitution and support the principles of civil and religious liberty on which American institutions are based, simply because he is a Catholic, neither can or should any Catholic be trusted with any public office." *The Commonweal* response, a calm and lengthy open letter, called the issue of alleged divided loyalty a "bugaboo which haunts and troubles you [Marshall] and other honest men."[3] Smith and thousands of other Catholics, they reported, had answered the practical aspects of the question over and over again by their daily life and activity. Quotations from various popes and others on Catholic church-state theory were misleading and not pertinent as they referred to a theoretical or ideal state. The essence of the Catholic idea of the state "as we of The Commonweal see it," was described as simply holding that the moral law may at times actually be superior to man-made law. In this sense, not only Catholics but all believers in the moral law were theoretically liable to conflict with the laws of the state. But was not this idea that moral is superior to man-made law, the most fundamental idea in American governance, they asked? As Jesus sought no civil authority to support the spread of his teachings, neither did the Catholic.

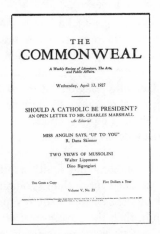

THE
COMMONWEAL

A Weekly Review of Literature, The Arts,
and Public Affairs.

Wednesday, April 13, 1927

SHOULD A CATHOLIC BE PRESIDENT?
AN OPEN LETTER TO MR. CHARLES MARSHALL
An Editorial

MISS ANGLIN SAYS, "UP TO YOU"
R. Dana Skinner

TWO VIEWS OF MUSSOLINI
Walter Lippmann
Dino Bigongiari

Ten Cents a Copy　　　　　Five Dollars a Year

Volume V, No. 23

A lead editorial in the following issue took up the topic again, and quoted at length from a 1909 article of Cardinal Gibbons who had been called upon to answer a number of questions quite similar to those now asked of Alfred Smith. "They [Catholics]," wrote the Cardinal, "accept the Constitution without reserve, with no desire as Catholics, to see it changed in any feature. . . ."

> The separation of Church and state in this country seems to them the natural, inevitable and best conceivable plan, the one that would work best among us both for the good of religion and the state. . . .

> No establishment of religion is being dreamed of here by anyone; but
> were it to be attempted, it would meet with the united opposition of
> people, priests and prelates.[4]

Still further discussion followed the next week as *The Commonweal* published a point-by-point response to Marshall by Father John
A. Ryan of Catholic University.[5] It was, however, the response
which Smith himself made in *The Atlantic* which probably communicated most clearly to readers, as in essence he stood on his record.

> I have taken an oath of office in this state nineteen times. Each time I
> swore to defend and maintain the Constitution of the United States.
> All of this represents a period of public service in elective office
> almost continuous since 1903. I have never known any conflict be-
> tween my official duties and my religious belief. No such conflict
> could exist. Certainly the people of this State recognize no such
> conflict. They have testified to my devotion to public duty by electing
> me to the highest office within their gift four times.[6]

In Houston in 1928, Smith won the Democratic nomination easily,
but was soundly defeated at the polls by Herbert Hoover. Hoover
received twenty-one million popular votes to Smith's fifteen million;
the electoral vote was 444–87. Smith failed to carry even his own
state, though he did quite well in New York City and in most of the
nation's larger urban centers. There is disagreement as to exactly
what factor caused his defeat. His political origins were associated
with Tammany Hall; he was not a college graduate; he was opposed
to Prohibition; and he was also a Catholic. Whether this latter was
the chief cause of his defeat or not, it is clear that there was expressed during the campaign a great deal of anti-Catholic feeling.[7]

The Commonweal was officially nonpartisan in the campaign.
Michael Williams, however, was an advisor to the Smith campaign
which was being directed by John J. Raskob, a distinguished member
of the Calvert Associates and a financial supporter of *The Commonweal*. Raskob took the view that the bigotry factor would work in
Smith's favor. George Shuster has recalled that Raskob felt that if it
could be shown that Hoover was being led by bigots, the generous
spirit of the American people would rise up and condemn him, and
bring home a Smith victory.[8] Shuster himself opposed the theory,
even to the point of feeling that the Marshall attack should be ignored. In no way, however, did Shuster feel that Smith could win.

One finds no evidence of *The Commonweal* being used as a tool in
the 1928 campaign, that is, no dishonest journalism appears nor is
any bigotry baiting evidenced. It did respond to and discuss the

campaign. Further, the Calvert Associates prepared and published the *Calvert Handbook of Catholic Facts*.[9] Compiled as an informational source, it takes up an interesting array of questions: do Catholics favor the liquor trade, is the doctrine of infallibility of the pope a menace to the loyalty of American citizens, were the pioneers of this country exclusively Protestant? Some thirty questions of this type are discussed, and then there is appended a thirty page Who's Who of Catholic relatives of the presidents from George Washington to Calvin Coolidge!

The depth and extent of bigotry manifested during the campaign proved greater and more destructive than almost anyone had anticipated. It shocked many Catholics and made them turn defensively inward. This was of course the antithesis of *The Commonweal*'s desire and purpose. Shuster has recalled that American Catholicism received a setback which hurt it for at least twenty years.

> It lost what I call the *élan* of the World War I thing, you know where so many soldiers came back and Catholic boys had been with Protestant boys in France and all over the place, and they came to know each other and make friends, whereas they wouldn't have done that at home. There was a lot in the air. The atmosphere of the Al Smith campaign made our position, our work, much harder.

Michael Williams seems to have received quite a personal setback from the campaign experience. He had conceived *The Commonweal* out of precisely the *élan* of which Shuster has spoken. Carlton Hayes has stated that Williams was "greatly disillusioned by the violent anti-Catholic forces at work during that time."[10]

While the experience of the Smith campaign did make more difficult *The Commonweal*'s goal of turning Catholics more creatively outward and did create a trauma for its founding editor, it also resulted in a substantially expanded readership for it.[11] This would be a help to the magazine in the difficult financial times which were ahead.

Turning the Decade

Between 1928 and 1932, the major event for *The Commonweal*, the United States, and the world was the stock market crash and the Great Depression. Another focal point for the magazine in these years, however, was at the organizational center of Catholicism, as the Lateran Treaty of 1929 finally unencumbered the Vatican of its territorial claims in an agreement with Mussolini, then at a high point of his influence. Also, two famous encyclical letters of far-reaching importance were issued from Rome during this period. *Quadragesimo Anno* presented some updated social doctrine in the midst of the economic crisis, and *Casti Connubii* addressed the always controversial question of birth control.

Generally speaking, the editors of *The Commonweal* were as unprepared and unaware of the impending financial crisis as were most Americans. In late 1927 they editorialized on the good health of the economy. They were pleased by the large number of freight car loadings, a popular indication of sustained business activity. There was also the steadily increasing purchasing power of the dollar. The stock market indicated nothing of particular significance for future business. "Some stocks go up as easily as others go down—from which we may say that the patient seems normal!"[1] They found some observers who were concerned over the amount of installment buying and speculative building construction, but they felt these comprised no stormcloud, as there was no large-scale business setback in view. A few weeks later, another editorial observed:

> Everyone sees now that economics has utilized the system of statistical inquiry so intelligently and patiently that it is able to claim for its conclusions a degree of probability. It has now actually become something like a barometer at which one can look to see what kind of industrial weather is likely to prevail tomorrow.[2]

The "weather" indicators all seemed to point to clear skies.

In May, 1929, the forecast also seemed good, as the editors observed in commenting on the report of President Hoover's Committee on Recent Economic Changes. But by this time they had become more critical of what might be called the statistical approach to evaluating the American economic system, stating that "it is futile to hurrah the status quo in a mood of bland indifference to dangers and evils."

> Chief among these is, we think, a willingness to reduce all human life to a series of figures—to be content with a civilization which shows a profit, regardless of the grossness of its outlook and the absence of generosity from its heart. If the poor were no longer with us, in the money sense, we should still be obliged to deal charitably with the pauperism of mind and spirit which everywhere crops out from under the veneer of comfort. But they are still here; and so the opportunity for genuine advance lies in concentrating attention upon them rather than upon the savings accounts of the successful.[3]

This same kind of human sensitivity prompted *The Commonweal* to speak up quite often on the problem of unemployment. At times, the editors seemed rather mystified by the complexity of the American economy and those who claimed to be expert in its affairs, but the problem of unemployment was very real and clear. In late 1927, they pointed out that over one million workers were unemployed and that the wages earned by an almost equal number were astonishingly small. They suggested that this was a problem that called for some kind of governmental action. In early October, 1929, in addition to the unemployment problem, they editorialized on the bankruptcy of American agriculture with the consequent decay of rural life, the failure to raise the real wages of industrial workers to a saving or cultural level, and an inability to consume what was produced while basic needs were still unmet. In the same issue, there was begun a series of four articles on unemployment written by Father John A. Ryan. It was a series which would conclude the week of the Crash itself, an event which would lead to far greater unemployment than Ryan or anyone envisioned. The lead editorial of the October 2 issue concluded with the following paragraph which seems rather haunting, although it is based more on social sensitivity than economic punditry.

> We need to measure the walls of our social house anew. We need to plan for the future. Above all, we need to be ready for a shock when that comes. As is usual in such instances, collapse is likely to be made impressive by the pressure of economic sacrifice and curtailment it would involve. But then we should certainly become aware that the process of undermining, or of decay, had been evident in a score of moral fissures too small and too little troublesome to worry about. It has been written that man shall be unconscious of the evil he does until it has been visited upon his head.[4]

While the economic collapse dwarfed most of the other news stories of 1929, there was an important development in that year which had implications for all Catholics, but particularly for Italian Catholics as Benito Mussolini and Pope Pius XI reached a settlement of the so-called "Roman Question." The development was editorially cheered by *The Commonweal* which pronounced it "a day of rejoicing—in every respect a day which the Lord hath made." They observed that Mussolini "has once more done excellent work for Italy" in that he had removed a cause of bitter dissension, improved the international position of his country, and won the support of Catholics. The Vatican for its part had made concessions which "would doubtless have been out of the question a generation ago," but which now freed its hands for the business of humanity. "The head of the Church now is free, not only of the intolerable restraints which followed the advance of Italian nationalism but verily also of handicaps which were attached to an outmoded world order."[5]

An earlier editorial was more caustic in its appraisal of Mussolini. While it granted that Americans might admire Mussolini's power to organize a people against economic and social ruin, it observed that there is a clear limit to the amount of "right-about face" that the world of men will stand for. "Mussolini seems utterly unconscious of this immemorial circumstance; and sometimes one is inclined to surmise that the end of all his tugging at the bootstraps will be a settling back to earth less pathetic, perhaps, than terrible."[6]

The Commonweal's early handling of the question of Italian fascism was an example of its forum style of journalism. Thus in 1927 it published in the same issue two contrasting views of fascism, "the most important political development in the world today."[7] The first article was a sympathetic review of the book *Italy and Fascism* by Don Luigi Sturzo, the Italian Catholic priest and exiled antifascist. The review was written by Walter Lippmann, the chief editorial writer for the *New York World*, who in expressing agreement with Sturzo stated that fascism was the logical and uncompromising development of the autocratic state, and that the supreme fascist theorist was Machiavelli. Lippmann quoted Lord Acton to the effect that the first Whig was Thomas Aquinas, "who laid the foundation of that reverence for natural law to which all who resist the overweening pretensions of the political state have appealed." The other article, by Columbia professor Dino Bigongiari was entitled "Mussolini: Servant of Italy" and supported the conclusions of a book which lauded the achievements of Mussolini. Whereas Sturzo saw the theory of the Fascists as saviors of Italy as a fable covering an aggressive and reactionary coup d'etat, the book by Guiseppe Prezzolini saw fascism as the victorious Italian resistance to the forces of disintegration, with Mussolini as "the best, beyond all comparison the most powerful and capable, servant of a great tradition, who had led to victory, not elements shaped by himself, but comrades who follow him as their best guide, as the supreme advocate of their cause, the embodiment of their best aspirations."

Within fourteen years the Fascist Il Duce, this embodiment of the "best" Italian aspirations, would see his regime in complete disintegration and meet death at the hands of the overwhelming hatred of his own people. But this was 1929, and with the settlement of the "Roman Question," he was at the summit of his popularity.

With the close of the decade of the 1920s, Michael Williams, George Shuster, and others on the staff could look with some pride on what they had accomplished with *The Commonweal*. It was now rather firmly established and was listened to carefully and with respect both in Catholic and non-Catholic quarters. Its courtesy and fairness were rather uniformly acknowledged. It had not failed to speak out clearly on issues, however. In international affairs it was antiisolationist, calling isolationism a "blindness" and a "stagefright in the presence of truth." It called for a creative internationalism and a generous settlement of the war debts question. On the national scene, it had consistently favored more equitable social and economic conditions in accord with the Bishops' Plan for Social Reconstruction of 1919, a very forward-looking document prepared by Father John A. Ryan calling for a minimum wage, unemployment insurance, progressive taxation on personal and corporate income, public housing, and control of monopolies. (Upton Sinclair had called it the "Catholic miracle!") It had fought for Billy Mitchell and for justice for Sacco and Vanzetti. It had made some brave ventures into ecumenism, and had provided a forum for some creative Catholic intramural exchanges on liturgy, education, and other topics. It had published articles by Henry Morton Robinson, G. K. Chesterton, Hilaire Belloc, Hendrik van Loon, C. C. Martindale, Lewis Mumford, Agnes Repplier, Fulton Sheen, Sean O'Faolain, Etienne Gilson, Don Luigi Sturzo, Michael Cardinal von Faulhaber, Leo Ward, Dorothy Day, Paul Hanley Furfey, John A. Ryan, and a host of others. In addition, the weekly poetry section had been well-received. George Shuster has recalled that one of the big jobs was to find the poetry every week, "but it helped to make a good many friends because we didn't publish only Catholic verse, but verse of all kinds. Poetry was one of the most successful features we had."[8]

In spite of its notable achievements, however, *The Commonweal* found itself in early 1930 in serious financial distress. Its original funds had been depleted (Michael Williams had spent money with the same style and flourish with which he had raised it), and despite a consistent growth in circulation to about eighteen thousand paid subscriptions, it had each year operated at a deficit which had been met by its patrons. Financial problems for *The Commonweal* would continue to be severe throughout the Depression, and would continue on in its history too. As a lay rather than clerical journal, editorial and business salaries had to be set mindful of the family and personal responsibilities of those filling these posts. Likewise, manuscripts had to be adequately remunerated if their quality was to remain high. The editors openly communicated these problems to their readers, though at this time no financial appeal as such was made to readers. They were encouraged, however, to assist in finding new subscribers for *The Commonweal* as it was felt at this time that an increase to twenty-eight thousand paid subscriptions would make the magazine self-sustaining.[9]

As the full depths of the misery of the Depression began to manifest themselves in 1930 and 1931, *The Commonweal* editors, like many other Americans, searched for signs of hope and direction. Thus they received with great enthusiasm the Catholic social encyclical *Quadragesimo Anno* issued by Pope Pius XI on Pentecost Sunday, 1931. Previously the editors had tried to promote a revival of Christian economics on the basis of the 1891 encyclical *Rerum Novarum* of Pope Leo XIII,[10] but the new encyclical presented an even more hopeful impetus. To this point in time, American Catholics, both clergy and laity, had barely been influenced by such social doctrine, seeing their social and political life as something apart from this kind of a religious perspective. Al Smith, for example, when challenged by Charles Marshall's attack on his Catholicism on the basis of the political teachings of Leo XIII, asked his advisers, "Will someone please tell me what the hell a papal encyclical is?"[11] The two encyclicals would form a touchstone of *Commonweal* editorial policy throughout the Depression and the New Deal era.

At about this same time another encyclical was issued which attracted the attention of *The Commonweal*; this was the encyclical *Casti Connubii*, on Christian marriage. It contained a scarcely veiled direct response to the Episcopal bishops' qualified admission of birth control in certain cases, which the Lambeth Conference had issued in London a few months before. In commenting on the encyclical which held that no reason or motivation could justify the use of artificial means of birth regulation, *The Commonweal* stated that "against the forces which would dissolve Christian morality, Rome has again spoken," and added in commenting on an Associated Press anticipatory report that "even secular journalists now know that Rome can only speak an unchangeable word in all that concerns the moral law." A week later another editorial reiterated: "Rome has spoken and the case is closed." While the editors acknowledged that "there are many Catholics who are disobeying the moral law in this particu-

lar phase of it," they accurately predicted that there would be no
public resistance among Catholics as a result of the encyclical. They
stated that those who violated the norms of the encyclical for the
most part were victims of "the terrible pressure of economic injustice" and they called on all the faithful to help remedy this situation.[12]

Three months later, the approval of artificial birth control by the
Federal Council of Churches occasioned the longest lead editorial
which *The Commonweal* had published since its inception. "Apparently, the main body of American Protestantism has surrendered
unconditionally to secularism," it commented. "If the Federal Council correctly interprets 'the corporate conscience' to use their own
phrase, of the majority of American Protestants, it has done more
than merely surrender the historic morality of Protestantism—it has
now joined the massed enemies of Orthodox Christianity and now
fights with them."[13]

Succeeding issues of *The Commonweal* offered a number of articles defending the Catholic position on birth control and explaining
the evil of contraception.[14] The discussion took an interesting new
turn some two years later, however, with the development of the
Ogino-Knaus or rhythm method of birth regulation. On March 8,
1933, *The Commonweal* published an article called "New Light on
Birth Control," a rather extensive review article of *The Rhythm* by
Dr. Leo M. Latz, a member of the faculty of the Loyola University
Medical School, Chicago. In a note accompanying the article, the
editors observed that it was unnecessary in their opinion to say more
than that the rhythm approach appeared "to be in harmony with
established Catholic teaching." In gauging the significance of the
development, the reviewer struck a cautious and rather accurate note
when he observed that "in the end the true worth of the theory may
prove to lie somewhere between the estimates of those who expect it
to revolutionize domestic life and sceptics who are uninterested in
it."[15]

The discussion of rhythm was a change of pace from earlier discussions on birth control. Ernest Dimnet in a letter to *The Commonweal* pointed out that the stress in earlier contributions was on the
immorality and dangers of contraception. In the rhythm article, on
the other hand, the stress was on the advisability and practical in-
evitability of contraception. "For the deliberate and scientific avoid-
ance of conception in marital relations may be called by any Latin or
Greek name, but to people unused to theological subtleties, it will

appear as mere contraception." Dimnet was chiefly displeased by the triumphant tone of the article. "Unquestionably the tone of the formerly abused resolution of the Anglican bishops on the same subject was more productive of the right atmosphere than this triumphant demonstration." His second point was perhaps even more fundamental as he observed that he missed in this article "as I always missed in theological disquisitions, the clear statement that there can be no legitimate marital relations without love, real love; that is to say, a sentiment antecedent and superior to sexuality, even if it leads to union. Intimacy that is not regulated by the heart is what Bernard Shaw says it is in terms which I do not wish to recall."[16]

In *America*, Wilfrid Parsons, SJ, wrote an article denying that rhythm was "Catholic birth control." He tried to cool the enthusiasm of some rhythm proponents by emphasizing the deficiencies and difficulties of the method. On the moral aspects of the question, he pointed out that the Holy See as long ago as 1880 advised confessors "that there was no reason to disturb penitents who in their use of marriage restricted themselves to days that are physiologically sterile." Doctors Ogino and Knaus had simply given some scientific predictability to an earlier theory.[17]

Another interesting feature of the birth control discussions of those days was the range of opinions it produced on the Catholic birth rate and world and national population predictions. A *Commonweal* editorial explained the necessity for a Catholic "back to the soil" movement in the following terms:

> Between 80 and 90 percent of the entire Catholic population of this country are city dwellers. They are thus exposed more than almost any other element of the nation to all the hazards inseparable from a wholly industrialized existence. Moreover, urban families, as vital statistics prove, do not long maintain themselves. The average urban family dies out in three to four generations. With immigration walls preventing the influx of Catholics from other lands, humanly speaking it is simply a matter of elementary arithmetic to deduce from these facts the steady decline in numbers of the American Catholic population, if the conditions now prevailing are not changed. It is therefore a vital necessity for American Catholics to return to the land and to plant their roots deeply in the soil of the country, even as it is a vital necessity for a proper portion of the whole nation to do likewise.[18]

This kind of thinking seems to have played a significant part in the development of the Catholic Rural Life Bureau of the National

Catholic Welfare Conference,[19] and in its editorials encouraging the work of the group, *The Commonweal* did not fail to mention that those Catholic bishops, priests, and farmers were not simply striving heroically and against heavy odds to improve the bad conditions confronting those Catholics who still clung to the soil, they were crusaders "whose great mission it is to save the great mass of their fellow Catholics from the decline and almost certain extinction which menaces the whole Catholic population of the United States unless they can be led back to the land."[20]

The concern expressed was not simply a Catholic concern, it was also a national concern. Dr. James J. Walsh in 1930 contributed an article entitled "Are We Due to Disappear?" which projected the outlook that by 1935 the death rate would be higher than the birth rate "and we shall be a disappearing people." *America* also expressed this view which was not limited to Catholic circles.[21]

Nineteen thirty-two was the cruelest year of the Depression. Unemployment was variously estimated at between 12 and 17 million; industrial production was less than half its 1929 volume; stock in the New York Central Railroad which had been at 256⅜ in September, 1929, and had dropped to 160 after the Panic, hit a low of 8¾ in 1932. *The Commonweal* commented that there was "peril of the most grievous kind that social disorder will ensue, if the pressure of hunger and cold and destitution and homelessness is not soon lifted from the bodies and souls of a multitude of unfortunate victims."[22] The story of one such victimized family the editors reproduced as it had appeared in the columns of the *New York Times*. It was the only time in the history of the magazine that they simply reprinted a news story, but it was so poignantly expressive of the human dimension of the economic collapse that it was quite appropriate. It related the experience of Josephine and Sylvio Giacinto, a couple so poor that they had to borrow from neighbors the twenty-one cents necessary to claim the telegram the city sent them—collect—to notify them their twelve-day-old daughter Josephine had died in Bellevue Hospital from the effects of rat bite. The incident had occurred just twenty-four hours before. As the family was sleeping, all in one bed, a rat jumped from the floor, bit the child on the forehead, ran over the mother's face and scurried into hiding. The article explained how the Giacintos, within three years, had gone from a comfortable middle-class existence to one in which they could not even afford to claim their child's body, nor indeed to even receive the terse telegram announcing her death.[23]

A few weeks after this, *The Commonweal* editorialized on the subject of rats, pointing up the national extent of the problem and the destructiveness and danger of the rodents. There was no doubt, they observed, that if a definite and well-organized effort were made, most of the rats in the country could be eradicated. They maintained that surely there was never a better time to do it, since it would give employment to a great many men and save a great deal of valuable food material that was wasted while many went hungry. "If the death of the little girl which touched so many hearts could be made a signal for a crusade that would rid us to a great extent of the rodents that are such a danger to health, then that child's life would not have been in vain."[24] The topic of rats, however, was one to which future editorial writers would have to return.

The Commonweal, the 1932 Election, and FDR

In this section, we will attempt to show some social and political currents of thought among Catholics at this time, by reporting briefly on how American Catholicism and *The Commonweal* reacted to the presidential candidacy of Socialist Norman Thomas, and the New Deal of Franklin D. Roosevelt. We will also indicate certain differences which developed with Roosevelt, namely on his Mexican policy and his decision to recognize Russia, and bring the story of *The Commonweal* itself to the mid-1930s.

The Commonweal declared its neutrality in the 1932 presidential campaign, stating that "as a journal of opinion, it will seek to evaluate what is offered the public as leadership or policy." At least one Hoover supporter, however, felt their editorial columns carried at least an implicit endorsement of Roosevelt. One of the most interesting features in the election, however, was the candidacy of Norman Thomas on the Socialist ticket, a development which sparked some interesting exchanges in the pages of *The Commonweal*. Charles Willis Thompson, a well-known New York journalist of political affairs and frequent contributor to *The Commonweal*, initiated the discussion with an article called "Will Catholics Vote for Thomas?" in which he asked if Catholics could vote for a Socialist, and answered in the affirmative so long as the Socialist was Norman Thomas and the country the United States. The article occasioned a flood of letters and a lead editorial the following week which stated that "the question is a more complicated one than is indicated by our political correspondent." Various reasons, they maintained, made it essential for the Catholic to proceed with "great prudence" in this matter. They agreed that a good deal of the Socialist platform expressed Catholic social doctrine, but a main question of disagreement was the extent of social ownership. "The Socialist perpetually seeks to extend the public ownership line into private ownership; a person speaking from the standpoint of Catholic social teaching tends to push the public ownership group into as few industries as possible." The Catholic social program was described as avoiding the danger both of excessive government control and excessive control by a minority of capitalists. Further, it had "the true philosophy of life in contrast to the false philosophy of socialism." The editorial concluded by stating that the proper place for a Catholic should be with Catholic Action rather than the Socialist party.[1]

Father Francis J. Connell, CSsR, a well-known moral theologian, was even more explicit in a letter which he sent the editors stating that "a Catholic may not vote for Mr. Thomas, whatever be the latter's personal integrity and abilities." Connell held that one voted not only for a man but for the party principles to which he was pledged; since Thomas had not stated that he was developing a new socialism, he therefore fell under the general condemnation of socialism expressed by Pius XI in *Quadragesimo Anno*. Other correspondents, however, felt differently. One wrote:

> May I ask you about those who regularly vote the Democratic or Republican ticket? Are the economic policies of the old parties, if you can discover them, of a character to be approved by Rome? Are they of the same pattern as the social teachings of the Church and Catholic Social Action? Your editorial would imply that they are, since the attack is centered on the Socialists and not on the old parties. If my deduction is wrong, what ticket, won't you please inform us, is a Catholic to vote, since, thank the Lord, there is no Catholic ticket?

The writer asked for a protest vote of five million for Thomas which he predicted would bring an infusion of progressivism into the national scene.[2]

Thomas received a popular vote of nearly nine hundred thousand, several times more than he would poll again in three subsequent presidential campaigns, while Roosevelt rolled up a victory over Hoover, the statistics of which were an almost exact reversal of the 1928 election.

Roosevelt presented to the nation what he called "a new deal," and for the most part the editors of *The Commonweal* were pleased with it. So were the great majority of Catholics and Catholic publications. Bishop Karl Alter of Toledo stated that the president's inaugural address "breathes the spirit of our Holy Father's recent encyclical." When speaking to Catholic audiences, Roosevelt himself referred to *Rerum Novarum* and *Quadragesimo Anno*. Richard Dana Skinner, drama critic for *The Commonweal* and an interested Democrat, wrote privately to party leaders that if Catholics "once understood clearly the identity of idea between the administration's efforts and the Pope's recent program of social justice, they would be more likely to give it enthusiastic support through thick and thin." Another staunch friend of the administration who was affiliated with *The Commonweal* was Father John A. Ryan, who had accepted an invitation to join *The Commonweal* editorial council in 1930. In later correspondence, Ryan would refer to Roosevelt as "the Miracle Worker in the White House." Another individual who joined the editorial council at the same time as Ryan was Thomas Woodlock, the former president of the Calvert Associates, then working with the *Wall Street Journal*. Woodlock was a critic of the president, and at editorial council meetings would engage in heated through friendly arguments with Ryan, whom he considered "pink."[3]

In an editorial in midsummer 1933, *The Commonweal* seemed to approach the New Deal cautiously, observing that while it was not at all joining forces with ultraconservatives who would fight every effort to interfere with the old "irresponsible" system, it agreed heartily with former Governor Alfred E. Smith in his admonition to "keep your eye on the Constitution." In succeeding months, however, *The Commonweal* gave a less reserved support to the president and to the National Industrial Recovery Act, a key part of the New Deal recovery program. While the NRA occasioned various criticisms, *The Commonweal* stated:

> Nevertheless, the really great fact which a thousand minor criticisms cannot alter, although they may disastrously conceal it for a time, still stands evident—namely that President Roosevelt has gloriously led this nation toward a real reformation of its entire polity, and that the nation as a whole is aware of that fact, and is determined to go ahead with him and under his leadership.

The Commonweal supported nearly all aspects of the New Deal, which is characterized as "this country's true, native, conservative effort" both to recover from the immediate effects of the Depression and to reform its social system.[4] Two questions on which it differed with the Roosevelt administration, however, were the Mexican policy and the question of the recognition of Russia.

In his youth, Michael Williams had visited Mexico and had formed a negative impression of the Calles regime, as not really having the best interests of the people at heart. As editor of *The Commonweal* he published an immense number of editorials on Mexico and the religious persecution which was being prosecuted there. American Catholics were keenly interested in the fate of their fellow Catholics south of the border and in 1929 Ambassador Dwight W. Morrow had participated in negotiations which resulted in a truce between church and state. The arrangement did not last long, however, as conflict broke out over rights in education. In 1933, Roosevelt appointed Josephus Daniels as ambassador to Mexico. Daniels had served as secretary of the navy under President Wilson and had been the chief of the young FDR who was serving as assistant secretary. The appointment of this eminent person, one who was close to Roosevelt, raised American Catholic hopes for the relief of their persecuted coreligionists. Wilfrid Parsons of *America* wrote an open letter to the new ambassador calling on him to use his position to influence the Mexican government to halt its persecution of the Church. He pointed out instances of the murder and torture of priests and nuns and other injustices and asked Daniels to "use your best influence to stop them."[5]

Soon, however, American Catholics were demanding the recall of Daniels. On July 26, 1934, in a speech in Mexico City he quoted General Calles on the importance of education to the future of Mexico. Calles had said, "We ought to enter into and take possession of the mind of the children, of the mind of the youth." On this statement Daniels commented: "In order to realize this ideal, which is the only one that can give Mexico the high place visioned for it by its statesman, the government has been making the rural schools a social institution."

Commonweal sharply criticized Daniels for his public praise of this educational policy, commenting that he apparently found himself in full agreement with "the dogma of the Totalitarian, Atheistic State. . . ." They quoted the Calles remark in context, which called for taking possession of consciences for the revolution, dispossessing them of the prejudices of religious belief, and forming the national soul. They stated that the remarks of Daniels "upholding the destructive central policy of the Absolute State will have a profound effect

upon the New Deal in the United States" as "millions of Americans
—Protestants, Jews, and Catholics—may well ask themselves how
soon they are to meet the same fate as their fellow religionists are
suffering in Russia, Germany and Mexico."[6]

There was a widespread chorus of Catholic criticism of Daniels
which then grew into a rather strong pressure group attempting to get
Roosevelt to intervene on behalf of the persecuted Church in Mexico. This Roosevelt refused to do as he considered it an internal
Mexican affair, the intrusion into which would be a violation of his
Good Neighbor Policy. *The Commonweal* commented rather caustically:

> Officially, the Totalitarian Tyranny, which now persecutes the help-
> less millions of Mexican Catholics, is a Good Neighbor of the Amer-
> ican administration. Officially, that Tyranny is of course immensely
> strengthened in its course by President Roosevelt's statement of the
> new policy of absolute non-intervention. Germany, Russia, and Italy,
> and all countries controlled by governments which deny or minimize
> religious liberty will also be comforted by this new policy.

Gradually, American Catholic opinion became split between those
who were reconciled to this position and those who were not. Those
who especially supported a "hard-line" on the Mexican situation
were Bishop Michael Curley of Baltimore and Martin Carmody with
the Knights of Columbus. On the other side were Rev. John J. Burke
of the NCWC; Rev. John F. O'Hara, president of Notre Dame;
Cardinal Mundelein of Chicago; and Professor William Franklin
Sands of Georgetown. Editorially, *The Commonweal* basically followed the Curley-Carmody position, although it did publish articles
on the affair by Sands. Eventually the Mexican situation subsided
internally and was upstaged by other events, but it has been described by one historian as "the most severe strain imposed on the
generally harmonious relationship between Roosevelt and American
Catholics."[7]

It was probably the greatest strain on the relationship between *The
Commonweal* and Roosevelt too, although another point of difference was the question of the recognition of Russia. This was a development to which *The Commonweal* had been opposed for some time
on the basis that the gain in prestige thus effected for the Soviets and
their organized atheism would outweigh all possible political and
economic advantage.[8] The Roosevelt administration, however,
weighed the values involved somewhat differently and in late 1933
was able to effect recognition rather quickly and without too much

strong Catholic opposition, by carefully listening to Catholic opinion on the matter and demanding religious liberty for Americans in Russia as a condition precedent to American recognition. A personal meeting between the president and Father Edmund A. Walsh, SJ, of Georgetown, considered the leading Catholic expert on Russian affairs, was a diplomatic move which flattered American Catholics. When the recognition of Russia was announced, *The Commonweal* commented that they felt the president "sincerely did what he could and secured reasonable conditions for civilized human intercourse between Russia and the United States."[9]

During these Depression years *The Commonweal* was in a real struggle to stay alive financially. In December, 1931, Michael Williams wrote to Father John A. Ryan:

> We nearly went on the rocks several times in the last six months, but with very timely and I hope to believe God-directed generosity on the part of Father Riggs, Mrs. Nicholas F. Brady, and Mr. John Moody, a recent convert to the Catholic Church and a man whom you should try to convert to your economic gospel (I think the moment a favorable one for the attempt), we have pulled through, although still feeling the storm.

In April, 1932, Williams wrote to Ryan informing him that *The Commonweal* needed $27,000 to continue, and asking him if he would "contact one or two good prospects." Ryan wrote back to say that he could think of no one, but was sending a gift of $100.[10]

Williams was not one who let his sense of style and class and his penchant for ceremony and extravaganza be impeded by finance. Only a few days before contacting Ryan for financial help he had presided at the Calvert Associates' annual *Ark* and *Dove* religious liberty celebration at the Waldorf Astoria. The evening included songs by John McCormack, and speeches by Governor Ritchie of Maryland, and others. Patrons for the affair included Cardinal Hayes of New York, Bishop Curley of Baltimore, Episcopal Bishop Manning of New York, the British consul-general, the minister to Washington of the Irish Free State, the Presidents of Columbia, Yale, Princeton, Georgetown, Fordham, Catholic University, James Gillis of the *Catholic World*, Wilfrid Parsons of *America*, Mr. and Mrs. Robert Shriver, Princess Catherine Radziwill, Mr. and Mrs. John J. Raskob, and many others, including a British Cooperating Committee of notables. On display at the gathering was a cross made of wood from the tree under which the first Mass was said at St. Mary's, Maryland, 1634. It had been given to the Calvert Associates by

W. Scott O'Connor and was destined to hang in the reception room of
The Commonweal.[11]

Williams seems to have thrived on these productions for the Calvert Associates and other affairs he arranged. He was remarkably
good at this kind of thing and had the instincts of a real showman.
Occasionally, however, something would go wrong as happened in
the following amusing story which George Shuster has told in recalling the friendship for *The Commonweal* of Dr. Nicholas Murray
Butler, president of Columbia.

> Among the many services which he [Butler] rendered the maga-
> zine was acceptance of an invitation to preside over a luncheon
> tendered the English writer, Hilaire Belloc. Our editor, Michael Wil-
> liams, had arranged for this great if sometimes bilious writer to visit
> these hospitable shores, and for a good two weeks the magazine's
> secretarial staff had done virtually nothing save attend to the business
> of our guest, who arrived when it suited him attired in a Napoleonic
> cloak and dictated letters to be dispatched thither and yon, together
> with whatever chapters of books happened to occur to him. The
> luncheon was designed to be the culmination of the journey, and the
> invited guests were of the requisite distinction. But when the ap-
> pointed hour came, everyone appeared save the lion. After an embar-
> rassing period of delay, a messenger was dispatched to Belloc's hotel
> to see if perchance he were ill. He was not. It had merely occurred to
> him that no honorarium had been suggested for his address at this
> luncheon, and why did British writers visit these shores if not to
> collect honoraria? Finally he was persuaded to come nevertheless,
> food was served nearly two hours after the appointed time, and
> Butler made a very gracious introductory speech. Belloc grudgingly
> got on his feet, said "Thank you!" and sat down. That was positively
> all the oratory he was prepared to deliver free of charge.[12]

While things thus occasionally went awry for Michael Williams he
was now in serious trouble as *The Commonweal*, that ship with
which he identified in an understandably personal way, was in danger
of sinking. In this financial crisis, it was first decided to appeal to a
select group of readers whose special interest in *The Commonweal*
was known either through their letters or personal visits to the office.
"They comprised a group of about six hundred men and women:
bishops and priests, heads of religious orders, both men and women,
and the laity." Within a few days, donations of almost $7,000 were
received. This was quite encouraging, and at a special meeting of the
board of directors of the Calvert Associates, held on April 21, 1932,
it was decided to continue the publication of the magazine and to
extend the financial appeal to all readers. This was done, as an open

letter appeared in place of a lead editorial in the issue of May 4. The appeal did not succeed in raising the full $27,000 asked for; working funds were received, but the debt remained almost the same. The publication did continue, however, and the editors were no doubt encouraged by the concern expressed by general readers and others such as G. K. Chesterton who wrote:

> Having heard with the utmost horror the suggestion of *The Commonweal* being in some peril, even of its most beneficent existence, I can only say that the loss of *The Commonweal* would be colossal, not only to America, but to England, and to any number of places where intelligent men want the real issue between a Christian and a pagan culture debated in an intelligent way.

John Tracy Ellis in a letter accompanying a financial contribution said that he knew of "no magazine which had done more to give intelligent and moral interpretation to the problems of current affairs than *The Commonweal*," and said he was sure there were "thousands throughout America who would echo the opinion of Chesterton in regard to the paper." Another financial appeal to readers was made in the spring of 1933 in an attempt to remove *The Commonweal*'s debt which remained at about $26,000. The appeal was quite successful, as nearly all of that amount was raised. Changes in typography and paper also helped reduce costs.[13]

One aspect of the fund-raising campaign of 1933, however, was very unsuccessful. Several priest subscribers had written privately to *The Commonweal* suggesting that a "Priests' Committee" be formed which would address its own appeal for *The Commonweal* to all the clergy. George Shuster took up the idea and outlined it in a letter to Father John A. Ryan in which he asked if he would be a member of the committee and permit the letter to be sent under his signature. Shuster said, "We have long since realized that the strongest support of our 'lay action' has been coming from clergy, many of whom not only subscribe for the magazine, but promote the habit of reading it among their parishioners." The number of priests they were reaching, however, was relatively small.

> The Commonweal goes to 3,221 rectories—about 26% of churches with resident pastors listed in the Catholic directory. We have done everything possible to reach the others, but some are afraid of us and many seem to regard our work as "just another Catholic magazine."

Shuster wrote that he and John McCormick, *The Commonweal*'s business manager, felt the plan had the great advantage of not coming directly from them, "and also of showing that our form of Catholic action is not in any sense contaminated by a desire to function independently of the clergy." Shuster concluded, "We have every reason to believe that the results would be most satisfactory."

Ryan agreed to the project. The results of the appeal by the Priests' Commonweal Committee, however, were very poor. Some twenty-nine thousand letters were sent out to priests. Two hundred replies were received and a total of $1200 was raised.[14]

At this time, Michael Williams was in Rome, having led a Calvert Associates' Holy Year pilgrimage there following the celebration of Calvert Day with a Mass and a Te Deum in St. Patrick's Cathedral, sung by the Calvert Associates "as a manifestation of their rejoicing in and gratitude for the great gift of religious and civic liberty enjoyed by the people of the United States of America." In Rome, Williams presented a letter from the group to Pope Pius XI which offered "the most loyal and devoted homage of their Catholic members, together with the respectful felicitations and greetings of their Protestant and Jewish friends, assuring you of their gratitude to you as the Vicar of Jesus Christ for your unceasing and fruitful labors on behalf of economic and political justice for and among all classes of society, and for the promotion of peace among nations." Pius received them privately and personally greeted each one of the more than fifty members of the party. *Osservatore Romano*, in a front-page article, reported that the Pope "gave this pilgrimage his special blessing because it came to him under the auspices of *The Commonweal* and of the Calvert Associates."[15]

A year later, in 1934, *The Commonweal* celebrated its tenth anniversary, receiving congratulations from innumerable well-wishers including Archbishop Amleto Cicognani, the apostolic delegate to the United States. Not all were pleased with *The Commonweal* of those days, however. One correspondent complained of its interest in current events and encouraged it to "supply the permanent things, the eternal explanations. . . ." Another wrote of "the shocking essay you published on depopulation and race suicide (I believe it was called 'New Light on Birth Control')" and said that *The Commonweal* had "been too willing to make concessions to liberal sentiments in its pages." Others, however, wrote to defend *The Commonweal* on these charges.[16]

In late 1934 Dana Skinner resigned as drama critic for *The Commonweal* due to the pressure of other commitments, but continued to take a keen personal interest in the venture and to contribute occasional articles and reviews. A few months before, two young men were added to the staff, having been selected by George Shuster. They were Philip Burnham and Edward Skillin; the former a graduate of Princeton, the latter of Williams. Their names did not appear on the masthead, however, and their work, at least initially, consisted mainly of a "Seven Days Survey" section, a noneditorializing survey of current events with a relative emphasis on religious affairs, which was added to *The Commonweal* in April, 1934. In a few years, Burnham and Skillin would come to play a very important role in *The Commonweal.*

During those Depression days, a number of movements or groups began to spin off from *The Commonweal*, or to receive a helpful nudge from it. For example, *The Commonweal* had been approached about funding a Liturgical Arts Society, which would concern itself with the improvement of religious art and architecture and publish a journal devoted to these interests. While unable to fund it due to its own problems, *The Commonweal* did support and encourage the Society which came into being and began publishing its quarterly journal. The Catholic Worker Movement also has roots in *The Commonweal*. Peter Maurin, a poor itinerant French philosopher, poet, and social visionary, visited George Shuster in 1933, described his ideas on social reconstruction to him, who then suggested that he talk to Dorothy Day, a free-lance writer who did work for *The Commonweal* and other Catholic publications. The result was one of the most interesting phenomena in American Catholicism. The Catholic Association for International Peace was another development of those days that had ties to *The Commonweal* and especially to Carlton Hayes and his colleague at Columbia, Parker Moon.[17]

The 1936 Olympics, Nazi Germany, and Father Charles Coughlin

By 1936, no man was as much an object of world attention as the German Nazi leader Adolf Hitler. For some years *The Commonweal* had been watching Hitler, evaluating him, and warning all who would hear. This was very largely the work of George Shuster. Shuster, who was fluent in German and French, had spent part of his Army service in World War I doing translation work in Germany. Then, during 1930–31, while continuing his writing for *The Commonweal*, he visited Germany on a fellowship and wrote a book called *The Germans*. In 1933, he went to Germany again, and wrote

Strong Man Rules, the first book to warn Americans of the ultimate menace of Hitler. There was probably not another magazine in the country during these years that was publishing more about what was happening in Germany. In 1935, Shuster published *Like a Mighty Army*, which told the story of Hitler's actions against established religion, Protestant, Catholic, and Jewish.

As the time approached for the 1936 Olympics, scheduled for Berlin, *The Commonweal* led an attempt at producing an American Catholic boycott of the games. Their editorial on the matter pointed out how the Hitler regime had violated the Concordat of 1933 with the Church, how German Catholic organizations had been viciously attacked, their property confiscated, their leaders jailed and slain. It concluded by asking,

> that no Catholic, and no friend of the sport activities of Catholic institutions, ought to make the trip to Berlin. We request each and every organization identified with the Church to make clear to its members that participation in the approaching games means endorsement of willful and violent persecution. And we respectfully petition the hierarchy to warn the faithful concerning the issues involved, so that no Catholic young man or his friends unwittingly give to enemies of our faith opportunity to question the sacred solidarity of Christian belief.[1]

Many Americans were opposed to participation in the games. *The Commonweal* editorial admitted it was simply making the case for Catholic nonparticipation. Other publications such as the *Nation* also called for a boycott, and the *Christian Century* called for the games to be moved to a site other than Berlin, as did the National Council of the Methodist Church. The American Federation of Labor opposed American participation because the Nazis were anti-labor and because there was "nothing noble" in the persecution by sixty million Germans of six hundred thousand Jews—one hundred to one was not fair odds. Many American newspapers including all the New York dailies opposed the continuation of preparations for choosing the American team. Damon Runyon wrote that "Germany's pagan putsch makes its acceptance of the real Olympic oath either an impossibility or a hypocrisy."[2]

The chief spokesmen for participation in the games were Avery Brundage and General Charles H. Sherrill. Brundage had competed in the 1912 Olympics in Stockholm and was sixth in the decathlon won by Jim Thorpe. Years later, when Thorpe was a broken drunk and Brundage a wealthy Chicago businessman, Brundage was adamant for the strict upholding of the principles of amateurism that resulted in Thorpe being stripped of his medals for having played bush-league professional baseball in 1909 and 1910. This was not personal opportunism on the part of Brundage. He was simply a man of intense, if at times narrow, principle regarding the purity of amateur athletics. In Brundage's world, nothing was more important than the Olympics and anyone who held that there could be something more important than these games was simply indulging his petty ego. General Sherrill, a former outstanding sprinter credited with being, in 1888, the first to use a crouching start in the dashes, was more the polemicist than was the platitudinous Brundage. Sherrill, a member of the International Olympic committee, felt that the crucial question was whether Hitler would allow at least one invitation to be sent to a German-Jewish athlete. He reported that not one but two invitations were being sent to German Jewesses and maintained that the point had been made. Others felt it was clear that Jews had been systematically excluded. (Earlier, for example, it had been learned that though twenty-one Jews had been "nominated" for the Olympic training camps in Germany, none had been "invited" to attend.) An official of the American Olympic Committee stated that the Germans were not discriminating—the Jews had been eliminated because they weren't good enough. After all, he remarked, there were "not a dozen Jews in the world of Olympic calibre." General Sherrill stated that "there was never a prominent Jewish athlete in history." Sherrill then failed to enhance his image as a diplomat when he was widely quoted from a speech in which he praised Mussolini as "a man of courage in a world of pussyfooters," and added, "I wish to God he'd come over here and have a chance to do that same thing."[3]

Since Sherrill's explanation of German concessions actually seems to have satisfied some people, George Shuster again outlined in an article the case against participation. He repeated that he was presenting the case from the Catholic point of view, and disclaimed any "communistic sympathies," something he had been charged with in some hate mail he had received on the publication of the editorial opposing participation in the games. He pointed out that the Berlin Olympics of 1936 were to be no ordinary athletic games, but were designed with an obvious political goal, that of glorifying and giving recognition to the Nazi state and system as the up-to-date "religion of youth." German Catholic youths could only participate as members of some Nazi group. Athletic effort had been made a strictly party function and the German Catholic athletic youth group, the *Deutsche*

Jugendkraft which Catholic authorities had particularly tried to keep intact when the Nazis had come to power, had been violently suppressed. Shuster concluded:

> It is not merely a question of the persistent violent hostility of Hitlerism to the Church—a hostility which has sent hundreds of the faithful to death or into exile; which has rendered the life of the clergy a continuous martyrdom; and which has impoverished and ruined hundreds of thousands. No—these games are to set the seal of approval upon the radically anti-Christian Nazi doctrine of youth.[4]

The opposition to American participation was strong and culminated in a rally at Madison Square Garden on December 3, 1935. George Shuster, recalling the opposition, has stated that "it may well be that one little shove more and the Führer's face would have been slapped resoundingly." That shove did not come, however, from the Catholic hierarchy. What was said editorially in *The Commonweal* was reprinted on the front page of the *New York Times*, and though *The Commonweal* had not mentioned the archbishop of Baltimore by name, it had said "a bishop" was pledged to support their stand. By the next day, however, the chancellor of the archdiocese of New York, Bishop McIntyre (later cardinal of Los Angeles), having conferred with Avery Brundage, released a public statement that the archdiocese thoroughly disapproved of *The Commonweal*'s stand, and in fact endorsed American participation in the Olympics. This action effectively killed the attempted Catholic boycott. In fairness to McIntyre, it should be pointed out that George Shuster has written that "later on Bishop McIntyre frankly regretted his action in this matter." Reflecting on the affair some thirty-five years later Shuster has commented: "It still seems to me that staying away from Berlin in 1936 would have been a good and glorious deed. Perhaps it might have even postponed the outbreak of the war."[5]

The Commonweal's campaign was a failure. Even among the Catholic journals of opinion there was not much support. Father James Gillis of the *Catholic World* supported the idea rather strongly, and so did the *Sign*, but the influential *America* ignored it as did generally the diocesan press. This was regrettable, but of no consequence in principle to Shuster, who was concerned more with integrity than pragmatic results. Writing in the midst of the controversy, he granted that a young athlete might not grasp the argument made against participation, but that a journal like *The Commonweal*, which did understand and appreciate the situation, "would lose every right to exist" if it didn't throw itself heart and soul into this cause.[6]

The campaign against the Olympics brought Shuster a great deal of mail, one day's pile of which contained three separate threats against his life. Death was predicted upon his leaving *The Commonweal*'s office that day. Shuster has recalled the story with some amusement, telling how his secretary, a stocky and devoted Sicilian girl, insisted on preceding him out the door, saying "If they're going to shoot you Mr. Shuster, they'll have to shoot me first!"[7]

A possible source for this "hate mail" was some extremist followers of Father Charles Coughlin, the radio priest of the 1930s, one of the most controversial figures to appear on the American political scene in those or any days. Commanding an audience of millions he was at first simply an advocate of the social reforms indicated in the encyclicals of Leo XIII and Pius XI. He then became a strong Roosevelt supporter in 1932, but gradually became estranged from the New Deal, organized his National Union for Social Justice in November, 1934, and his own political party in 1936.[8]

As early as December, 1933, *The Commonweal* had cast a wary eye on him in an editorial entitled "Dangers of Demagogy" which upbraided him for a baseless personal attack on Al Smith and urged him to "drop the two-edged sword of personal abuse" because he was otherwise "the greatest apostle of social justice and the moral law that has appeared in this country. . . ." By May, 1934, George Shuster dealt with him somewhat more coolly when in the course of an article on the growing irrationalism in the country he observed:

> The people clamor for action rather than thought. Men who have studied least are listened to most. I predict that if Mr. Roosevelt should be threatened with defeat in 1936, he could stave it off by ousting Professor Tugwell and putting Father Coughlin in his place. Whether that would be a good thing is beside the point. It is merely obvious the Professor Tugwell is an intellectual while Father Coughlin is not.

In March and April, 1935, *The Commonweal* published two editorials on Coughlin, justifying his right as a citizen to political activity and pointing out that millions of Catholics opposed him and that he did not himself represent Catholicism.[9] At this time Michael Williams wrote privately to John A. Ryan:

> I should be greatly obliged to you if you would give me, in confidence, your views concerning him [Coughlin]. I at no time have unreservedly upheld him—but I have believed—and still believe, unless good reasons are given me to change my opinion—that his influence on the whole is beneficial.

That very month, however, Ryan had outlined his views on Coughlin in an article in the *Catholic Charities Review*, "Quack Remedies for the Depression Malady," which discussed the views of a "radio orator" and observed that "one of the greatest obstacles to the progress of industrial recovery at the present time is the misinformation and unsound economic doctrine diffused among the masses by the advocates of pseudo-remedies masquerading as currency and credit reforms." Williams had possibly been prompted to contact Ryan by correspondence from Father T. Lawrason Riggs in which he dissented publicly from *The Commonweal* editorial treatment of Coughlin which he considered much too gentle. Riggs strongly denounced Coughlin as a demagogue who was doing great harm to the nation and the Church. Another editorial a few weeks later emphasized that Coughlin did not speak for the Church, but did not denounce him as such, holding that the merits or demerits of his economic views were a separate matter. An editorial in August, 1936, held that "the censure which his reckless language deserves can only be modified by the hope that he is actuated by the great charity of wishing to aid the poor and disinherited."[10]

The Commonweal, as it had done in previous elections, declared itself nonpartisan as the time for the 1936 election came near. In early October, the campaign took an interesting twist when Monsignor John A. Ryan took to a nationwide radio hookup provided by the Democratic National Committee to attack Coughlin. Coughlin at this point in the campaign was reminding his followers that their candidate William Lemke needed only 6 percent of the total vote to throw the election into the House of Representatives. Ryan denounced Coughlin's charges of communism against Roosevelt as calumnies and defended the New Deal as "mild installments of a too delayed social justice." Coughlin then devoted an entire radio broadcast to responding to Ryan. He maintained that he had never called Roosevelt a communist, but had held and still held that his theories were communistic.

The emergence of the Ryan-Coughlin controversy brought *The Commonweal*'s strongest statements yet on Coughlin.

> The rank wizardry of his illogical yet crudely fascinating oratory may continue to obsess the unthinking portion of his diminishing audience; but the appeal to reason made by Monsignor Ryan will increasingly be heeded by those Catholics who use their head.

The editorial did not maintain that there were not substantive issues for discussion in evaluating the New Deal and social justice, but pleaded for real debate and not simply ranting, as it felt Coughlin had done. It also pointed out that the 1936 campaign had at least exploded the myth of Catholic political solidarity, what with Ryan advocating Roosevelt, Coughlin shouting for Lemke, and Al Smith supporting Landon.[11]

Lemke received some nine hundred thousand votes out of a popular vote of about forty-four million. Coughlin discontinued his radio broadcasts for a time, but later returned, became quite anti-Semitic, for which he was taken to task by *The Commonweal* and other Catholic publications, retaining to the end only the support of the ultraconservative *Brooklyn Tablet* and his own *Social Justice* publication.[12]

The Commonweal and the Catholic Layman

Perhaps no topic was more appropriately of concern to *The Commonweal* than the role and function of the Catholic layman, especially the American Catholic layman. Though well-articulated reasons for it were rarely made explicit, this question was generally referred to in Catholic circles as the "problem" of the Catholic layman (and the masculine form was used appropriately, for the female side was not even considered). The term "problem" was used rather vaguely. On the one hand it referred to the problem of trying to get Catholic laymen concerned about matters of Church and society. Catholicism has long been organized in an essentially clerical and professional (nuns, sisters, brothers) way, with rather precisely defined functions and lines of authority established. How to get much of a rise out of the nonprofessional class, the laity, has been one problem. On the other hand, if the laity were responsive and concerned, that was frequently a "problem" too, especially if they were responsive and concerned in a way that didn't coincide with whatever the particular Church authority figure in question had programmed or decided. The great majority of the Catholic laity, however, were content to leave "church matters" to their priests, whom they regarded benevolently, and to pursue, devoutly or not so devoutly, the rather individualistic notions of Catholic holiness. Catholic Action— which was defined as the participation of the faithful in the apostolate of the hierarchy—and the social encyclicals were considered "church matters" by many of those who weren't aware of what the terms "Catholic Action" or "encyclical" meant.

According to George Shuster, the roots of *The Commonweal* were in the National Catholic Welfare Council (the successor to the National Catholic War Council) and the great vision which Father John J. Burke, CSP, had for the layman in the scope of its activities. The organization was the first really comprehensive Catholic vehicle, and it offered great possibilities. Shuster has reported that "In Burke's original magnificent diagram, his view of the whole thing had a marvelous role for the laity." The council, however, had internal problems with squabbles among American bishops, and external problems with Rome which feared a too autonomous American church and had the name changed to the National Catholic Welfare *Conference*. In this conflict, "Burke began to be shoved more and more aside and what remained of all these Burkean insights was incorporated in *The Commonweal. . . . The Commonweal* was probably the only thing that survived."[1]

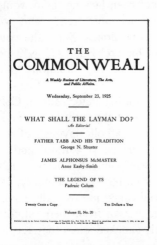

THE
COMMONWEAL

A Weekly Review of Literature, The Arts,
and Public Affairs.

Wednesday, September 23, 1925

WHAT SHALL THE LAYMAN DO?
An Editorial

FATHER TABB AND HIS TRADITION
George N. Shuster

JAMES ALPHONSUS McMASTER
Anne Easby-Smith

THE LEGEND OF YS
Padraic Colum

Twenty Cents a Copy   Ten Dollars a Year
Volume II, No. 20

The Commonweal's handling of the problem of the layman, however, was generally nonmilitant, and consisted, for the most part, in calls for the laity to work for Catholic Action and especially as the Depression came, to work for the practical implementation of the social encyclicals. An early editorial on "What Shall the Layman Do?" did, however, refer to the National Council of Catholic Men as the "least satisfactory" department established by the National Catholic Welfare Conference.[2] Shortly afterward, an article chronicled the failure of the National Council of Catholic Men. The plan was that it would be organized in each parish.

> The plan was good but the human element interfered. Parochial organization put the local pastor in position to dominate the local unit; he could kill or cure. Too many, I believe, unhappily chose to kill.

The plan also was unapproved by many bishops who did not countenance such a union of laymen and did not permit it in their diocese. Also, rumors of the impending collapse of the whole NCWC were of course harmful to any kind of growth.

The fundamental problem, though, was the "exaggerated spirit of parochialism so widely prevailing—the determination not to have within a parish any organization or activity coincident with parish lines and associated with the parish and with the Church, over which the pastor would not have at all times absolute dominion and control." The writer, Mark O. Shriver, observed that "with pastoral support" a Catholic lay union could and would be a great success. "Had that support not been lacking there would be today a splendid body of energetic laymen able, ready and willing to do all those things so necessary to be done." Since the councils "sought only to aid as active allies of hierarchy and clergy, working under them and with them," Shriver found the situation "pitiable" and "unnecessary."[3]

In February, 1926, Father Peter Moran, CSP, sent a letter to *The Commonweal* that praised the publication and also praised the patience of the American Catholic layman, of whom he thought some might have sung: "Come all ye faithful and bring your duplex envelopes." Another correspondent, however, rebuked him for implying that laymen might be restive. In January, 1933, however, when a *Commonweal* editorial called in especially vigorous terms for laymen to awake to Catholic Action from their "slothful stupidity," the editors seemed genuinely shocked when they received an unusually large number of letters, several running to fifteen hundred words, well-written, clearly expressed, full of a "most evident sincerity" suggesting that the major blame for the failure of Catholic Action should be placed on the clergy. As one correspondent wrote:

> Are our Catholic men and women taught from Sunday to Sunday what their duties as Catholics are regarding social and political and economic reform, for instance, from the pulpits of our churches? . . . Is there not a great deal of timidity among the clergy in denouncing political corruption and social injustice?

The editors decided not to publish the letters, stating that however true or false the charges, "such facts in no way excuse the laity for not participating fully in many forms of Catholic Action already functioning, or in creating new developments when and where such seem to be needed."[4]

The Commonweal did, however, take up some specific problems of the layman. One of these was the question of some measure of security for those laymen who had staked their whole career on lay service to the Church. For example, what security, they asked, did a professor in a Catholic college have? With no other job in prospect, "a little note from the authorities" could effectively land him in the poorhouse. "You can make a gifted but inconvenient priest a bishop of Timbuctoo," they commented, "but apparently the only thing that can happen to a layman is more or less graceful obsolescence and starvation." The editorial, written by George Shuster, then related the fate of Friedrich Dessauer:

> In the turbulent Germany of our time [1935], no man stood out as more selflessly devoted to the social and religious mission of the Church than Professor Friedrich Dessauer, the last remnants of whose fortune have just been confiscated by the Nazis. By reason of his zealous advocacy of the peace encyclicals, Dessauer—one of the great medical specialists of our time—suffered about all that persecution had to offer, excepting death. But when he had to live in exile and seek a new field of activity, was it any Catholic organization which, as a tribute to his life-long devotion came to the rescue? No, indeed. It was the government of his majesty, the Sultan of Turkey.

What Catholic organization in the United States, asked Shuster, even knew where Heinrich Bruening was? The problem of the layman in the Church, wrote Shuster, could not be solved in a day, but it could at least be referred to. He concluded:

> Nobody has any right to expect that those who labor for the Church ought suddenly to look and live like stockbrokers in the days of yore, forgetting even that theirs is a cross to carry. But they cannot function either if their function is that of tramps who have been given a morning's employment. Or is that really the point? Is it not, rather, that good-will should abound among brethren?[5]

In other matters touching in some way the problem of the Catholic layman, *The Commonweal* served as a forum for a discussion of the quality of sermons—a topic on which they received letters for almost a year, until they finally called a halt. They also tried to emphasize the role of the layman in the liturgical movement through the publication of articles by Virgil Michel and others. In 1936, they published an article praising the nineteenth-century Bishop John England of Charleston for his diocesan constitution with its strong representative role for the layman. There is really nothing, however, in these 1924–38 years that could be called anticlerical in the pages of *The Commonweal*.[6]

The Spanish Civil War

The Spanish Civil War has been referred to as that "tragic prelude" to World War II in which Hitler played only a secondary part, while the chief actors and sufferers were the Spanish themselves.[1] It was a fascinating and grim struggle that had a remarkable ability to divide people in their evaluation of it, and even today there are differences concerning who was right and who was wrong—something that few wars clarify. It is clear that the war resulted in a defeat for democratic values. Britain, France, and the United States showed a vacillating attitude which did not significantly influence the affair, while the Fascist forces—Franco, Italy, and Germany—stood strong and united.

American Catholics were not divided by the war along the same lines as were most Americans, a majority of whom supported the Popular Front. The violent anticlericalism evidenced early in the conflict, plus later on the aid of Moscow to the Popular Front, settled the question in favor of Franco for most Catholic church officials and publications, almost all of which were either under Church control, or were sponsored by religious orders, the editors of which had Spanish confreres who had suffered loss of life or property. Polls, however, showed that four out of ten Catholics supported the Popular Front.[2] *The Commonweal* for various reasons became divided by the question to the point of it becoming a transitional point in its history, from which a newly constituted magazine emerged.

In July, 1936, the eruption of the Spanish Civil War brought horrors of destruction and violence to that country. It is reliably estimated that within the first month of the war, nearly one hundred thousand people were murdered by the forces of the Right and Left. Thousands of priests and nuns lost their lives, often amid the cruelties and atrocities of what may stand as the most passionately expressed hatred of religion and all its works the world has seen.[3] The causes of the war were in the working class movement which came late to Spain; the growing demand for autonomy in the Basque provinces and Catalonia; the strong surge of anticlericalism attacking church wealth and power (according to popular rumor, the Jesuits alone controlled one-third of the capital of the country); and the hypocrisy of the spiritual front with which many Spanish workers felt churchmen endowed the affluent and power-holding class.

The immediate context of the outbreak of the war was in the deteriorating order in society which followed the narrow Popular Front victory in the elections of February, 1936. Throughout the spring of 1936 the extreme left parties in the Popular Front drove toward social revolution, as land seizures, revolutionary strikes, and murder became daily occurrences and outrages against clergy and churches were frequent. In July, following an exchange of murders of highly placed political and military figures both by the Falangists (Spanish Fascists), and extreme left groups, the war began from a military standpoint on the 17th with the revolt of an important garrison of troops in Spanish Morocco and the arrival of General Francisco Franco from the Canary Islands to take command.

A few days after the outbreak of the war (July, 1936), Father Francis X. Talbot, SJ, editor of *America*, called a meeting of New York's Catholic journalists to determine what common editorial position, if any, could be taken.[4] At the meeting which was attended by an agent of Franco's junta, George Shuster urged that they study the situation carefully, and that Gil Robles who had headed the Catholic party in Spain and who had sought a haven in Portugal, be invited to confer with them. Shuster recalled a clear impression "that this suggestion had been endorsed, but it soon became obvious that it had not. Many were far beyond needing any advice."

America's first commentary on the Spanish situation, far from being searching or tentative, placed it strongly in support of Franco and the insurgent legions. "Whatever the nature and the policies of the government that would be established after a victory of the Right army, they could not possibly lead to greater disaster than those already perpetrated by the Red Government now in control. . . ." If, on the other hand, the Madrid government were to achieve victory, it "would not stop until the whole of Spain was Sovietized."[5]

The earliest *Commonweal* comment expressed the hope that the "nightmarish incident" would pass, and stressed the root problem of social justice for Spanish peasantry and proletarians, "a uniquely depressed lot." With the violence continuing, a succeeding issue offered a more detailed appraisal. It pointed out that relations between Church and society in Spain had not been simple, with efforts for social reform consistently defeated as "right and wrong were too cleverly mixed, as is so often the case in lands where the state has rendered age-old lip service to the Church and vice versa." The editorial held that there was no reason for stridently applauding the rebels under Franco. The victory of Spanish Fascism would produce the antithesis of the radical social change needed. Superficially, it would oppose anticlericalism, "because Fascism is traditionalistic and there is only Catholic tradition in Spain," but it would not liberate creative Catholic social energies that had struggled to emerge during hundreds of years.[6]

The editorial produced a strong reaction, but not as great as did events which began in March, 1937, with the magazine's publication of "European Catholics and Spain," by Barbara Barclay Carter, who was closely identified with Catholic lay leadership in Great Britain. It spoke against those who presented Franco's cause as a "holy war" and reported a recent protest signed by nine eminent Spanish Catholics against the barbarity of the war and especially against the ruthless bombardment of Madrid by the Francoites. She pointed to the fervent Catholics of the Basque provinces, supporters of the Popular Front, and gave a sampling of recent articles in Catholic journals in England, France, and Switzerland, holding a condemnation for both sides and an opinion that the triumph of the Fascists would not be for the greater good of religion. The article aroused a great furor, and attacks on it were numerous and vociferous.[7]

On April 2, 1937, George Shuster published an article in *The Commonweal* entitled "Some Reflections on Spain." The article was prefaced with a note by editor Michael Williams which said that he wished to "express my agreement with Mr. Shuster's views concerning the Spanish situation after making one reservation, namely, that I believe facts are producible which prove that Communism and Anarchism played a far greater part in provoking the revolt led by General Franco than his article shows. . . ." As Shuster has recalled, "This amiable pat on the back was to cause him a lot of grief in the days that ensued."[8]

The article was an endeavor to answer criticisms of *The Commonweal*, particularly those which had been directed at the publication of "European Catholics and Spain" by Barbara Barclay Carter. The article was a summary of pro-Franco sentiment among U.S. Catholics, and a critique of it. The summary portion stated:

> A republican government fell under the sway of Communists who began to perform every kind of injustice; and thereupon some fine old soldiers rallied all stanch Catholics to safeguard religious and

national rights against tyranny. This act of rebellion was legitimate, since the government overthrown was elected through fraud and was later guilty of violating the Constitution. If General Franco had waited another month, all the priests and religious in Spain would have been shot. Proof of this is found in the fact that hundreds have been massacred wherever the Reds have gained control. Catholics everywhere ought, therefore, to support the Insurgent cause and to hope for the speedy destruction of all Marxists. Of course a few benighted persons have ventured to differ from these conclusions. But it can easily be shown that they are tainted with "liberalism," or guilty of French patriotic emotions, or singularly unfamiliar with logic or moral theology.

The critique portion held that while this analysis was in part correct, it suffered from three major faults. The first was that a great many unimpeachable Catholics did not believe all of it, nor were they guilty of "French patriotic emotions." Veteran journals in France, Austria, Switzerland, and Germany were critical of the Franco movement as a champion of religion and culture, and all pointed out that no authoritative verdict on the situation was available, and that evil had clearly been done on both sides. Shuster indicted simplistic analyses on both left and right. In a comment on a statement issued by ninety-two American writers supporting the republican regime, Shuster stated:

> Perhaps only in America are there many naive enough to believe that the present Valencia government is anything much better than an aggregation of oratorical mortals trying to get the bull populace to see something besides a red flag. It is shocking to think that ninety-two writers—no matter how idealistic and intelligent—could be found in and about New York to underwrite what honest French radicals have repudiated in their journals.

In comment on the apparently official Catholic opinion of support for Franco, however, Shuster added:

> But shall we also be obliged to witness the equally shocking fact that Catholics are ready to ignore the manifest brutality, reactionary political method and intellectual simplicity of the Francoites? No history of the blunders of the Insurgents need be written. It must suffice to declare that the person who set the wheels in motion to grind out propaganda for Franco as the saviour of religion and culture was that eminent defender of the faith, Herr Goebbels.

The second point in Shuster's critique pointed out that the present dilemma was whether the Church should again live under the thumb of a reactionary, militarist regime? Was such a policy, historically responsible for a decline of faith, to be relied upon now as a missionary enterprise? While one could reasonably argue, said Shuster, that a fascist state in Spain might be induced to give some guarantees and liberties, one could also argue that in the end a sufficient peace might be made with the republic to ensure at least a modicum of religious and cultural freedom. This view, he stated, was as deserving of a fair presentation as the other.

Shuster's third point of critique was that the pro-Franco view failed to consider adequately "all the shadows which fall upon the scene from without." Questions to be asked were: Why had Mussolini been induced to strike the bargain with Franco at the start of the insurgent uprising? What kind of pact was it, and what were the ultimate objectives the bargainers had in mind? Why was it that little by little Germany was drawn into the fray and great efforts were made to get people used to believing that the Hitler-Mussolini combination was saving Europe from Bolshevism?

> Perhaps there are people who do not find all this a hoax. But they ought at least to explain why it is that a dictator who places Herr Rosenberg in the saddle in order to destroy the Catholic Church in Germany feels it his duty to sacrifice men and money in order to save that Church in Spain.

The week which followed the publication of the article was a nightmare for Shuster. The criticism which had followed *The Commonweal* campaign against U.S. participation in the 1936 Olympic games in Berlin had been severe, including threats against life, but the onslaught that followed the publication of "Some Reflections on Spain" was a different kind of thing. Shuster's parish priest in Glenbrook, Connecticut, a good friend, called him in amazement to say that New York's Chancery Office had telephoned to inquire whether he went to Mass on Sunday. Much denunciatory mail poured in to *The Commonweal*, though the mail also included a letter from Van Wyck Brooks, a leader in the statement by ninety-two writers, in which he said he regretted his earlier statement and agreed with Shuster's analysis. Shuster has recalled that this was one of the very few pleasant things that came his way in the aftermath of "Some Reflections." The general situation, however, was now starkly revealed to him: "It now dawned on me that for Catholic New York the world outside the United States was either Communist or Fascist and that therefore they had opted for Fascism."[9]

What Shuster has recalled as being in many ways "the unkindest blow of all" was Father Francis X. Talbot's "Answer" to "Reflections" which appeared as the lead article in *America* on April 10, 1937. Shuster had assumed that until the Catholic editors had their meeting with Gil Robles, which incidentally was never held, they were on their own regarding their attitude and were in no way violating the agreement they had entered into in their meeting. Father Talbot saw things differently.

The "Answer" article seems to have been a collective effort, and in Shuster's opinion, "expressed the solidly united opinion of the Archdiocese of New York." The article stated that the "propagandists," that is, the writers who had signed the manifesto against Franco, had sought to split the "corporate influence of Catholicism" and that with the appearance of Shuster's article it appeared that the editors of *Commonweal* had fallen into their "snares" and a breach in the "corporate" position was opened. The "corporate position" in Talbot's view was world-wide. He stated that Catholic periodicals in France, "with the exception of a few terrorized by Hitler fear," the major Catholic papers of Great Britain and Ireland, and every Catholic publication in the U.S. "with the exception of *The Commonweal* and one or two minor sheets"[10] had put their "faith" in the nationalist "movement" as against the communist "aggression" in Spain. Shuster made a "poor impression" on Talbot by saying "the person who set the wheels to grinding out propaganda for Franco as the saviour of religion and culture was that eminent defender of the Faith, Dr. Goebbels." That phrase, Shuster has recalled with some wryness, "was quoted from a letter written by one of his fellow Jesuits at the Vatican."[11]

The key element in the Talbot attack, however, was in the following paragraph:

> I believe that Mr. Shuster's stand against Nazism and Fascism is to be commended. But I rather believe that his preoccupation with them is clouding his vision of that other more dangerous form of the totalitarian state, Moscowism. But why does he assume, and rabidly, that General Franco is a Fascist and committed to Fascism? Franco never was a Fascist, and I judge that he never will be.

Shuster responded to the Talbot article with an essay that was his swan song as managing editor of *The Commonweal*.[12] In brief summary, the article affirmed that what was happening in Spain was a great tragedy rather than any victorious crusade. Conservative people, it maintained, frequently failed to see what they were doing when they ignored the evident perils of a fascist state on the ground that it was after all preferable to communism.

With the help of swarms of Moors, 150,000 Italians and as many Germans as can be packed into Bremen, the "march on Madrid" is being carried on. But: the condition of labor is worse in Spain than it is anywhere else in Europe, and it is assumed that Catholicism (for the first time) is backing the other side. These things mean that if the Fascist state wins out, the cleavages will be extraordinarily great, and (automatically) that antipathy to the Church will grow.

Another passage from the article should be noted for its prophetic character:

One has only to look around and see that Fascism is rapidly being converted into what has been termed National Bolshevism. In Germany for example, a system is coming into being which differs so little from "Moscowism" that the eventual alliance between the two states is no longer the fear of just a few dreamy mortals. The fourth partition of Poland has ceased to be a mirage. Very probably a large number of Nazis wish no such development. It is merely the inevitable finale of their system. The most elemental moral principles are discarded. A deep and bitter social antagonism is engendered. War for war's sake gradually becomes the only reliable recipe. In short there remains of Christian eithics less than enough to press between the pages of a book.

It was, indeed, the Stalin-Hitler Pact and the partition of Poland which made many Catholics take a more critical look at the world situation. While the pact shocked American Communists and their supporters, it had an equally marked impact on the thinking of American Catholics who, as Shuster has stated, "had preferred one system of totalitarianism to the other."[13]

The Commonweal in Transition

To explain how the article was Shuster's swan song, we must shift our spotlight to editor Michael Williams and the rather perilous state of *The Commonweal*'s condition at this point. Circulation stood at about fifteen thousand, but the continuing problem of adequate financial resources was severe. Just a week before the publication of Shuster's finale, a *Commonweal* editorial had announced that the assistance of Mr. Joseph P. Kennedy had been secured to sponsor a plan for the adequate financing of *The Commonweal*, and that "already steps have been taken to bring it to the attention of our numerous well-wishers."[1] Throughout its history, the magazine had been dependent upon such "well-wishers" as circulation and advertising had never been sufficient to sustain it, but now in the midst of the Depression, it was perhaps particularly dependent on them.

The magazine had taken a position in the Shuster articles which was very unpopular with the Catholic establishment, especially in New York, the home of a number of financial supporters, and the diocese in which it operated. A very influential journal, it was now suffering an onslaught of abuse stronger than at any other time in its history. Also, it was quite isolated, holding a point of view shared among national Catholic publications only by the *Catholic Worker*, the pacifist newspaper of Dorothy Day and Peter Maurin. It was hardly a good time for a new fund-raising campaign, but money had to be obtained. The demise of *The Commonweal* was quite possibly at hand. Weighing the various factors, as well as his own partial reservations on the Shuster view of the Franco affair, Williams, whom Shuster recalls warmly as "a marvelous combination of pragmatism and morality,"[2] decided that the magazine would come out strongly and unmistakably for Franco and do so with all the public relations expertise and gusto he could command, which was considerable. Shuster, for his part, felt he could not remain with the magazine if Williams insisted on the demand for editorial reversal. Thus, though he had envisioned a lifetime career with *The Commonweal*, Shuster for reasons of intellectual integrity left his position as managing editor. He exited with a generous fellowship for study in Europe from Columbia University and the Social Science Research Council, and would go on to a career as president of Hunter College, a post-World War II military governorship in Germany, and, after his retirement at Hunter in 1959, a position as assistant to the president of Notre Dame.

Meanwhile, Michael Williams was pulling out all of the stops. On April 30, 1937, he published a long lead editorial supporting the Catholic Charities Appeal of the archdiocese of New York, replete with generous quotations from Cardinal Hayes. The May 7 issue announced that a new organization, *The Commonweal* Spanish Relief Fund, would hold a mass meeting and rally in Madison Square Garden on May 19. The issue also contained a lengthy "Open Letter to Leaders of the American Press, On Spain" by Michael Williams. An accompanying editorial note added that the "Open Letter" had been sent to "several hundred" key editorial and news service individuals throughout the country, and had been given in a condensed form to news agencies supplying material to the religious press. The article complained of a "deplorably one sided—and therefore a false

—picture of the situation in Spain" which he felt prevailed in the press. The *Nation* and the *New Republic* were denounced by name, as were the Scripps-Howard papers.

The lead editorial in *The Commonweal* for May 14 announced that forces preparing for the May 19 rally had been merged and were now under the name of the American Committee for Spanish Relief. The magazine contained a processional hymn of thirty-four stanzas which Williams composed to be sung by "Father Finn's chorus of one thousand voices" during the "Pageant of Spain's Sacrifice" at the mass meeting. The hymn traced the history of Spain and on the current situation intoned:

> Now again over Spain,
> Hangs the Hammer of Hell,
> And the Sickle of the Bolshevik,
> And the Anarch's evil spell.
>
> Ave! Ave! Ave! Jesus Christ!
> Ave! Ave! God scourges Spain!

Commonweal's issue of May 21 continued the barrage with "Open Letter to the Press: No. 2," which challenged a press report on a speech which Williams had given in Philadelphia on the Spanish situation. He denied a reporter's published allegation that he had changed his former stand on the affair and threatened legal action unless there was a retraction. The letter also charged a distortion of his views by the *New York Evening Post*, whose publisher he challenged to an open debate at the Garden Rally, with a wager of $1,000 that he would win. He suggested a list of prominent journalists from among whom a judge and jury could be chosen. A contributed article in the same issue claimed that "an immense majority in Spain is with Franco."[3]

The assault in the pages of *The Commonweal* reached a climax in the issue of May 28, the lead editorial for which was written the day of the rally, May 19. "Open Letter to the Press: No. 3" was addressed by Michael Williams to H. L. Mencken, for whom he had a high regard. In essence, it asked Mencken's help and influence in changing the biased views of the American press. It contained the following postscript:

P. S. As I write (12 o'clock, noon, May 19, the day of the Mass Meeting for Spanish Relief in Madison Square Garden, New York), some twenty members of a group calling itself the "Spanish Anti-

Fascist Committee" . . . are picketing the offices of *The Commonweal*, as a protest against the action of the Editor, myself, in planning and directing the Mass Meeting of tonight under the auspices of the American Committee for Spanish Relief, of which I am secretary-general, in cooperation with the American Association against Communism.

Under hysterical slogans printed on banners, the demonstrators are loudly denouncing *The Commonweal* as they parade in front of the office building at 386 Fourth Avenue. . . .

Williams complained of such groups showering the Catholic churches of New York with pamphlets and again issued a challenge for a debate, saying that he would post any amount up to $1,000 of his own money to guarantee the hiring of a hall or the purchase of radio time.

The rally proved to be something of a disaster, both in itself and in its effect on Michael Williams. Edward Skillin has recalled that Williams, who had been working at a high emotional pitch toward the event, was tremendously let down and was never again quite the same person.

As a spectacle, it was up to Williams's imaginative standards. Speakers included Allison Peers, author of *The Spanish Tragedy*, Father Bernard Grimley, editor of the London *Catholic Times*, Michael Williams himself (no debaters appeared), and Father Edward Lodge Curran, president of the American Association against Communism, who was an associate of the "radio priest" Father Charles Coughlin. "Democracy Imperiled: A Spanish Pageant" conceived by Father Leonard Feeney, SJ, was enacted by players of Father Conrad's "Veronica's Veil" Company, and, of course, a huge combined choir under the direction of Father Finn, the Paulist, sang the hymn the *Commonweal* editor had composed for the occasion.

Commonweal's published report on the affair indicated "a capacity audience," but Edward Skillin has recalled a sparse crowd, and Father H. A. Reinhold who attended the rally with *Commonweal* staff member Philip Burnham has recorded it in his autobiography as "a wild affair, as entertaining as a circus, yet the Garden was only half filled."[4]

Previous to the Garden Rally, while plans for it were being promulgated, Professor Carlton Hayes had voiced to Michael Williams his personal objections to his "unauthorized association of *The Commonweal* and the Calvert Associates with the pro-Franco mass meeting in Madison Square Garden." Hayes requested that his name be withdrawn from the editorial council of the paper and from the board of directors of the Calvert Associates as a protest against what he considered Williams's "high-handed" action. It seems that Williams promptly heeded Hayes's objections for before the Madison Square demonstration he had already ceased to announce its sponsorship by *The Commonweal* or by the Calvert Associates. On the other hand, it may be that this was more a product of Williams's having succeeded in affiliating other groups with the promotion. One recalls here that by rally time Williams had become secretary general of the American Fund for Spanish Relief. Hayes, however, felt his protest had to some degree been heeded.[5]

On the afternoon of Friday, June 11, 1937, a meeting of some members of the editorial council of *The Commonweal* and of the board of directors of the Calvert Associates was held in the office of *The Commonweal*. Williams felt the meeting was called primarily by Hayes and with the concurrence of Father Lawrason Riggs to discuss Hayes's objections.[6] Hayes has denied calling the meeting.[7] Business manager John McCormick sent notice of the meeting, which was standard procedure.

Those present at the meeting were Monsignor John Ryan, Father Riggs, Professor Hayes, John McCormick, Bancel La Farge, Professor Karl Herzfeld, Dana Skinner, Grenville Vernon, Thomas Woodlock, John J. O'Connor, the new acting managing editor, and Michael Williams.

As a result of the discussion which lasted from 5:30 to 7:00 P.M., when it had to be concluded because Williams was obliged to give a scheduled broadcast address, it was decided to adjourn the meeting to the evening of Wednesday, June 16. At this meeting the question of whether or not Hayes would withdraw his resignation was to be decided by him, and Father Riggs was to express his opinion as to the desirability of holding a regular monthly meeting of the editorial council in order that the editor "might be better guided" by the opinions of the members of the council and of the members of the board of directors than had been the case up to that time.

On Wednesday, June 16, when Williams reached the office of *The Commonweal* a few minutes past eight, he found that a meeting of certain members of the editorial council and the board of directors was in session, and on entering the room was informed that it was an executive meeting from which members of the staff were excluded. Retiring to his own office, he was summoned at 10 o'clock and handed a copy of a communication which ran as follows:

The majority of the members of the Board of Directors and of the Editorial Council consulted recognize very deeply the meritorious service which you have given for many years to _The Commonweal_, but feel distinct misgivings about the rather arbitrary manner of management and the financial situation of _The Commonweal_. In their opinion, it would be to the advantage of the paper if you would retire from the editorship for the present without any commitments for the future. If financially possible, they would like to continue paying part of your salary at least for several months.

Williams was asked to take up discussion of the document with those present, but responded that for a decision of such grave importance he wanted time for consideration and consultation. Monsignor Ryan expressed the view that this was an entirely reasonable statement and the meeting adjourned without motion or further deliberation.

One week later, June 23, Williams sent a letter to all of those who had been at the meetings. He asked for more information than had been provided by the "anonymous" communication above. Were all the members of the editorial council and the board of directors consulted by those who wanted him to resign "without commitments as to the future and with no guarantee as to salary, or as to the conduct of the editorial policy" of the paper in his absence, a point he considered "of paramount importance." Furthermore, he wanted specifics as to what they had called "the rather arbitrary manner of management and the financial situation of _The Commonweal_." Concerning editorial policy, he asked, "On what points am I criticized, or, rather, condemned?" The financial situation was bad, but how far was it just to attribute blame for this to him? On such points, he said he had decided views which, whether right or wrong, he felt in justice he should be permitted to express before those concerned, including "the general membership of the Calvert Associates" before he could resign even temporarily his position. He closed by asking for a meeting of the entire membership of the board of directors with provision made for those who could not get to the meeting to be informed of the issues and asked for their vote by mail or telegraph. He reminded them that on more than one occasion he had previously expressed his readiness to resign as editor if a majority of the board of directors gave good cause for such a request or demand, but added that he did not consider that "the ambiguous communiction handed to me after a meeting from which I was excluded represents a position which I can properly meet save by a request for further and more definite information." A final paragraph spoke of a plan on his part, "already partly formed" which could be worked out offering a satisfactory solution as to the present situation.

What Williams's plan was is unknown, though it may have had principally to do with the financial situation and specifically with the cooperation of Joseph P. Kennedy and Judge Burns in raising funds for the magazine by sending a letter seeking support for the magazine to a number of people of liberal views, many of whom had never been reached before in campaigns for financial support for the paper.[8]

Whatever Williams's plan was, it seems it was never presented, as the *coup de grace* seems to have been administered to him by a circular letter sent in response to his letter of June 23, by Carlton Hayes.[9] Hayes denied that the Madison Square Garden incident was *the* cause of his critical attitude toward Williams's conduct of *The Commonweal*. Rather, it was "only one of a series of regrettable incidents, which have gradually borne in upon me the conviction that you are too ill a man to pilot alone such an important ship as *The Commonweal* and to keep it on an even keel." The word "alone" is probably significant here in Hayes's assessment, as it must be remembered that the departure of George Shuster, who had borne the major responsibility for the conduct of the journal, especially during Williams's frequent and at times extended absences from *The Commonweal* office, had placed greatly increased responsibilities upon Williams's shoulders, even though he had hired John J. O'Connor, a history professor at St. John's University, as acting managing editor.

> I must say, quite frankly, that I was inexpressibly shocked, as many intelligent non-Catholics were scandalized, by your drunken behavior at the Williamstown Conference two years ago, and that I was even more shocked (if possible) by the story told me by a very fine Catholic woman of your conduct on shipboard while returning from the pilgrimage you had led to Rome. I cite these distressing incidents (and you know there are many others of the same sort), neither for moral nor for personal ends (I would be the last one to pass moral judgment on anyone), but simply because they are clear signs of a physical ailment which, I feel sure, has had (and increasingly has) most deleterious effects upon both the policies and the finances of *The Commonweal*. It is highly important for the paper and above all for yourself, that you should devote major attention to curing the ailment rather than attempting to preside over *The Commonweal*.

This was the reason, stated Hayes, why he concurred in the action requesting his retirement as editor. He expressed the hope that Williams would not appeal to the general membership of the Calvert

Associates as had been hinted, as *The Commonweal* was in a precarious situation and "any washing of dirty linen in public will be sure to ruin and destroy it."

> Most members of the Board know as well as you and I know the real reason why you should retire from the editorship, but none of us wishes to explain it to the general public or even to a limited public.

Williams was urged to "face realities and accept the advice of your friends." On the other hand, Hayes stated that neither he nor in all probability other members of the board would enter into a fight to force him from the editorship should he choose to cling to it, but clinging to it would sacrifice present support and weaken *The Commonweal*. He suggested that business manager John McCormick be entrusted by the board with dictatorial powers, that he constitute a small advisory committee on finance and personnel, that they name an acting editor, and that Williams be engaged as a contributing editor, whereby he would continue to do some writing for a stated regular stipend. Hayes closed with a personal comment and an observation about the founding editor's work.

> I have written very frankly. I may have hurt you and if so I am very sorry. I have tried to write as my conscience and reason dictated.
>
> You should know that I have only the greatest admiration and respect for the heroic work you did in establishing *The Commonweal* and for the many brilliant constructive contributions you have made to it since that time. It is only because I have a real devotion to the ideal you have set before the paper and because the paper itself is well worth saving and perfecting that I have ventured to write so frankly.

In the face of this letter and appeal Michael Williams cooperated and the Hayes suggestions were followed almost to the letter, though Williams's name remained listed as editor for another nine months until John McCormick had come up with a satisfactory change.

It is clear that Michael Williams had some rather serious emotional and physical problems—and his alcoholism. But there is evidence that his difficulties on this score were well-known during the entire fourteen years he had been working for *The Commonweal* and that there was no more intrinsic reason to be afraid of them then than there had been five or even ten years previously.[10] Two factors, however, made the situation different. First, George Shuster was no longer with the magazine, and with his departure had gone the assurance that pretty much no matter what Michael Williams might do, or perhaps more pertinently, might not do, the magazine would function intelligently and wisely. This could no longer be counted on. Second, *The Commonweal*'s editorial handling of recent issues had managed to offend simultaneously both liberal and conservative camps, giving virtually everyone some grievance. Thus, when Williams's editorial supporting the "court packing" plan appeared, Al Smith called him up to, in Dana Skinner's words, "put on the heat," and *Commonweal* director Thomas Woodlock was also offended. When a year previously Michael Williams had offered to resign, Woodlock dismissed the idea as absurd, but since the Supreme Court editorial and in spite of his approval of the Spanish stand, Woodlock ceased to regard the proposed resignation as absurd. The liberal side had been offended by the way the editor had started out on his Spanish crusade. Thus Professor Hayes did not want to be identified with any militant support of Franco, and Mr. Woodlock did not care to be identified with any support of Roosevelt's Supreme Court proposal.[11]

However much one cares to weight some of these other issues, it does seem clear that all parties had a sincere concern for Michael Williams that was operatively present in their decision. He exited as the premier Catholic journalist and as one who had brought a remarkable assemblage of talents to his task. He was a first-class reporter and journalist, an acclaimed lecturer, an accomplished fundraiser, confidant and adviser to bishops, politicians, and others, and perhaps most of all a conceiver and executor of endless projects, all effected with a remarkable flair for symbol and drama. As special editor, he contributed a column of "Views and Reviews" for several years, before giving it up. After a lengthy illness, he died in Westport, Connecticut, on October 12, 1950, at the age of seventy-three. The man who in his travels had gone from his home in Nova Scotia to a newspaper career in Boston, New York, and San Francisco, to Upton Sinclair's utopian colony, to a Catholic journalistic career which had him leading Te Deums on more than one occasion in St. Patrick's Cathedral, was buried quietly, attended by no bishop or politician, nor indeed by his colleagues in the Catholic press save Father James Gillis of the *Catholic World* and members past and present of the *Commonweal* staff.

II. THROUGH IMMIGRANT CATHOLIC COMING OF AGE: THE COMMONWEAL, 1938–59

The New Commonweal

The departure of George Shuster and the termination of the editorship of Michael Williams mark the end of the first major period in the history of *The Commonweal*. During that period, the Catholicism which *The Commonweal* and its staff represented was essentially an assimilated and upper class Anglo-American Catholicism, having its roots ultimately in some of the founding Maryland families. Thomas McAvoy has maintained that the continued existence and growth of the Anglo-American Catholic group in the larger Catholic group is the chief connecting link between the history of the Catholic immigrant and that of the native Protestant and is the basic element in a distinctive American Catholic culture.[1] This element was strong in the origins of *The Commonweal* and thus offers some corroboration for McAvoy's thesis. Backers of the project were not infrequently members of a recently dubbed group of Papal Knights of Malta, the first in the United States. One of George Shuster's first tasks at *Commonweal* was the research and preparation of a special brochure on the Knights. *The Commonweal* was also heavily Ivy League. There had been discussion in Harvard circles for the founding of a journal like *The Commonweal*, and when Michael Williams came along in his organizing and fund-raising tour between 1922–24, co-operation was given to him. Members of the early editorial council were almost all of an Ivy League background with Harvard, Yale, and Princeton predominating. George Shuster was from a Catholic college, Notre Dame, but was receiving his doctorate from Columbia. The unique Michael Williams, a maverick genius, was a graduate of no college.

John McCormick, in his search for an answer to the editorial and financial difficulties of *The Commonweal*, tried to organize what Edward Skillin recalls as a "conservative" group to take over the magazine, with New York publisher Martin Quigley as one of the chief financial backers.[2] There were also negotiations with Professor Ross J. S. Hoffman about becoming editor of the magazine. On November 18, 1937, Carlton Hayes wrote Father Riggs that Hoffman "seemed *much* interested"—and that he was "pretty sure he would accept the Editorship at least for a trial year if the salary could be guaranteed him." He added, that "young Burnham and Skillin are eager to have Harry Binsse as Editor" but that he doubted whether that would solve the financial problem.[3] Hayes, Riggs, and McCormick seem to have been the principals in effecting the transition of the magazine. The situation, however, was quite unstructured and the powers of the editorial council were vague. One wonders why Riggs didn't assume financial control. His wealth, derived from his family's financial holdings in Washington, was great. Perhaps he thought it unseemly for a cleric to hold financial control of this lay operation, or perhaps he was simply not that interested. Ross Hoffman, a distinguished professor of modern European history, was at New York University at this time, but had become a Catholic convert and would shortly move to Fordham.

Meanwhile, during the fall of 1937, Edward Skillin, Philip Burnham, Harry Binsse, and a group of lay professors at Fordham including William O'Meara, James Vaughan, and Harry McNeill were meeting a couple of times a month, wringing their hands about the Catholic press on a number of issues, but especially the Spanish War. Skillin has stated that they were going to issue a "manifesto," had various chapters assigned, and were starting to figure out the cost of printing five thousand copies, when Harry McNeill suggested that it would be better to obtain control of *The Commonweal* and to show what a Catholic journal should be.

All were enthusiastic about the idea, and Burnham and Skillin approached John McCormick who seems to have been unsuccessful in working out the magazine's financial difficulties sufficiently, to conclude arrangements with Ross Hoffman for the editorship.[4] The two young men then met Carlton Hayes at an inn midway between New York City and the Hayes farm in Afton, had dinner, discussed the matter with Hayes and his wife, and received the professor's blessing.

The Commonweal owed a total of $30,000 to three major creditors: the paper supplier, the printer, and the landlord. They made an agreement with these that they would give them their trade and pay on a thirty-day basis, and the creditors settled for 30¢ on the dollar. The magazine was thus purchased for $9,000. Stock was sold in the magazine to get up enough funds, but 85 percent of the stock was held by Philip Burnham and Edward Skillin.[5]

Burnham at twenty-seven was the younger of the two. Born of a wealthy Illinois family, he had been educated at the Canterbury School and Princeton, and following graduation in 1931 took a position with the Illinois Emergency Relief Commission for two years, before being hired by George Shuster to work for *The Commonweal* in 1933. Skillin, six years older than Burnham, was hired by Shuster at the same time. Both Burnham and Skillin were Phi Beta Kappa. Skillin, while not as wealthy as Burnham, was financially comfortable. A native of New York, he was raised a Catholic after his mother's death by his Protestant and somewhat anti-Catholic father. Though he was accepted in Yale at sixteen, his father sent him to Philips Academy for an extra year of prep school and maturity, from which he decided to attend Williams College, graduating in 1925. Following this, he worked for Henry Holt publishers for seven years, and in addition obtained an M.A. from Columbia in political science, before coming to *The Commonweal*.

Burnham and Skillin were socially and culturally in continuity with the earlier *Commonweal* period, but were a generation removed from it, and with their youth, contacts, and concerns would bring the magazine to a position where it expressed a Catholicism more of a "grass roots" than an elite quality. In this development, they were to a large degree reflecting the growing maturity of American Catholicism itself, which by 1938 was a good bit removed from the more immigrant character it had had at the magazine's beginning in 1924. Joining them in this venture as their managing editor was Harry Lorin Binsse, who had attended Williams for two years while Skillin was there, but then switched to Harvard, graduating *magna cum laude* in 1926. Since 1931 he had been the managing editor of *Liturgical Arts* and the executive secretary of the Liturgical Arts Society. A relative of the LaFarge family, he was not, however, wealthy. A generous person, he at one point in life adopted all four children of deceased friends rather than see their family broken up.

Philip Burnham, Edward Skillin, and Harry Binsse were then the new stewards of *The Commonweal*. Michael Williams, listed as special editor, could say what he chose in his "Views and Reviews" column, but was no longer active beyond that in the magazine. There had never been much communication between Williams and the two junior members of the staff, Burnham and Skillin, who "lived in a world apart" as Skillin has recalled.[6] Williams had dealt with George Shuster and John McCormick, but that was it.

The new *Commonweal* emerged in April, 1938, but was much the same in format and conception. They reaffirmed the editorial of the first issue of *The Commonweal* from 1924 that the magazine was "not the organ of any political party or of any single school of economic or social theory," nor was it "an authoritative or authorized mouthpiece of the Catholic Church." It was simply "the effort of a group of American Catholics to observe affairs and opinions about affairs." In addition to the small staff, some nineteen contributing editors were announced, names that were familiar to regular readers of *The Commonweal*, and also included some members of the Fordham discussion group. Two months later, the names of George N. Shuster and Carlton J. H. Hayes, who had each been traveling in Europe, were added to the list.[7]

The first issue published under the new management included "Terror in Vienna," an article which Shuster wrote as a witness of the entrance of the Nazis to that city. He was there when Cardinal Innitzer had the bells of St. Stephen's Cathedral ring out in welcome as Hitler entered Vienna, and wrote: "I do not wish to judge harshly, but I doubt whether in all history there is a more shameless incident. It was for many of my acquaintances who sensed the full moral ignominy of what was happening round about, just as if Christ had really made a pact with Satan in the hour of temptation." The situation was the result, said Shuster, of Hitlerism and a certain "National Catholicism." Just as certain extremist Catholics had turned much too far to the Left under the impact of communism after World War I, so now others had moved to the Right without reservations "under the spell of chauvinism and Hitlerism." American Catholics, he observed, should learn a lesson from the experience in Vienna, so that at least any possible emergence to victory of destructive forces in this country would not come "through the Catholic gate."[8]

The article was not well-received by Archbishop John T. McNicholas of Cincinnati. McNicholas, a Dominican, was in many ways a rather enlightened man, but one thing he couldn't stand, recalled Skillin, was any criticism of the hierarchy. "When this [the article] came out, his Chancellor wrote us and said if you ever do anything like this again, steps will be taken." Sure enough, another grievance was found some two months later when at long last the new editors finally got to publish their statement on the civil war in Spain and the lessons to be learned from it by Americans. Their position was one of "positive impartiality," which they defined as "a search for the right, unblinded by that passionate partizanship which simplifies the problems that confront us to the dimensions of a slogan, and claims the right as the complete and exclusive possession of one warring party." Americans should try for a "sanity of judgment" based on specific actions and should cease labeling everything they don't like whether in Spain or America as either "fascist" or "communist." This time, a letter from McNicholas's chancellor told them that from now on their magazine couldn't be sold in the back of the churches in the archdiocese of Cincinnati. This was not a great loss, however, as only one or two churches sold it anyway. Furthermore, it was interesting that shortly after this, Father Mark Carroll, the chancellor who had under orders written the letters, was made a bishop in Wichita, Kansas, and as soon as he got there, sent in a subscription to *The Commonweal*.[9]

The overall reaction to the publication of their statement on Spain, however, was nearly disastrous for the magazine in its new and fragile condition. Within a year they lost more than 20 percent of their subscribers, and as Skillin has recalled, "got some of the most violent letters I have ever seen in my life." The loss of subscribers among priests was especially great, dropping from twenty-five hundred to about nine hundred. All of this was perhaps predictable, but it shocked the young editors. Michael Williams, as they had expected, strongly disagreed with them in his "News and Views" column in the same issue in which they published their statement. *America* attacked them and praised Williams's view. The Jesuit publication pointed out that theirs was a magazine that prided itself on its partizanship in every important issue of the times and expressed amazement that *The Commonweal* editors could be impartial between "the champions of a Christian social order" and "the protagonists of a Sovietized state." The problem with them, the *Catholic Worker* group, and "Maritain and his historico-philosophers and French nationalists" was that they had willed not to consider the Spanish conflict "comprehensively." *The Commonweal*'s statement received almost no support in the Catholic press, and *America* editorialized that all that had been done was to give "comfort to the Loyalists, Leftists, and Liberals," who will quote it interminably against "the" Catholic opinion. An American Institute of Public Opinion poll, however, in December, 1938, showed Catholics seriously divided with 42 percent sympathizing with the Loyalists.[10]

The Commonweal managed to survive the crisis over this matter, though its finances were strained. The expenses of operation were actually quite minimal. There were only three editors and of these,

Burnham and Skillin were drawing little or no salary. Each was unmarried and was living in his family's home.

In 1939, the magazine celebrated its fifteenth anniversary with a special issue containing articles by Michael Williams, Lawrason Riggs, George Shuster, Bishop Francis Kelley, Ralph Adams Cram, Dr. James Walsh, Mary Kolars, Helen Walker Homan, and others who had played a part in the history of the magazine. Letters of congratulations were published from President Roosevelt, Alfred E. Smith, Henry Wallace, Walter Lippmann, Father John A. Ryan, Robert Hutchins, Dorothy Day, Arthur Sulzberger, and others, and among the Catholic bishops, Mooney of Detroit, Cantwell of Los Angeles, Muench of Fargo, Noll of Fort Wayne, and many others. Notably lacking among the well-wishers was Bishop Francis Spellman, who six months previously had become archbishop of New York. At that time *The Commonweal*'s lead editorial had promised him their "loyalty and devotion." Twenty-eight years later, on the death of Spellman, *Commonweal* commented that it was not easy for them to write an editorial on his death. "Apparently he made an indelible impression on those who met him. We never did. Neither he nor his office ever contacted us about anything, either to praise us or blame us. He let us alone and we more or less let him alone."[11] Such then was the relationship of *The Commonweal* to this powerful churchman.

Liturgy and Life, Capitalism and Labor

To understand *The Commonweal* during this period, it is necessary to appreciate the place which the liturgy occupied in its thinking.

A key belief of the editors of *The Commonweal*, particularly at this time, but in the earlier period too, was that genuine liturgical renewal and an appreciation of what should be the social impact of liturgical renewal, was the way to a program of general renewal for Catholicism. The liturgical "movement," as it was called, was not particularly concerned with the rules and rubrics of worship, as many erroneously supposed, even after 1926 when *Orate Fratres* (later *Worship*), the monthly journal of the unofficial movement, began publication with Father Virgil Michel, OSB, as editor. At the root of the movement was an appreciation of the Church as the Mystical Body of Christ, a notion long obscured, and especially so since the days of anti-Protestant polemics. Today, the term "Mystical Body of

Christ" is a household word among American Catholics, but this was not always so. A survey and complete bibliography of thought on the Mystical Body for the years 1890–1940, showed only eight articles in the more important English, Irish, and American periodicals before 1926 when *Orate Fratres* was founded. In 1952, a priest professor ordained almost fifty years, was asked what he had learned of the Mystical Body in his seminary days. The reply: "Mystical Body? Why, not even the Pope then knew there was a Mystical Body!" The *Catholic Encyclopedia* of 1911 had a half column bearing the interesting title "Mystical Body of the Church." Pallen and Wynne's *New Catholic Dictionary* of 1929, which was based on contemporary Catholic life, didn't even mention the Mystical Body in defining the Church; a legal and juridical definition was given.[1]

In addition to the Mystical Body of Christ, some of the other major themes of the liturgical movement were the *active* liturgical participation of the faithful, their participation in the priesthood of Christ, and the intimate connection between liturgy and life. The Mass was not simply something one went to, but something one lived. The liturgical spirit was to touch every aspect of the daily life of the Christian.

It was this stress in particular that drew *The Commonweal* and *Orate Fratres* and the liturgical movement together. A 1929 editorial by George Shuster on "Catholic action" drew a letter of congratulations from Father Michel. Shuster pointed out the "gradual decay of the communal aspects of our spiritual life. The liturgy is prayer in common, but we have forgotten the liturgy." The "supreme spiritual danger" of America, he observed, was that "the sacred ministrant should become not a mediator, but a functionary." Michel wrote him:

> A layman (alas!) must still be very cautious in writing such an editorial, and this editorial could hardly have put things more diplomatically and yet tellingly.—My hearty congratulations! Some day an "official teacher" will have to re-utter the age-old Catholic doctrine that the layfolk are not merely trained dogs but true living members of the Church. . . .

A year later, in April, 1930, with the financial collapse having intervened, Virgil Michel wrote to Michael Williams commending an article he had published, and inquiring as "to what extent the *Commonweal* may become an instrument of fostering a new social order based on strict Catholic principles." He expressed the hope of coming to New York to discuss the matter and added: "I believe with you that it is most important for us to come out plainly and openly with our views else the future will be in the hands of Communism as much as the past has been in the hands of unbridled capitalism."[2]

A lengthy illness struck the young Benedictine before this meeting could be held and it is unknown whether he and Williams met personally at a subsequent date, but an exchange of advertisements between *The Commonweal* and *Orate Fratres* was established. Of it, *Orate Fratres* commented that it represented the conviction of "a community of ideals and aims, with the *Commonweal* approaching the problem of the integrally Catholic mind and life more from the secular, *Orate Fratres* more from the specifically religious angle."[3]

When Edward Skillin and Philip Burnham took over *The Commonweal*, they were very close to Father Michel and in the midst of the crisis following the publication of their Spanish Civil War stand he wrote them a letter for publication in defense of their stand.[4] At the time, Virgil Michel had already created quite a controversy in the pages of *The Commonweal* with his article "What Is Capitalism?" The article was, in part, written as a response to an essay in the *Catholic World*, which had called Christ "the first preacher of Capitalism." For Michel, this was blasphemy. There was nothing really Christian about modern capitalism. Indeed, the capitalist system was "finished," because of its "failure to attain the social ends proper to any economic system." It had "reduced hundreds and thousands to a state of chronic malnutrition and even of starvation," and had "prostituted culture to the seeking after material gain." What the Christian had to do, however, was to look not backward but forward and not allow "iniquitous capitalism to lead to its logical conclusion in either communistic collectivism or the equally totalitarian fascism." Various Christian distributist, agrarian, and cooperative movements were suggested as being the beginnings of viable alternatives to capitalism, and they were recommended in that they were opposed alike to capitalism, communism, and fascism, and had principles and aims in harmony with the Christian ideal of life.[5]

Attacks such as this on capitalism were by no means unknown in the Catholic periodical literature of the 1930s. In 1933, an *America* editorial commented: "Capitalism, as we have known it in this country, has ever been a stupid and malicious giant. Even the Depression may have brought it no enlightenment." The *Catholic Mind, Catholic World*, and others also presented critiques, at times associating capitalism with Protestantism. Competition was said to be "far more

Protestant than Catholic in origin. Catholicism has in mind the welfare of all."[6]

Catholics were more populous in the laboring ranks than were Protestants, which may account for the earlier expression of critical views among Catholics, but by the mid-1930s Reinhold Niebuhr, the tireless preacher, journalist, teacher, and theologian, had brought "Christian Realism" to a creative presence in society and Protestantism could not be considered as an enemy of labor.[7]

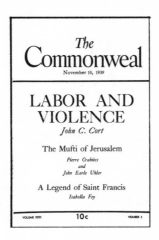

In 1937, John C. Cort, at first a contributing editor of *The Commonweal* and later a full-time editor, was among the founders of the Association of Catholic Trade Unionists, a group which grew out of the Catholic Worker Movement when he, Ed Squitieri, Martin Wersing, and eight others decided to do something about "the good brains and muscle rotting away on the Catholic Worker bread-line for want of work." The immediate impetus for founding the group was the death of a friend of Wersing and Squitieri, who was fired for union activity, couldn't get another job, and finally, mad from despair, hanged himself in the bathroom of a five-room tenement flat, leaving a sickly wife and seven small children.

In one of their first projects, they decided to back the miserably paid girls striking at the Woolworth stores in New York, and to picket the big Woolworth store on Fourteenth Street off Union Square. An item in the newspapers had reported that Barbara Hutton wasn't so bad because she had given heavily to charity. Also, at about that time Pius XI had just written his encyclical *Divini Re-*

demptoris. The group put the two together and produced a picket sign reading:

> BABS GAVE $11,000,000 to CHARITY, *BUT* "THE WORKER IS NOT TO RECEIVE AS ALMS WHAT IS HIS DUE IN JUSTICE"
>
> POPE PIUS XI

As John Cort recalls, "Maybe we were a little unfair to Babs, but the main thing is that we had put the pope—perhaps for the first time—on an American picket line."[8]

The group did not try to set up Catholic unions. Rather, their purpose was to build an organization of Catholic men and women who were at the same time active members of the established AFL, CIO, or independent unions. Catholic labor schools for workmen and labor publications by Catholics followed under the group's inspiration.

These were the kind of things *The Commonweal* of Edward Skillin, Philip Burnham, and Harry Binsse tried to assist and relate to. John Cort was soon contributing a special section on labor to the magazine. This development symbolized as well as anything a gradual and perhaps subtle shift in which *The Commonweal* was coming to express a Catholicism no less intellectual, but more of a grass roots variety, and also more activist.

Isolationism-Interventionism and World War II

One of the most vigorous periods in *The Commonweal*'s history occurred during the isolationist-interventionist controversy which divided the editors of *The Commonweal* as it divided much of the nation, and resulted in some bristling exchanges in its pages.

American isolationism was at its peak in 1938. It was the natural product of a period of intense preoccupation with domestic affairs. France and Britain, however, were much like the United States in this. Japan expanded in the East, Italy conquered Ethiopia, Hitler left the League of Nations, tore up the disarmament clauses of the Treaty of Versailles, built up his forces for aggression, entered the demilitarized Rhineland, and in 1938 conquered Austria. All of this was observed, and no effective means were employed to stop it. In the fall of 1938, Hitler demanded from Czechoslovakia the cession of the Sudetenland. The Munich Settlement, which granted this, has become, with hindsight, synonymous with capitulation and appeasement, but at the time the vast majority of the British and French welcomed the agreement. In March, 1939, six months later, Hitler violated his solemn promises, proclaimed the extinction of the Czechoslovak state, and extended his annexationist drive to non-German peoples. With this action, the attitude of the European democracies swung around sharply to a policy of resistance to Hitler. They realized the necessity of taking a stand against further aggression. This change in attitude that came in Europe in 1939 was not, however, accompanied by a similar change in American opinion. The American people did not as yet feel insecure.

In *The Commonweal*, George Shuster had denounced the Munich Settlement as "a ghastly bargain—just another entry into the ledger of those who, wherever they be, have helped make Hitler what he is today." Donald Attwater, however, writing from England in the same issue, thanked God for the agreement and the peace it would bring. The editorial position was that while Munich hadn't finally settled anything, war was no lasting solution either, nor would it produce good, and on these grounds Chamberlain was to be applauded. When the Munich Settlement was violated in March, 1939, they wrote that "the only hope seems to be to allow Hitler to expand to the point of collapse, for everyone stands to lose by another European war." They felt that the only way to overcome Nazism was for the people under that regime and under the threat of that regime to undergo a personal revolution and then reorganize their society on a human enough basis to counter the totalitarian system of Hitler. When Poland was invaded in September, 1939, and Britain and France went to war, the editors would have none of it, commenting that "our place is not beside Britain and France or even invaded Poland, but with the neutral nations of the world." They felt we should be neutral not merely in a formal sense, but in a genuine sense, and should, in concert with other neutrals, prevent the expansion of the war, limit its intensity and duration, and serve as arbiters of peace. When President Roosevelt called Congress into special session that month to undertake a revision of the neutrality laws, they urged Congress to hold fast, praised Colonel Lindbergh's radio speech upholding neutrality, and expressed happiness with the results of a Gallup poll showing 84 percent of Americans opposed to the sending of our army and navy abroad to fight against Germany.[1]

In February, 1940, C. G. Paulding joined the staff of *The Commonweal* as associate editor. An American, he had for the five years previous been with the French personalist review *Esprit*, and earlier had lived in Rome during the growth of fascism following his service as an intelligence officer in Paris during World War I.

Within a short time after the arrival of Paulding, the four editors were split on the question of American action with regard to the war. In the Isolationist-Interventionist Controversy, as it is generally called, Paulding and Harry Binsse supported the latter, while Philip Burnham stood for the former, with Edward Skillin agreeing with him. There was a large measure of agreement on many aspects of the war: aiding the needy and refugees, condemning totalitarianism and the amorality manifested by the totalitarian camp; but as they commented, "such things do not exhaust the issue." The decision was that some editorials would be followed by the initials of the writer.[2]

The so-called "phony war" of the fall and spring of 1939–40 gave way to the unambiguous grimness of war more clearly evident in April, May, and June, as Denmark and Norway, Belgium, and shockingly enough, France, fell before the German armies. With all opposition driven from Europe, the peril of the situation was more evident to most Americans. When *The Commonweal* spoke of the Burke-Wadsworth bill for peacetime conscription as a "startling proposal" without demonstrated justification for "the grave evils involved in so complete a militarization of the United States," public opinion polls showed the bill receiving 59 percent approval. A month later, on July 20, approval was 69 percent, and in late August, it was 86 percent.[3]

The
Commonweal
November 22, 1940

Children's Books
1940
Harry Lorin Binsse

Can We Justify
Neutrality?
William M. Agar

VOLUME XXXIII   10c   NUMBER 5

Public approval of the draft was one thing: approval of active participation in the war another. Few people favored the latter course, though debate on participation was vigorous. Contributing editor William Agar wrote:

> Can we watch nations fight and go under for our beliefs, for our kind of civilization, for Christianity, without raising a hand to help them and still have any virtue left in us? I suspect that our moral standards will rot so rapidly if we continue to do this that, in the end, we will not even be fit to conduct a decent burial service for those who died that we might live.

Others, however, pointed out how such language was similar to that found in the Catholic press during World War I, exhorting to a war for "civilization" and saying that religion was being "restored" by the war. Philip Burnham said that personally he could not conceive that there was any comparison between the goodness of the two sides battling in Europe, but still the disillusioned arguments of the isolationists must be given some weight. Whatever the Nazi regime was, it was subject to possible internal change.[4]

As the 1940 presidential election approached, *The Commonweal* declared its neutrality, saying that neither party had presented a program worth partisan enthusiasm. John Cort had no such feelings, however. True, Roosevelt had his faults, "but who else is going to protect the poor man's hard earned gains? Who else is going to save us from the robber barons?" When Wendell Willkie said, "Get government off our backs, and we'll put the unemployed back to work in no time," the real meaning was, "Let us raise prices and profits and lower wages!" Cort wondered how anyone who had read the social encyclicals could vote Republican. A survey of some of *The Commonweal*'s contributing editors showed eight for Roosevelt, two for Willkie, and three fence-sitters. Philip Burnham supported Willkie; C. G. Paulding, Roosevelt. In the Catholic press, *America* came out strongly against the third term for Roosevelt and so did Father Gillis of the *Catholic World*, who employed canon law in his argument, showing that certain religious superiors were limited to one or two terms. The anti-third term views of Archbishop Schrembs of Cleveland and Father John LaFarge were read at public meetings. *Our Sunday Visitor*, a publication halfway between a diocesan paper and a journal of opinion, was content at investigating whether Willkie's father had been a death-bed Catholic convert.[5]

The victory for Roosevelt was decisive, with the vote based mainly on domestic concerns. It seems clear that millions of lower- and middle-income Catholics strongly supported Roosevelt, and were simply not seriously concerned about his becoming the first third-term president in the nation's history.[6]

By the time of the presidential election, Britain was in serious difficulty in the war and public sentiment was gathering for more substantial action on her behalf. Two months after the election, Roosevelt submitted to Congress a program to make American war material immediately available to the fighting democracies. This Lend-Lease Act, which made the United States the "arsenal of democracy," was debated for two months and passed by substantial majorities in both the House and Senate, becoming law on March 11, 1941. A few weeks later, the United States seized all Axis shipping in American ports, and *The Commonweal* expressed reservations about the momentum of events drawing the country toward war, stating that "we can oppose the succeeding steps down this desperate line without weakening our opposition to the spiritual, political and economic evils of national socialism." Contributing editor William Agar saw things differently. With a lengthy quotation of Reinhold Niebuhr from the first issue of *Christianity and Crisis*, Agar carried forward the argument he had been presenting for some months: the immediate task was the defeat of Nazi tyranny; not to act would betray a cause to which we owed allegiance.[7]

A few weeks later Agar wrote again of how disheartened he was over *The Commonweal*'s "inability to distinguish light from darkness" with regard to the war.

> A few of our bishops and a growing number of priests and laymen are outspoken for the defeat of Hitler, but, so far as *The Commonweal* indicates, there is no reason to believe that we cannot be just as merry under Hitler as under any other form of government. There is no use in your pointing to numbers in which you may have called Hitler names. That is not what I mean. One is either for Hitler or against him. If one is against him one cannot help but advocate doing something about it.

In response, Philip Burnham acknowledged his preference for another policy than all-out war, and stated that admittedly, compared to all-out war, any other conceivable policy appeared "pale and negative in tangible action and emotional force."[8]

For Burnham, the crucial concern was how peace would or could take shape. An editorial that seems to have been written by him (the initialing of editorials was rarely done in practice), stated on July 18, 1941, that the editors had, throughout the war, attempted to see beyond it to the peace it would effect. "For us the question has always been where will mankind find itself when this violent motion subsides." War exposed societies to change, and the purpose of intelligent men was "to influence and determine the nature of this change in society." According to Edward Skillin, Burnham felt that the United States could best contribute by staying out of the war, remaining strong, working toward a peaceful settlement of the conflict, and, from a position of strength, influencing the shape society would take in the settlement.[9]

The debate on the proper response by the United States to the war continued vigorously in the pages of *The Commonweal*, but its editorial position was one of opposition to participation. This position continued steadfast right up until Pearl Harbor. *The Commonweal* was not pacifist in its argumentation and thus differed from the *Catholic Worker*, which held in June, 1940, and throughout World War II that the conditions for a just war were impossible of fulfillment in the modern period. But it does seem that *The Commonweal* was influenced by the *Catholic Worker's* position. It may be recalled here that the two publications had shared a like view of the Spanish Civil War a few years previous to this, and were the only national Catholic publications to take a stand critical of Franco. In addition, *The Commonweal* had great respect for the communitarian movement, the critique of capitalism, the emphasis on international and interracial brotherhood, and the Christian personalist philosophy which was embodied in the Catholic Worker movement. Insofar, however, as a reaction against the evils of technology and capitalism led to an emphasis on the individual and the creation of what the English artisan-philosopher Eric Gill called a "cell of good living," it ill prepared one for the kind of collective action Reinhold Niebuhr saw as necessary under "Christian realism" in dealing with the menace of Hitler. Rather than strong collective action, *The Commonweal* seems to have clung to the thought it expressed on March 24, 1939, when it said that the only way to overcome Nazism was for the people under the Nazi regime and under the threat of that regime "to undergo a personal revolution" and then reorganize their society on a more human basis. Whether the situation was really open to such inner dynamics flowing from personal change on the part of individuals seems highly questionable.

On October 31, 1941, *The Commonweal* reported on a "Catholic Clergy War Poll" showing 91.5 percent of Catholic priests opposing a shooting war outside the hemisphere and 90.5 percent opposing aid for "the Communistic Russian government." The poll, conducted by an organization called the Catholic Laymen's Committee for Peace, obtained replies from 13,155 of the 34,616 priests contacted. Philip Burnham commented that although the questions were somewhat weighted toward the result obtained, and would more ideally have been posed to whole parishes rather than simply to the clergy, it was reassuring to see that those opposed to U.S. entry into the war were "not in opposition to any overwhelming tide of wisdom."[10]

In February, 1939, *The Commonweal* had warned that the American public must not become so concentrated on Europe as to "lose sight of ampler but looser drama of the East," but *The Commonweal*, like most Americans, was shocked by Pearl Harbor. Its first editorial comment on it did, however, perceive the ultimate significance of the tragedy, namely that the attack had brought the United States into the war in a way that gave the country the "maximum possible political strength."

> No one in the country, no matter what committee or school of thought he has belonged to during recent debates, wants a condition which permits Pearl Harbor to be bombed. We are locked in a unity to beat off a naval and military threat which our enemies themselves have made a physical fact that no argument, theorizing or political viewpoint can remove from reality. Disastrous as the opening of the war may be to military and naval effectiveness at the disposal of the United States government, it is highly doubtful if Japan gained an advantage to compensate for the unity she gave this country in return.[11]

While *The Commonweal* was thus now in support of the war effort, it still saw the war as an important area for rational reflection and decision-making. During the war years, it consistently sought to get the aims of the war clearly stated. It also forthrightly condemned the change in the Allied bombing policy to area bombing, lamenting that the "sensitiveness of a nation at war is dulled."

> Again and again we have protested against the change in our bombing policy. When the war started, the bombing of open cities, the massacre of civilians was a German crime. When we started bombing the continent our "precision" bombing was our great pride. It still is, but it has become the precision bombing of entire inhabited areas. . . . It is no longer the factories we are bombing; it is the areas in which the factory workers must live that we bomb. It is the cities and the towns. It is the women and the children, the old and the young whom we burn alive, suffocate, bury and destroy. By the hundreds and thousands. This policy which Mr. Churchill announces

will not be abandoned by the United Nations, is in our opinion murder and suicide. It is the murder of innocent people and the suicide of our civilization.

The occasion of this comment was an article by Vera Brittain entitled "Massacre by Bombing: The Facts Behind the British-American Attack on Germany," published in *Fellowship*, February, 1944. The article had a foreword signed by Dr. Harry Emerson Fosdick of Riverside Church, New York; Episcopal Bishop Appleton Lawrence of Massachusetts; Oswald Garrison Villard, former editor of the *Nation*; and twenty-five other prominent Protestant leaders. *The Commonweal*'s editorial strongly recommended the article. It pointed out that while *Fellowship* was a pacifist magazine and *Commonweal* was not a pacifist magazine, it would be "an appalling and disastrous thing if the argument against the 'saturation' bombing of cities is carried on by pacifists exclusively." The *Fellowship* article and its signatories were denounced, with letters to the *New York Times* lined up fifty to one against them. Many suspected the signers of being outright Axis sympathizers or at least victims of its propaganda. The Reverend Daniel A. Poling warned that every minute of delay in winning the war was death for yet other men, women, and children. William Shirer doubted Miss Brittain's report. *America* ignored the whole affair. A correspondent to *The Commonweal* reacted to their editorial by stating that "all those who are not pacifists cannot suddenly at a certain point in the logical course of total warfare interfere by bringing up religious or moral considerations."[12]

The "logical course of total warfare" was to lead the debaters all a large step further on, however, with the dropping of the atomic bomb. In June, 1945, two months before the dropping of the bomb, C. G. Paulding editorialized on a proposal by Major George Fielding Eliot that poison gas be used to shorten the war against Japan. Eliot maintained that there was no real difference in killing people one way or another. Paulding granted that "when aviation fuel jelly, flaming and inextinguishable, roasts men alive it might even be kinder to let them gasp quickly and die." There was a case for the use of gas against Japan—a technical case. But "that is why the case must not be left to technicians. . . ."

> To the Orient we are bringing the latest inventions of our civilization. There is only one we have not brought. It is gas. If we use that we will have brought them all. Gas is no worse than flame. It is only that it is one more weapon. The last one we have to use. Until we invent a new one.

But, said Paulding, "the time has come when nothing more can be added to the horror if we wish to keep our coming victory something we can use—or that humanity can use."[13]

Then on August 6, that which no one could have imagined or dreamed happened. And then it happened again. Eric Goldman recalls some Americans joking that the Japanese were suffering from "atomic ache"; or that "when God made Atom, he sure created a handful for Eve." For *The Commonweal*, however, Hiroshima and Nagasaki were names for American guilt and shame. Victory was defiled. Rotterdam and Coventry symbolized German shame; Pearl Harbor symbolized Japanese shame. Now America had its own unique shame.

> The war against Japan was nearly won. Our fleet and Britain's fleet stood off Japan's coast and shelled Japan's cities. There was no opposition. Our planes, the greatest bombers in the world flew from hard won, gallantly won bases and bombed Japanese shipping, Japanese industry and, already, Japanese women and children. Each day they announced to the Japanese where the blows would fall, and the Japanese were unable to prevent anything they chose to do. Then without warning an American plane dropped the atomic bomb on Hiroshima.

In exasperated anger, the editorial concluded: "Once we have won our war we say that there must be international law. Undoubtedly."[14]

Most of the leading Catholic periodicals expressed feelings similar to *The Commonweal*'s. The *Sign* said that before the bar of future generations America would stand as "the nation that vaporized the last shred of humanity from warfare when she annihilated without a warning masses of unarmed citizenry." The *Catholic World* called the bombing "the most powerful blow ever delivered against Christian civilization and the moral law" and asked civilized peoples to reprobate and anathematize the action taken by the American government. *America*, however, somewhat weakly temporized that the moral issues raised by the bomb were so grave that moral theologians were hesitating to give a forthright decision as to whether or not its use could be justified for any reason. The American Catholic bishops had no comment either at the time of the dropping of the bombs nor at their annual meeting in November. Father Daniel Berrigan has asked if the bishops might not have been more apt to speak if eighty thousand contraceptive devices had been dropped on Hiroshima rather than eighty thousand lives taken. Patrick Scanlan of the

Brooklyn Tablet in a front page editorial called the bombing "a form of annihilation . . . devised in utter contempt for the Christian teaching that man is a creature made to the image and likeness of God." Much of the diocesan press, however, failed to offer any editorial discussion of a moral issue being raised by the bomb, and Hanson Baldwin of the *New York Times*, a graduate of the Naval Academy, offered more discussion of the moral question than did diocesan editors.[15]

Some Issues during the 1940s

The events on which *The Commonweal*, a weekly magazine with a specialized audience, will comment, are a combination of major issues of concern to almost everyone, and minor issues which will never find their way into history textbooks, but which are of concern at least to the specialized readership. In this section, we will present a cross-section of these two kinds of interests. We will speak of racism in society and church, of labor and the Taft-Hartley Act, and of the stunning political achievement of Harry Truman in 1948. We will also speak, however, of a rather minor novel and the discussion it engendered, of a gross injustice against a professor in a Catholic university, and of a German immigrant priest who was perhaps best known by the initials H. A. R. We will also continue to report on certain changes in *The Commonweal*.

During the war years *The Commonweal* took up anew the problems of domestic racism about which *The Commonweal* of the Williams-Shuster era frequently editorialized, but which were now more evident against the backdrop of a war against foreign racism. The forcible removal, on the plea of military necessity, of one hundred ten thousand Americans of Japanese ancestry to "relocation centers" only served to demonstrate, said *The Commonweal*, "that citizenship can fail to hold the primacy over race which the ideals of this country assign to it." On the occasion of a particularly atrocious lynching, it asked: "Who are we to reproach the Nazis with their concentration camps for Jews if we ourselves can drag a Negro through the streets and then ignite him with gasoline for the pleasure of a crowd of three hundred acquiescent spectators?" In 1942, it stated that it was "high time" some baseball owner or manager gave "a boost to his country and his team" by signing up Negro ball players.[1]

The Commonweal also raised the question of institutional racism in Catholicism. In June, 1947, it published Alice Renard's "A Negro Looks at the Church," which said amid specific charges that it required "supernatural folly (the folly of the cross) to sign up for life in a Church whose clergy and institutions can practice race discrimination with impunity." The article was denounced as having "all the earmarks of the work of an anti-clerical, non-catholic professional agitator" by a correspondent who expressed shock that such a thing could appear in *The Commonweal*. The editors responded that while the incidents recounted by Miss Renard might not obtain generally, the specific cases she mentioned had been carefully checked and authenticated before publication. The incidents that Renard reported, however, were more widespread than it is pleasant to recall. A 1949 survey of the Chicago archdiocese showed Catholic Negroes confined to membership in three Jim Crow churches, no matter where they lived in the city. Also there were cases of Negro children being refused admission to the nearest parochial schools, in violation of canon law.[2]

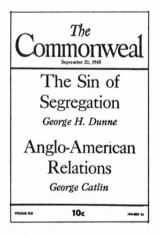

The
Commonweal
September 21, 1945

The Sin of Segregation
George H. Dunne

Anglo-American Relations
George Catlin

VOLUME XLII   **10c**   NUMBER 23

In 1945, George H. Dunne, SJ, had written "The Sin of Segregation," which proved to be one of the most widely reprinted of *Commonweal* articles. That same year, the editors applauded the admission of Negroes to St. Louis University, an event followed, however, by a dispute about whether the Negro students might attend a university-sponsored formal prom. Authorities of the university seem to have felt it would be dangerous to permit it, but Father Claude

Heithaus, SJ, who had led the student movement that had successfully integrated the school, fought hard and forced the issue into the
open before public scrutiny. It was successfully settled, with four
Negro couples attending the dance, but Father Heithaus was trans-
ferred from the school as a troublemaker. *The Commonweal* expressed pleasure at the settlement of the dance issue, but added that
it could understand how his immediate superiors felt that "he would
no longer be useful on the university's faculty," a comment it is
difficult to understand from the perspective of the 1970s.[3]

During the war years there were many interesting discussions
about Catholic life in *The Commonweal*. In 1941, A.J. Cronin's best
selling *Keys of the Kingdom* became a source of controversy. Its
story was that of Father Francis Chisholm, a Scottish missionary,
who for his time, 1895–1935, might have been considered radical.
Harry Binsse found the book contrived and melodramatic, and felt
that it showed the Church in a false light in that most of the priests in
the book, save Chisholm, were stuffy, pompous caricatures. John
Cort, a Harvard graduate not lacking in sophistication, felt, however,
that the book deserved "at least two and a half cheers." While not
great, it was a very fine book that told an engaging story and even
managed to make sanctity seem a desirable thing, and comfort-
worship and phony piety undesirable things. Another correspondent
wrote to say that Cort was in essence saying the book was good
propaganda, something which he as a labor organizer might be sensitive to, but in truth the book was "one vast stinkerola." In Cort's
attitude, he said, was the fallacy that had cursed Catholic criticism of
the arts and emasculated Catholic writing. Art and propaganda must
not be confused. A badly written book was a badly written book no
matter if it converted millions! Novelist Katherine Burton commented that perhaps one reason for the popularity of the book
among Protestants and some Catholics too was that there was
throughout the book "a sense of flouting authority as represented by
the Church." The book presented the Church in an unbalanced light,
and, further, Father Chisholm seemed "to interpret the Scriptures
to his own way of thinking sometimes."[4]

Jacques Maritain was a very frequent contributor to *The Commonweal* after he arrived in the United States in 1940, having trav-
elled here on ship with C. G. Paulding. Paulding himself had added
immeasurably to *The Commonweal* and his signed editorials in each
issue were sensitive, substantive, and polished essays that Michael
Williams found too poetic but which John Cogley grew up admir-

ing.[5] François Mauriac, Etienne Gilson, Robert Penn Warren, Georges Bernanos, George Dunne, and Thomas Merton were among contributors during the 1940s, with the latter's poems frequently appearing.

Financially, *The Commonweal* struggled under Philip Burnham and Edward Skillin much as it had under the earlier editors. In fact, the enterprise almost sank in its first few months. A large number of people dropped their subscriptions, mostly as a result of the Spanish stand. The two young editors got to the beginning of the summer of 1939 facing the realization that financially they couldn't get through the lean summer months. In their plight they sent wires to all the bishops in the United States saying "Help," and enough of them did come through that they were able to carry on. Edward Skillin recalls that they contacted the bishops two or three times in this way, in addition to turning to some known generous supporters and contributors. During the war years the financial situation improved and it stands as the one time in its history that *The Commonweal* actually made ends meet.[6]

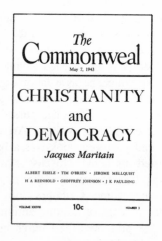

The

Commonweal
May 7, 1943

CHRISTIANITY
and
DEMOCRACY

Jacques Maritain

ALBERT EISELE · TIM O'BRIEN · JEROME MELLQUIST
H A REINHOLD · GEOFFREY JOHNSON · J K PAULDING

VOLUME XXXVIII   10c   NUMBER 1

The war years were also a time during which death came to a number of early *Commonweal* editors and supporters. In 1941, Dana Skinner died prematurely at the age of forty-eight. Others, all older than he, followed: Ralph Adams Cram, Grenville Vernon, James J. Walsh, Lawrason Riggs, Cardinal O'Connell, William F. Sands.

As in every period, *The Commonweal* was criticized by both the Left and the Right. One correspondent wrote of "the anaemic brand of

Catholicity served up by the Skillins, the Corts, the Maritains, the Justice Murphys, and their lily-livered ilk." In somewhat the same vein Patrick Scanlan charged that of all the periodicals claiming to be Catholic, *The Commonweal* offered "the sole consolation of the anti-God forces." The problem was that it was "liberal" and "soft on communism." But *Pravda* wasn't pleased either. For the Communist organ found *The Commonweal* and the *Catholic World* to be outstanding examples of "the warmongering Catholic press."[7]

For their twentieth anniversary issue, in 1944, the editors invited Michael Williams to write an article in letter form stating frankly what he thought of the then editorial policy in general and in particular. To Williams, some of the editorial utterances sounded more like the examination of conscience of idealists afflicted with scrupulosity, rather than the workmanship of realistic journalists, but he preferred that to the brand of partizanship he saw in most Catholic publications. On particulars, Williams touched two points, the 1944 election, and his "now" point of view on the Spanish Civil War. On the former he preferred a more vigorous support for Roosevelt over Dewey rather than the "mild and allusive" support they now gave. On the latter, he granted that the attitude of refusing to support either side was "sounder" than his in supporting Franco, but the actual circumstances, i.e., provocative persecution, made the war "humanly speaking" both inevitable and necessary. The tone of Williams's appraisal was on the whole positive and fraternal.[8]

On July 24, 1945, Harry Binsse sent Michael Williams a letter suggesting that the ambiguous title "special editor" attached to his name on the masthead be dropped so that it might be clear to readers that he was in no way responsible for editorial policy. Binsse suggested that instead, the masthead would contain a line that read "Founded by Michael Williams in 1924." Williams assented to changing the masthead but suggested that it read "Founded by the Calvert Associates, Inc.; 1924; Michael Williams, President and Editor." He pointed out that the founders had really been a number of men—and women—something which shouldn't be forgotten in "our masculine-muddled America." (Very few women, however, have played much of a role in the history of *The Commonweal*, either in the Williams period or later. Helen Walker, Mary Kolars, and Anne Fremantle are perhaps the only names to mention.) Williams then added to his response a blistering attack on the editors' idea of founding editorial policy by committee. The problem with this was that the sum of opinions too frequently equaled zero. They should drop the plan, elect or hire an editor, and then eject or fire him if he didn't make good. On specifics, he was angry that *The Commonweal* wasn't fighting for the cause of Poland, Lithuania, and other countries being gobbled up by Russian power.[9]

In response, the editors stated that the picture of a headless committee wasn't true. In practice, individual editors wrote editorials and that since Pearl Harbor they hadn't had any real differences, and that previous to that, when they did have differences, they signed their editorials. (John Cogley, in reflecting on his experience with *Commonweal* had said that he thought the idea of having one person, unhindered, writing editorials in the name of the group was unusual, but that for the most part, he found the same system with the *New York Times*.)[10]

On the charge of being soft on Russian expansionism, they said that while it might seem a noble thing to invite the nation to fight Russia over Poland, it was not a policy which they could in conscience advocate. Their policy toward Russia, they said, was that the United States should combine "firmness with true understanding" and work out a way of living in the same world with them. Edward Skillin has conceded that *The Commonweal* was "not very active" in the Cold War. Harry Binsse, he stated, "was convinced that the Russians were scared to death of being invaded again, and that that was why they set up the buffer states."[11]

Michael Williams no longer contributed his columns to *The Commonweal* after the publication of this open letter. His suggestion on the masthead was followed until the twenty-fifth anniversary issue in 1949, which contained "Notes for an Unfinished Article," the next and last piece he contributed to the magazine before his death in 1950.

The Commonweal of the 1938–49 period ran somewhat less theological material than it did in the earlier period in which George Shuster made an attempt to introduce American readers to some of the progressive European Catholic theologians, and considerably less theological material than it did in an increasing crescendo from 1950 on. "After George Shuster left," Edward Skillin has recalled, "we tended to feel we were not theologians, and things that were straight theology, we wouldn't go in for." (Later, they consciously sought and still seek to have a certain portion of material deal with theology.) They did, however, run a good number of articles on the liturgy: the Mass, the sacraments, the liturgical seasons, etc. Most of these were written by Father H. A. Reinhold, a German priest in the apostolate to seamen who had to flee his native land because of his opposition to the Nazi government. He was bluntly received in New York in September, 1936, by its new chancellor, Monsignor Francis McIntyre, who saw him not as a refugee from Nazi persecution but as a priest who might say something against Franco. He was told that the New York archdiocese was "loath" to grant him any faculties except permission to say Mass and that he was not to speak in any fashion in favor of Spanish Loyalists. A few weeks later, for the grave evil of addressing some striking seamen in the privacy of Dorothy Day's soup kitchen, and not about Spain, he was informed by the chancery that he was not to speak about anything, anywhere in New York. Meanwhile he was befriended by George Shuster who discussed the Nazi situation with him, and by a number of people in the *Commonweal* and *Catholic Worker* circle, Edward Skillin, John Cort, Phil Burnham, and others. Shuster arranged with Thomas Molloy, the bishop of Brooklyn, for a place for him to stay in that diocese, for, as Shuster said, the very fact that he was ill-treated in New York was reason enough for him to be welcome in the Brooklyn diocese. Thus began the close relationship between *The Commonweal* and Father H. A. Reinhold, who rapidly became a very influential figure in the liturgical movement in the United States.[12]

The liturgical movement was by no means concerned simply with obtaining a vernacular liturgy. In fact the question did not arise in the first years of the liturgical movement in the United States. All efforts were extended in trying to make it understood that the liturgy was more than rubrics and ceremonial. In 1929 and 1930, however, Virgil Michel enthusiastically reported in *Orate Fratres* papal permissions for the use of the vernacular in some European countries. It was 1938, though, before he thought it prudent to make what seems to have been the first public call in the United States for the introduction of English into parts of the liturgy. The question was the subject of discussion in *The Commonweal* in early 1939 with a correspondent pointing out that it was scandalous that the liturgy was intelligible to so few. John Cort strongly agreed and added that it was difficult to see how the Church could hold the working class in America or realize the revival of faith necessary for a Christian reconstruction of the social order without somehow breaking down "the terrible wall of incomprehension" that stood between the altar and so many of the Catholic congregation. *America* as early as 1937 had pointed out that the chief reason for the adoption of Latin, namely, that it was the language of the people, now militated against its retention. It was not self-seeking on the part of Catholic intellectuals which drew them gradually to lead a drive for a vernacular liturgy, for they were members of that small group for whom comprehension of the Latin liturgy was not difficult and some were personally rather attached to it. Even H. A. Reinhold in 1945 stated that it would be a "sad day" for him when he could not hear his voice at the altar recite the beautiful and familiar Latin.

> But who shares my grief? Not one percent of my people. Of course they never ask for a translation. As a matter of fact they may be opposed to it, what with the education they have had, the ignorance in which they live as to the beauty of it all, and the aversion to any change in what seems to them unchanged since Christ's day.

It was not for novelty's sake that the issue had to be advanced, but because of the specter of a *religio depopulata* (Church without a people). While this specter was as yet rather dim, it was necessary to realize that ecclesiastical wheels might run smoothly for years "after the power has been turned off."[13]

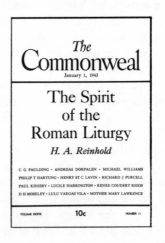

The
Commonweal
January 1, 1943

The Spirit
of the
Roman Liturgy

H. A. Reinhold

C G PAULDING · ANDREAS DORPALEN · MICHAEL WILLIAMS
PHILIP T HARTUNG · HENRY ST C LAVIN · RICHARD J PURCELL
PAUL KINIERY · LUCILE HARRINGTON · RENEE COUDERT RIGGS
D H MOSELEY · LULU VARGAS VILA · MOTHER MARY LAWRENCE

VOLUME XXXVII   10c   NUMBER 11

An insight into the state of Catholic higher education and American Catholic attitudes toward it is gained by recounting an unfortunate incident which occurred in November, 1943. At that time it was announced that Dr. Francis E. McMahon's connection with Notre Dame University had been severed. Father Hugh O'Donnell, the president of Notre Dame, made it quite clear in his statement on the matter that Professor McMahon's views on faith and morals were not heterodox, and paid him tribute for his competence as a teacher.

The reason he was being fired was that "Dr. McMahon's individual pronouncements . . . were being interpreted as the University's stand." Earlier, McMahon had spoken out strongly against Father Coughlin, had clearly called Franco a fascist rather than a savior, and had pushed for American intervention in the war when such a position enjoyed little favor. There seems to have been no immediate cause for the action against him but the growing resentment of those whom he had offended by advancing his ideas in an articulate way. President O'Donnell requested that McMahon, as a condition of his remaining a member of the faculty at Notre Dame, "submit a list of his speaking engagements, an account of his press releases, and the contents of his addresses" to the university administration in advance. As Ralph Barton Perry wrote to *The Commonweal* editors, "No action could have been taken better calculated to identify the private and personal opinion with an official opinion." *The Commonweal* in an editorial with the weak and revealing caption "Better to Grin and Bear It," did come out and support McMahon, with whom they had quarreled on interventionism, and pointed out that the incident established a precedent "unfortunate for academic freedom in Catholic institutions of learning." Neither McMahon nor any university professor could be expected to accede to such a proposal as had made by Father O'Donnell. O'Donnell meanwhile was pointing out that there was no intent to violate freedom of speech or academic freedom "rightly understood." Ralph Barton Perry asked if the result of the affair was not to disseminate widely grave doubts as to whether academic freedom was "rightly understood" at Notre Dame? Perhaps the most interesting feature of this episode, however, from the perspective of the 1970s, is that *The Commonweal* was the only Catholic publication to touch the McMahon story, although it had appeared in the *New York Times* and elsewhere. Further, even among *Commonweal* readers, the story seems to have aroused little concern, as the only published communication on it was from Professor Perry of Harvard, himself not a Catholic. The issue of academic freedom in Catholic higher education would dominate the late 1960s, but in the 1940s few Catholics seemed interested at all, and those who were contented themselves to comment "Better to Grin and Bear It."[14]

The war years had stimulated a massive and unprecedented productivity with industrial production nearly doubling between 1940 and 1944. Roosevelt's critics had called him romantic when in 1940, a year in which twelve thousand planes were produced, he spoke of a possible productive capacity of fifty thousand in a year, but in 1944, ninety-six thousand planes were produced! In this expansion, labor was virtually forced to subordinate its interests to the goals of the prolonged national emergency. There was some dissatisfaction. In May, 1943, John L. Lewis had led his United Mine Workers out on strike against the pay-rise formula that had been decided by the National War Labor Board. But, generally, labor did not press demands for better wages or working conditions in such a way as would slacken production. Within less than a year after the cessation of the war, however, the United States saw serious strikes in automobiles, steel, and railroads. Management was not inclined to grant raises without compensatory price increases. A period of rapid inflation began. Eggs that were 33¢ a dozen in 1940 were 58¢ in 1945 and 72¢ by 1948. Consumer goods were unavailable, but stored-up purchasing power was. Housing was inadequate and there were long waiting periods for cars. "Had enough?" the Republicans asked the country. For the first time in fourteen years they had captured the national mood, and in 1946 America had its first Republican Congress since the days of Herbert Hoover. By 1947, that Congress was passing—over President Truman's veto—the Taft-Hartley Act, which outlawed the closed shop and secondary boycotts, gave the president power to postpone threatened strikes, and declared that unions could be sued in the courts. It was legislation born of resentment since there was widespread feeling that labor was irresponsible. In 1946, 4.6 million workers were on strike at some point, with a loss of 116 million man-days of work. Also, there were charges, with some substance, of featherbedding, corruption, and communist infiltration.

According to *The Commonweal*'s John Broderick, it was "foolish" to maintain that the bill was all bad. The provisions against featherbedding, secondary boycotts, and jurisdictional strikes, for example, were good. Provision by provision, one could give the bill "a fairly decent score," but the bill's details made a long, happy wedded life between labor and management less probable. The rhetorical exchanges over the bill produced images on the one hand of sweat shops and slave labor and on the other of congressmen picturing themselves as protectors of neighborhood grocers threatened by labor's wild driverless team of firehorses charging madly down the American street upsetting pyramids of oranges and apples on every side. They were merely protecting society from its most frightening anarchic element—organized labor. *America*'s Benjamin Masse felt that irrespective of the bill's merits or demerits, it was seen by labor as a symbol of oppression, a threat to its survival. It was doubtful that the law would be accepted in practice by labor, and it would be better to repeal the law and try to get labor and management to jointly make legislative suggestions. The Social Action Department of the National Catholic Welfare Conference called for veto of the bill, but when it passed a second time, encouraged labor to learn to live with it. *Look* magazine in a poll of union members' attitudes toward Taft-Hartley found 64 percent opposed, but when given ten of the bill's most controversial provisions singly, a majority of opposition was not recorded even on the provision against closed shop. The lesson of this, *The Commonweal* editorialized, was not that T-H was necessarily a good thing nor that it really had the implicit support of labor, but that we are all in danger under a political dispensation such as ours, of "taking a stand on the basis of personalities, slogans, catch-phrases or fire-tinged epithets."[15]

Like many people, *The Commonweal* editors didn't think Harry Truman stood much chance of winning the 1948 presidential election. In August, 1948, John Cort spoke of "the almost certain victory of the Republicans." In July of the previous year, he had called Truman "singularly unimpressive," but felt that he was sure to be nominated and that it was better for labor to stick with him than to think of Henry Wallace or the building of another third party. A third party would mean Republican landslides for about the next ten elections, and "somehow that just doesn't seem very appealing." Editorially *The Commonweal* was nonpartisan. Dewey-Warren, it observed, would constitute a "formidable team" against even the stiffest opposition, and there seemed to be an inference that the Democratic ticket, at that point unknown, but surely to include Mr. Truman, would not constitute the "stiffest opposition."[16]

The stunning victory of Harry Truman, probably the greatest upset in American political history, left *The Commonweal* editors, in their own words, "flatfooted." The American people, they commented, "not only clearly preferred Mr. Truman and the Democrats (and whatever remains of the New Deal) . . . they also repudiated most of the actions and inactivity of the Eightieth Congress."[17] The country had had a chance to catch its breath, step back, and take a look at the great social changes that had come especially since the "New Deal"; on the whole it wanted continuity with those changes. Harry Truman had won because of overwhelming backing from labor, blacks, and most white minority groups, plus a good share of the farm vote and nearly all the newer middle classes. The Catholic voters, like many of those in this grouping, had benefitted considerably by the progressive social legislation of nearly two decades, and when they went to the polls they didn't forget it. In his State of the Union message delivered shortly before Inauguration Day, Truman called his program the "Fair Deal." It was, he explained, fundamentally an extension of the New Deal. Both meant "greater opportunity for the mass of the people." The differences were not of principle but of "pace and personnel." There would be "a steady pace without the gyrations of certain early New Dealers." For many Americans, the speech was a perfect combination of progressivism and conservatism, and the Catholic mood generally was typical of the nation's.

In the fall of 1949, *The Commonweal* celebrated its twenty-fifth anniversary with a special issue. A group of distinguished contributors, familiar to *Commonweal* readers, was assembled, including Jacques Maritain, Thomas Merton, Dorothy Day, Michael Williams, George Shuster, H. A. Reinhold, and J. F. Powers. The time, however, was one of change, both for *The Commonweal* and the nation.

Philip Burnham, who had taken over the magazine in 1938 with Edward Skillin, now left it. Called for military service early in 1942 to participate in a war that he had, previous to Pearl Harbor, argued against extending, he served with distinction, but returned a man more conservative socially, politically, and later religiously. He was more convinced than ever, especially as the Cold War developed, that his idea of allowing fascism and communism to expend themselves in a war the United States refrained from had been correct. He differed with C. G. Paulding and Harry Binsse after the war as both wanted to give the Russians far more benefit of the doubt than he, and he was unsatisfied on this and other scores even after Paulding and Binsse left the magazine. He differed with John Cort whom he felt was excessively prolabor. The personal relationships of the group were friendly enough—there is a way in which gentlemen can differ that has been a hallmark of *The Commonweal*—nevertheless, questions of integrity were posed for Burnham. Helping to move Burnham to the right, according to Edward Skillin, was his relationship with his brother James, a one-time Communist turned polemical anti-Communist, whose strong writings drew upon himself violent attacks. A sensitive person, devoted to his family, Burnham increasingly identified himself with his brother.[18] He withdrew to contributing editor, but did little or no writing. At this time, however, he maintained his *Commonweal* stock.

A year before this, in 1948, Paulding left the magazine and went with the *Reporter* which was then being launched by Max Ascoli. His reason for leaving, however, was principally that he was marrying a divorced woman and felt that his staying at *Commonweal* would thus have been embarrassing for the magazine. American Catholics at this time took an intense interest in the marital and family life of Catholic public figures who had "made it to the top" such as Bing Crosby, Stan Musial, or Irene Dunne, all of whom were exemplary, but Catholics were at least as interested or concerned about those who were deemed less than exemplary. Paulding as a quasi-public figure would have attracted some of this interest, especially against the backdrop of *The Commonweal*. There was never any notion of dismissing him on this account, though.

The departure of Harry Binsse from *The Commonweal* in 1947 was almost accidental. Having taken his sick and elderly mother to a summer home in Canada, he found that she was not really capable of the return trip. He had a couple of contracts to translate books, and decided simply to stay in Canada and to do translating and writing from that base of operations, while dropping his editing responsibilities which obviously he could not fulfill from there.

John Cogley was hired to replace Philip Burnham, and within a relatively short time was joined on the staff by James O'Gara. These two men, who would come to influence the magazine greatly, symbolize a further step in the evolution of *The Commonweal*. *The Commonweal* of Michael Williams and George Shuster was, in its roots at least, a heavily literary and somewhat churchy magazine of high church Catholicism. It was cut off from the masses of Catholic opinion culturally and was intellectually attuned to Anglo-American Catholic and European Catholic centers. From the beginning, however, a dynamism was at work between the magazine and American Catholic intellectual life; both were changing and developing, but with the magazine clearly leading the way, albeit in a searching and tentative fashion. The magazine quickly moved from churchiness to creative religious concern, especially through the influence of George Shuster, a remarkable man, ahead of his time, who has comfortably spanned the magazine's fifty years. When Philip Burnham and Edward Skillin took it over in 1938, however, it was still rather representative of an upper-class cultural Catholicism, though a younger generation was now at the controls. By continuing the initiatives begun by Shuster of relating to the emergent Catholic intellectual, religious, and social movements, Burnham and Skillin helped these movements toward maturity. Within these movements, in a special way, the immigrant American Catholicism was coming of age.

John Cogley and Jim O'Gara were representative of this. Each was born of working-class parents. O'Gara's immigrant father had an eighth grade education. He and Cogley became friends in 1940 when O'Gara, who had gravitated from a minor seminary to the Young Christian Workers Movement, joined Cogley, two years his senior at twenty-four, at the Catholic Worker's House of Hospitality in Chicago. Cogley was running the House, which slept fifty men and served about one thousand meals a day. O'Gara assisted him with this and with the editing of the *Chicago Catholic Worker* newspaper, which, contrary to its New York counterpart, was not pacifist, and was in fact interventionist. Each at that time had a year or more college credit at the Jesuits' Loyola University, but had dropped out partly through financial pressure and partly because of their attraction to the *Catholic Worker* activity. O'Gara was drafted in September, 1941, and the newspaper was dropped. Cogley married in 1942, and was drafted shortly thereafter. The House kept going for a month or two and then closed down completely.

During the war, Cogley and O'Gara corresponded about starting a national Catholic publication, which O'Gara has described as "something between *Commonweal* and the *National Catholic Reporter* as it now exists." After the war, Father H. A. Reinhold through a friend raised $1,000 for them as "seed" money. The idea was that with this they would go to New York to try to interest the "big Catholic money" in the project. In New York, they saw money on a scale to which they were not accustomed—maids, butlers, townhouses. "I remember," said Jim O'Gara, "being told at one such house which impressed me very much—'Tomorrow we're going to take you where the real Catholic money is.' Then, however, the cautions came: downplay your interest in the racial question; be careful not to be too pro-labor or too liberal." The two young men listened to the homily in silence, went to their taxi, got in, and simultaneously turned to each other and "uttered a vulgar expression." Returning to their hotel room, they wrote notes cancelling the rest of their appointments, and gave the project up on the basis that if they had to pull punches, they wanted no part of the action.[19]

Back in Chicago, they met with Father Martin Carrabine, SJ, a friend from their *Catholic Worker* days who was in charge of Catholic Action programs in the city's Catholic high schools and colleges. Adapting their idea a bit, they asked him if he'd like to publish a national Catholic student publication primarily aimed at college students. He liked the idea and spoke to a group of Catholic Action moderators, asking them to support three issues on a trial basis. The trial proved successful and *Today* magazine was launched. In addition to this activity, the two used their G.I. Bill benefits to complete their degrees at Loyola, with O'Gara going on for a master's degree in sociology and Cogley leaving *Today* and going to the University of Fribourg, Switzerland, where he studied philosophy and theology and was the first layman to matriculate in the theology school.

Cogley was returning from these postgraduate studies in 1949 when he stopped by the *Commonweal* office at 386 Fourth Avenue to pick up a check which was due him for the *Catholic Digest* having reprinted one of the articles he had published in *The Commonweal* while free-lancing to help support his wife and two children during their stay in Switzerland. His writing had been well-received, and as Edward Skillin chatted informally with him, he offered him a job at *Commonweal* filling a gap in the editorial staff created by the departure of Phil Burnham. Cogley accepted and within a couple of years was joined at *Commonweal* by his friend O'Gara who had meanwhile served as editor of the *Voice of St. Jude* (later it became *U. S. Catholic*), supporting his family after his marriage to Joan Smith, Father Carrabine's secretary. William Clancy came to *Commonweal* shortly after Jim O'Gara. He had graduated from the University of Detroit, the son of an auto worker who had seen hard times of unemployment during the Depression. William Pfaff joined *Commonweal* a month before John Cogley in 1949. A southern Catholic and graduate of Notre Dame, he was still fulfilling a promise he made his father not to smoke till he was twenty-one, when he began work with the magazine. The group in essence was an Irish-Catholic intellectual Mafia, unabashed both in their liberalism and their Catholicism. They marked the emergence of a grass roots intellectuality for American Catholics and a discernibly new development in *The Commonweal*'s history.

The Commonweal and McCarthyism

Only rarely does an event occupy center stage in both church and political circles, but this was precisely what happened in the case of Senator Joseph R. McCarthy. Communism and communist infiltration became an issue which was both religious and political. Because of this, and because of the way in which the American Catholic community was especially involved, McCarthyism was an issue made to order for *The Commonweal*.

The beginnings of it were actually in 1949, which as we have seen was a year of change for *The Commonweal*, but a year of shock for American society. First was the defeat and retreat of Chiang Kai-shek—the "loss" of China. Second, the Soviet detonation of the atomic bomb. This was followed in 1950 by the Korean War. Many Americans were baffled as to how we could lose China, our atomic monopoly, and then almost lose the Korean War.[1] Could Soviet scientists be as good as American scientists? Could communism win on its own in China? The explanation must lie somewhere else. Could there be some kind of treason and monstrous conspiracy at work?

Some found support for the conspiracy view in the Alger Hiss case and the treason of Klaus Fuchs. In August, 1948, Whittaker Chambers, who had been an editor of *Time* magazine, accused Alger Hiss of being a Communist spy, at least between 1934–38, and of passing secret government documents to the Russians. By the close of 1949, after two trials, Hiss was found guilty of perjury and sentenced to five years in prison. The case was a source of great controversy, with many, whether for or against Hiss, deciding on *a priori* grounds. Hiss was a Harvard Law School graduate of a wealthy and social Baltimore family. He had been with the State Department and at Yalta with Roosevelt before becoming president of the Carnegie Endowment for International Peace. He was dapper, urbane, and well-spoken. To many he was an "egghead" New Dealer and international "do-gooder" whose very name suggested perfidy. Others just as superficially ruled out the possibility of guilt. He had in any event been a minor official in the State Department and it was doubtful he ever influenced policy, but he made a convenient major villain.

Two weeks after Hiss's conviction came news of the conviction of Klaus Fuchs, an atomic physicist who had worked at the Los Alamos laboratory, now found guilty of giving atomic information to the Russians. At about the same time, eleven top Communists of the American Communist party were brought to trial under the Smith Act of 1940, which made it a crime to conspire to advocate and teach the violent overthrow of the government. This then was the background of the phenomenon known as McCarthyism which dominated the early 1950s: the triumph of communism in China, the Russian possession of the bomb, the Hiss affair, the treason of Klaus Fuchs, the Communist trials, and the Korean War.

On February 9, 1950, Senator Joseph McCarthy of Wisconsin alleged that he had the names of two hundred five "card-carrying Communists" in the State Department. This was three weeks after Hiss was convicted, ten days after President Truman ordered work on the H-bomb, and six days after the British announced the Fuchs confession. It was also thirty-three days after a dinner meeting at the Colony Restaurant in Washington at which McCarthy met Father Edmund A. Walsh at a get-together arranged by Charles H. Kraus, a professor of political science at Georgetown, and William A. Roberts, a well-known Washington attorney.[2] Father Walsh, vice-president of Georgetown and regent of its School of Foreign Service, had authored *Total Power*, a strongly anticommunist volume. It was with Father Walsh, considered the leading Catholic expert on Russia, that FDR had met in the 1930s in the rather successful diplomatic effort at defusing Catholic opposition to the recognition of Russia. McCarthy, a graduate of Marquette, asked the well-known Jesuit and Kraus and Roberts for help in coming up with an issue that would stir Wisconsin voters, as his term was running out in two years. Within months, Kraus, Roberts, and Walsh would all repudiate McCarthy, but at this time they wanted to help. After dinner, the discussion was continued in Roberts's office in the adjoining DeSales Building. Father Walsh pointed out the world power of communism and the danger that it could infiltrate any democratic government. In his opinion, vigilance against communism was an issue that would be important for at least the next two years and beyond. The issue of Communist infiltration rang true with McCarthy. He told Walsh the government was full of Communists and that the thing to do was "to hammer at them." The group warned that such a campaign would have to be based on facts, but the senator said offhandedly that he would get them.

McCarthy's speech in Wheeling on February 9 was followed by similar ones in Salt Lake City on February 10 and Reno on February 11, after which he wired President Truman demanding that the White House do something. His facts were flimsy, but he kept swinging away, and much of America was ready to believe his charges of "traitorous actions" by "bright young men born with silver spoons in their mouths."

The Commonweal's reaction to all this could hardly be called wildly leftist. There was no reaction at all until the March 31, 1950, issue, where an offhand comment in an editorial on the census referred to Senator McCarthy "shooting away at political records and personal reputations like a drunken sailor attacking rotary ducks at Coney Island." A week later an article on "The McCarthy Muddle" maintained that the senator only confused the cause he tried to defend. If we were to deal successfully with Communist actions in the Cold War, a middle way would have to be found between the reckless smearing of honest liberals, and ignoring the dangers of Communist infiltration. On related issues, Jim O'Gara, in a review article on *Seeds of Treason*, a pro-Chambers version of the Hiss-Chambers affair, spoke of his personal conviction of Hiss's guilt, while critically evaluating the book. The article—"These Gentle Traitors"—began with the quotation "He that trusteth to lies feedeth the winds: and the same runneth after birds that fly away" (Prov. 10:4), in a play on the bird-watching habits of Hiss and Chambers. The next week, a lead editorial blasted the views of Owen Lattimore on Asian policy and stated that there was "some fire behind the McCarthy smoke screen," though the context was not such as to make *The Commonweal* agree with McCarthy's charge that Lattimore was "the top Russian espionage agent" in the United States. None of this is right wing on the part of *The Commonweal* but it is at least a long way from knee-jerk liberalism. For example, an editorial on communism at this time, citing J. Edgar Hoover on the presence of fifty thousand known Communists in the United States, drew a letter of congratulations from the FBI director.[3]

By June of 1950, however, *The Commonweal* in a lead editorial referred to McCarthy as a "reckless, irresponsible bogey-man" and counselled against emotional and blind reactions in the period of fear and suspicion. In late May, however, McCarthy was receiving a standing ovation for his speech to the members of the Catholic Press Association, having been introduced by Pat Scanlan of the *Brooklyn Tablet* who described McCarthy as a courageous victim of slander and a national smear campaign.[4]

Earlier, *America* had spoken of McCarthy as "pretty irresponsible," but the Catholic press generally was in support of the senator throughout the 1950–54 period. The *Sign*, for example, stated that McCarthy had "stumbled upon the Leftist nest in a speech he gave in Wheeling, West Virginia, and ever since he has doggedly tried to carry through the unmasking of Leftists in the State Department." *Ave Maria* maintained that McCarthy fought communism "the way you fight rattlesnakes: without a rulebook." Later they maintained, "We fail to see anything wrong with his methods," and commented that the American public was not wasting its breath over McCarthy's methods. "They are wondering how such a vocal minority [Mc-Carthy opponents] can be so obtuse or even treasonous as to contradict good sense and right conduct. The methods? Let's stop worrying about what is going to happen to American freedom."[5]

The diocesan newspapers and columnists were virtually unanimous in their praise of McCarthy. The *Brooklyn Tablet* was probably his greatest promoter and in addition to favorable editorials published many letters from readers praising the senator. Typical was one reader who wrote: "McCarthyism to me is one hundred percent Anti-Communism; I glory in my McCarthyism."[6] McCarthy seems to have represented in the minds of many American Catholics wearied of having their true Americanism and patriotism challenged, a chance to show that they were both one hundred percent Catholic and one hundred percent American and patriotic. The issue of communism was at once both religious and political.

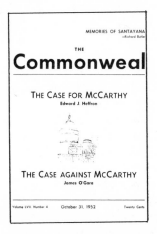

John Cogley came to play a leading part in the debates of these years as perhaps the most articulate anti-McCarthy Catholic. This was carried on chiefly through his column, a feature which developed in *Commonweal* somewhat by accident. A year or so after his arrival at the magazine in 1949, Cogley went to Ed Skillin and told him that although he enjoyed his work, he felt he would have to resign because he could not adequately support his family on his $60 per week salary. Cogley has recalled that Skillin said he "didn't want to start any bad tradition of paying large sums like $75, but if you write a column, I'll pay you $15 extra for the column."[7] Thus began the long-running career of John Cogley as a columnist, and, some would say, as "pope" of "Commonweal Catholics." Through his column, John Cogley debated the McCarthyites and other personalities of the period, such as Paul Blanshard.

In 1953, McCarthy, in the style he followed with many critics, inferred that *The Commonweal* was communist. The charge concerned Thomas Davin, a writer and editor who once worked on *Cosmopolitan* and later on the short-lived Manhattan daily *PM*. Appearing before Senator Jenner's subcommittee on internal security, Davin took the Fifth Amendment to many of the questions put to him, including whether he had been in charge of Catholic work for the Communist party, whether he had sought to influence the policy of *The Commonweal*, and when he had last visited its offices. He denied that he was then a party member, but declined to answer whether he ever had been. The day the report from the Jenner Committee was released, Ed Skillin, editor-in-chief, gave a statement to the Religious News Service. Skillin stated that Davin was a college acquaintance of a former assistant editor who left the magazine in the 1930s, that he had never published anything in *The Commonweal* and had visited the office only two or three times, the last visit being in 1938.

He pointed out that he was the only present staff member who had been with the magazine in 1938, that none of the others knew Davin at all, and that Davin had had "no influence whatsoever on *The Commonweal*." Skillin added that he had no way of knowing whether or not Davin had been assigned by the Communist party to influence the policy of *The Commonweal*, but if he was, "his failure was monumental, as our consistently anti-Communist policy of almost thirty years will show."

Two months later, in early August, 1953, in the course of an interview, McCarthy was asked to comment on the general complaint that regardless of who criticized him, the inevitable McCarthy answer was: "He's pro-Communist." McCarthy asked them to be specific on who the critics were, and when *The Commonweal* was mentioned he commented:

> I never said *The Commonweal* was Communist—I just said that in front of the Jenner Committee, one of its writers refused to say whether he is a Communist or not. From that you can draw your own conclusions.

Note that in the McCarthy comment, Davin is made a *Commonweal* "writer" and it is inferred that he was at that time a Communist—

something he expressly denied before the Jenner group. The interview was released by the North American Newspaper Alliance and fed to its affiliates around the country. John Cogley wrote the senator and asked for a public correction of his remarks, and he responded with a note inquiring as to the relationship of Thomas Davin to *The Commonweal*. The information was forwarded to him as it had been stated in the Skillin release two months earlier and published in the *Brooklyn Tablet*. Five weeks later, on November 12, McCarthy "replied" with no real reference to the Davin issue that had been so crucial.

> You inquire what I said before the North American Newspaper Alliance. In view of the fact that I had no prepared manuscript, it would be rather difficult for me to give you a verbatim quote. As I recall, I did mention Davin's testimony as well as the fact that considerable material in your paper constantly follows an extreme left-wing line. I should have pointed out that in your book the traitor is not the Communist but the Senator who dares to expose Communists.
>
> I may have also pointed out that while you referred to your publication as a Catholic magazine, as far as I know, you have no right to use that title unless the fact that your editors feel that because some of them attend the Catholic church they are entitled to call *The Commonweal* a Catholic magazine. So that there will be no doubt in your mind as to how I feel about your magazine, I feel that you have done and are doing a tremendous disservice to the Catholic church and a great service to the Communist Party. As you well know, papers like the *Daily Worker* and other well-known Communist and party line papers can be of little benefit to the Communist Party. However, a magazine which falsely and dishonestly masquerades under the title of being a mouthpiece for the Catholic church can perform unlimited service to the Communist movement.
>
> Trusting this answers your inquiry, I remain
>
> > Sincerely yours,
> > Joe McCarthy

McCarthy thus ignored the point in question (whether a *Commonweal* "writer" had been called before the Jenner Committee), ignored the request for correction of the false implications of his widely publicized comments on *The Commonweal*, and resorted instead to his familiar method of personal attack. The editors published the McCarthy letter and commented that they were "indebted to Senator McCarthy for one thing: He has again demonstrated, more effectively than we could ever hope to do, the level of his 'crusade.' "[8]

Just how strong was Catholic support for McCarthy? He certainly never received any official endorsement in the sense of a collective public statement by the country's Catholic bishops. On the other hand, except for Bishop Bernard J. Sheil, auxiliary bishop of Chicago, no member of the American Catholic hierarchy ever publicly criticized Senator McCarthy or his methods. In April, 1954, Sheil told an audience of twenty-five hundred CIO auto workers that it was time to "cry out against the phony anti-Communism that marks our way of life, flouts our traditions, and democratic procedures and sense of fair play. . . ." He called for a clarification of the difference between treason and nonconformity, and stressed affirmative anti-communism.

> If a man is truly anti-Communist, he is interested in such matters as seeing to it that people get enough to eat, have decent homes, are able to raise their children in dignity. His scope is broad. He is interested in measures to share the wealth of "have" nations with "have nots." He is interested in breaking down barriers that separate people—national barriers, religious barriers, class barriers. He is interested in making a better place of his own little corner of the world and of doing all he can to see that others are not in want.

> I judge an anti-Communist—the real thing, not the cops and robbers version—by how well he does these things. . . . By this standard a number of famous anti-Communists, I'm sorry to say, simply don't measure up.

Sheil pointed out that he was speaking as a citizen, not as a spokesman for the Church. He noted that other Catholics took a more kindly view of McCarthy and his effect on the nation. "That is their privilege," he said, "as it is my privilege to speak as I have. Time will tell which of us is right."[9]

The Commonweal warmly praised his speech and stated that it had been delivered by "one who was vigorously and positively anti-Communist long before it became fashionable."[10] The speech was news from coast to coast, especially since it was delivered in the same week that McCarthy spoke at a Communion breakfast attended by six thousand Catholic members of the New York City police force. Cardinal Spellman, who was at the breakfast, shook hands with McCarthy and applauded his speech. In August, 1953, when Spellman received the Bernard M. Baruch Distinguished Award from the Veterans of Foreign Wars, he was asked at a press conference what he thought of McCarthy. He replied:

McCarthy is against Communism and he has been doing something about it. He is making America aware of the dangers of Communism. He was elected and re-elected Senator from his native State and no one is better known than by his neighbors. I am willing to accept the verdict of the citizens of Wisconsin concerning Senator McCarthy.

A few months later, when in Brussels, Spellman was reported in the press as saying that Europe was unduly alarmed over McCarthyism. He remarked that "the loss of American prestige in Europe and Asia because of McCarthyism is a reflection not upon America, but upon European standards of honor and patriotism."[11]

Catholic laymen, however, were not nearly so unanimous in their approval of McCarthy as an examination of the Catholic press and hierarchy would indicate. The Gallup Poll of January 1954 showed 58 percent of American Catholics favorable to the senator as compared to 49 percent of American Protestants. The *New Republic* in analyzing Catholic opinion on McCarthy six months before this, had estimated that McCarthyism was not representative of Catholic thought, but it did worry about the possibility that McCarthy had the balance of power in states with large numbers of Catholic voters. In April, 1954, at the time of the Army-McCarthy hearings, the Gallup Poll showed a drop to 46 percent approval among Catholics. A national tide had begun to turn against McCarthy, and on December 2, 1954, after an investigation of his activities, he was censured by the Senate by a vote of 67 to 22.[12]

While Catholics were split on the McCarthy issue, it is clear that pro-McCarthy sentiments prevailed among Catholics who spoke out on the issue. For those few who spoke out against him, their situation could be made difficult. During this period, John Cogley was prevailed upon to accept the Democratic nomination for Congress from his largely Republican district in Nassau County, New York. The incumbent was a pro-McCarthy Catholic and the key issue in the race was how one stood on Senator Joe McCarthy. The Sunday before the election, the pastor of Cogley's parish church, with Cogley, his wife and six children assembled in the congregation before him, homilized: "What can you say of a man who is opposed to Senator Joe McCarthy? The best you can say is that he is a fool." He then went through some of the worst things you could say. Cogley ran a strong race in losing.[13]

For Catholic admirers of McCarthy, an anti-McCarthy Catholic was a clear contradiction in terms. The Church was anti-Communist and Senator McCarthy was anti-Communist; therefore, anyone who was anti-McCarthy was pro-Communist and anti-Catholic. The absurdity of this reasoning did not cut short its longevity. Later in the 1950s it was still essentially present. Jim O'Gara wrote an editorial on the American Civil Liberties Union in which he distinguished issues on which he agreed and disagreed with their stands, and was somewhat shocked when he received a call from the ACLU national office—he was not a member of the group—thanking him for his thoughtful critique, and asking him if he would accept a nomination to run for their national board of directors. He agreed, and was elected, becoming the first Catholic since the death of Monsignor John A. Ryan to serve in that post where he could influence ACLU policy. He was then treated to an anonymous mimeographed sheet which was passed out at all the Masses in his parish church denouncing him by name as procommunist. It was a difficult period. Cogley, Skillin, and O'Gara all had children in parochial schools at the time and as Jim O'Gara has commented, "You could never be sure what some over-zealous nun was going to do or say in class that would hurt your little kids."[14]

The Liberal Catholic and Cultural Freedom

Two issues around which a number of concerns of *The Commonweal* at this time clustered were the question of the "liberal Catholic" and the related question of Catholic cultural freedom, particularly in regard to motion pictures. They were issues that aroused a great intensity of feeling, and which must be considered if we are to understand the developing history of *The Commonweal* and American Catholicism.

What did it mean to be a "liberal Catholic" at this time? William Clancy attempted to articulate what the species was, although he acknowledged that to do so was to run the danger of seeming to set up a kind of "pseudo elite" within the Church. "Liberal Catholic," he commented, "could sound as insufferably smug as 'Catholic Intellectual.' " But the term was widely used to describe "a type of Catholic whose world-view is marked by an enthusiastic acceptance of certain ideals for which liberalism has waged its great battles—maximum human freedom under law, social progress, and democratic equality." There was an unfortunate historical antipathy which the terms "liberal" and "Catholic" had acquired toward each other, but this was the result of "the accident of liberalism's having struggled for some things which should properly have a Christian name." The "liberal Catholic's" efforts were aimed "not at compromise but at recovery and redemption." The Catholic liberal was, however, frequently suspect. Those whose theology he shared frequently distrusted him because of his politics, and those with whom he felt at home politically at times doubted him because of his theology. What the "liberal Catholic" pleaded for was that Catholics would become as passionately dedicated to human dignity and freedom as many liberals had been. Catholics had better philosophical reasons for so doing, said Clancy. Perhaps a world could emerge that went beyond labels. The "liberal Catholic" for his part would be "more content to be thought of as a Catholic who tries to be *catholic*."

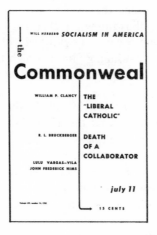

Others had different notions of what a "liberal Catholic" was. To some he was one who thinks:

> that his soul's salvation is a part-time work; that the Church ought to make a concordat with him personally. The "liberal" Catholic likes: the company of the faithless more than the company of the faithful; the catch phrases of the day more than eternal truths; both God and Mammon, but is more at home with the latter; to solve in minutes problems which stagger the Church for years, to be an outstanding Catholic, without being outstandingly Catholic.

This was the way the conservative Catholic weekly, the *Wanderer*, conceived the "liberal Catholic," but *America* editorialized that the Clancy exposition was a very successful attempt at disentangling confused ideological strands, and the Jesuit editors reproduced his article in their documentary publication, the *Catholic Mind*.[1]

In such a period of conflicting Catholic ideologies, the issue of Catholics and cultural freedom became a vexing one for *The Commonweal*. It was especially occasioned by the controversy surrounding the Rossellini film, *The Miracle*, which New York Catholic pickets, political power, and court tests sought to suppress, losing only in the U. S. Supreme Court. Similar controversy at about the same time followed efforts to censor and suppress the Rutgers undergraduate magazine *Anthro* for publishing a short story which certain elements in the local Catholic community considered immoral and blasphemous, and the successful attempt to remove certain Charlie Chaplin comedies from movie and television screens in New Jersey because the Catholic War Veterans suspected Chaplin of having "Leftist sympathies." Catching the spirit of things, a Queens Council of the Knights of Columbus threw a picket line around a theater showing *The Bicycle Thief* because it "glorified a thief"—an unusual way of summing up a prize-winning film of which the Legion of Decency had approved. But the management bowed and cancelled the run of the film.[2]

In an editorial on *The Miracle* and the flurry surrounding it, *The Commonweal* stated that what the affair showed was that American Catholics, especially those in heavily Catholic metropolitan areas like New York, were numerous, influential, and powerful. In addition, "we are burdened with an ancient siege complex and are keenly sensitive to slurs, real or imaginary." The editors wished that when the film appeared with the blasphemy some Catholics attributed to it, they might have spoken their piece about it, relied upon persuasiveness to clarify whatever was found objectionable, and allowed the community to decide whether or not they wished to patronize the film. Instead, there was a resort to picket lines and state power. They commented:

> We may be respected and our opinions kowtowed to, but too often it is our pocketbooks rather than our principles, our votes more than our virtues that win respect. And certainly no one can deny that we have our victories. But whether these are really victories for the cause we are supposed to represent is sometimes highly questionable.

The result of the whole affair, they concluded, in their editorial which was cited by one of the Supreme Court justices in the final case, was merely to make those outside the Church "feel as if they were being treated like children by an alien force that didn't give two cents for their personal liberty." William Clancy wrote that the Catholic War Veterans and other sincerely intentioned groups seemed only to be bent on proving that Paul Blanshard was correct in arguing the incompatibility of American freedom and Catholic power.[3]

Walter Kerr, drama critic for *The Commonweal* during the early 1950s, wrote an article on "Catholics and Hollywood" that argued that the power which Catholic spokesmen had come to wield over the motion picture had helped to make the motion picture even more commonplace than it need have been. He was distressed that the most publicized Catholic "art" award of 1952 had been the Christophers' selection of *Quo Vadis* as best film. The Christophers saw it as a "creative work of enduring significance," but it was for Kerr an "essay in calculated vulgarity." The Christophers' problem was that they made proselytizing content their aesthetic norm. This truth, said Kerr, slipped out when Father Keller in presenting the award immediately launched into praise of the film for showing "how a handful of human beings, fired with the love and truth of Christ, were able to overcome the might of Pagan Rome." When there was no recent film of obviously Catholic sympathies—"no priest in the pulpit, no nun in the backfield, no early-Christian Deborah Kerr in the jaws of a Technicolor lion"—the next best bet in the practice of Catholic criticism was to play it safe. Because of this, and the economic weaponry of the Legion of Decency, Catholic taste in motion pictures was "frozen at the 'unobjectionable' or purity with popcorn level, a level which if pursued down the ages would have called into question nearly every literary or dramatic masterpiece ever produced." A penalty of the relationship between Catholics and Hollywood was that it tended to discredit the entire Catholic intellectual tradition.

> The man who has been to see *Quo Vadis*, and who then read the Christopher citation, reaches certain conclusions: that the "Catholic" concept of art is a decidedly primitive one; that it probably rests on similarly primitive philosophical principles; that the Church, when its true colors are showing, is essentially antipathetic to the creative spirit, essentially in league with the vulgar.

> The fact that each of these assumptions is false, and would seem strange indeed to an Augustine, an Aquinas, or a Newman, is nothing for which the contemporary observer can be held responsible; the impression is thrust upon him, paraded before him, drummed in his ears by the most vocal Catholic spokesmen in the field.

Kerr said he had no illusions about Hollywood being a "seething ferment of crushed genius" which would produce great numbers of magnificent films the moment the production code was liberalized. However, as things were, Catholics had talked themselves into a corner, and into a code, which would automatically prohibit filming certain works of the most influential Catholic creative voices of the time, such as Mauriac, Claudel, Bernanos, and Greene.[4]

Discussions on cultural creativity and freedom continued throughout the 1950s as did discussions of the "liberal" Catholic, with John Cogley commenting that there was something wrong with a situation in which non-Catholics felt it necessary to make some kind of distinction when they described a Catholic who showed a deep concern for the state of "secular" culture and the common good, or who was ready and willing to cooperate in civic undertakings. When such people appeared—a Bishop Sheil or a Monsignor Ryan, among the clergy; a George Shuster or Jacques Maritain among the laity—why was it that they had to be explained away by the qualifying "liberal" added to the "Catholic"?[5]

Korea, Presidential Politics, Theology, and Commonweal

In this section, we will report briefly on some issues of nation and church to fill out our description of *The Commonweal* in the 1950s. We will consider the Korean War and the presidential elections of 1952 and 1956, and then touch on matters theological, including a formal charge of heresy against John Cogley. Then we will bring the story of *The Commonweal* to the close of the 1950s.

The Commonweal supported President Truman in his response to the North Korean invasion of South Korea, and supported him later on his dismissal of General MacArthur who the editors stated had "clearly exceeded his authority, and in defying the normal processes of the democratic code . . . placed himself outside the cause and the ideology we are trying to defend." At the height of the surge of Communist Chinese intervention in December, 1950, they counselled that "we should withdraw our troops from Korea on the best terms we can make and concentrate on the defense of Western Europe." That which could enable communism to subjugate the world was the heavy industry of the Ruhr and that of Great Britain and other sectors of Western Europe. Unless we concentrated our forces where they would do the most good, we would "not succeed in defending anybody."[1] The situation in Korea and throughout the world did not, however, develop as disastrously as the editors feared at that time. Under General Ridgway, UN forces fell back slowly to below Seoul, regrouped and in a spring counterattack retook Seoul and by mid-April were once more across the thirty-eighth parallel where the war ended after a long, bloody stalemate.

In 1952, for the first time in its history, *The Commonweal* expressly endorsed a candidate for president. Of General Eisenhower and Governor Stevenson, they commented that they had "been increasingly impressed with the level of one candidate's campaign, and depressed and disillusioned by the progressive deteriorization of the other candidate's promise." Eisenhower's treatment of the critical issues in the campaign "revealed a disarming ignorance of them." His vague references to "the mess in Washington" were hardly satisfying. Stevenson, on the other hand, was informed, specific, and even brilliant. Skillin, Cogley, O'Gara, and Clancy expressed their hope that the "positive and rational approach of Governor Stevenson" would win over his opposition's "dependence on frustration and fear."[2]

In 1956 the candidates were the same, but this time *The Commonweal* did not endorse Stevenson. For one thing, the editors had changed. James Finn and Philip Scharper had replaced John Cogley and William Clancy, Cogley going to Robert Hutchins and the Fund for the Republic, Clancy to *Newsweek* and later to the priesthood. For another, the editors felt Stevenson was open to serious criticism for his promise to end the draft as soon as possible. It was irresponsible to contemplate such a thing for the foreseeable future "until we can think that limited wars are a thing of the past, and land troops a luxury." But they weren't greatly pleased by Eisenhower either, whose image they felt shifted awkwardly from speech to speech and emerged fully only in press conferences "where he candidly acknowledges occasional ignorance of major issues, uncertainty of Administration policy, and confidence in the future." When Eisenhower won a great personal victory in the election while his party lost both the House and Senate, they spoke of the Eisenhower "magic" and commented that even strongly partisan followers of Stevenson were motivated less by the belief he would win than by the conviction that he should win.[3]

In the area of theology, the 1950s found *The Commonweal* only infrequently treating expressly theological matters, and then almost always by a priest-contributor. John Cogley has recalled that "there was a feeling that only priests knew any theology, that no layman should ever discuss anything theological at any time, and that even whatever knowledge ex-seminarians had, had been cancelled out by the 'sad' turn they had taken. We observed this to a certain extent, but now and then would veer over into some question." At these times, Ed Skillin, impressed by Cogley's Fribourg studies, would defer to him, though the latter never oversold his academic studies in theology.[4] Cogley, for example, reviewed Henri de Lubac's celebrated *Catholicism* at about the time the eminent French Jesuit and four of his colleagues were removed from teaching, the action being part of the move by Church authorities to suppress what was abusively called the "new theology." The big blow in this move was the 1950 encyclical *Humani Generis* which warned against historical-developmental and existentialist theologizing and emphasized a more static and authoritarian theological model.

An editorial by Cogley on the theology of the Church-state problem produced some grimly humorous reactions. The occasion for the editorial began with a speech by Alfredo Cardinal Ottaviani, secretary of what was then called the Sacred Congregation of the Holy Office. Ottaviani's address defended the thesis that a Catholic state had a duty to grant special privileges to the Church and to restrict the religious activities of non-Catholic groups. It also chided certain "liberal" Catholics, especially in the United States, who had questioned that view and advocated a religiously neutral state. The *New York Times* investigated how authoritative Ottaviani's remarks were and was told by the Vatican that while his address was "not official or semi-official" it was nevertheless "unexceptionable." Hence the *Times* for July 23, 1953, carried a front page story with the head "Vatican Justifies Views of Prelates on Curbing Protestant Minorities." The *New York Times* story caused great apprehension. In an editorial on the affair, Cogley wrote that no one had ever denied that the view expressed in Cardinal Ottaviani's address was the traditional Catholic view, and hence was therefore described as "unexceptionable." Nonetheless, it was in need of revision. Perhaps it was once suitable to a sacral civilization, but it seemed to many Catholics "out of date, and useless and even harmful if applied in the twentieth century—and this whether it be applied in the United States or in Spain." The editorial closed by exhorting the continuance of the effort among Catholics to formulate a church-state position which had "some relevance to the world they live in." The editorial was forthright and strong and certainly expressed the view of the majority of ordinary Catholics in this country, as developments in the 1960s would show, but it was not received kindly in some quarters. When

Cogley came to the office a few days later, he found a telegram from the editor of a Catholic diocesan weekly with whom *The Commonweal* had tangled over *The Miracle*, summoning him to an ecclesiastical trial for heresy and for having the effrontery as an untutored layman of having theological opinions. Cogley responded with a private letter that said he didn't know anything about whatever kind of trial was being contemplated, but they shouldn't wait for him to arrive for it.[5]

The incident was unique in the magazine's history. It was, of course, essentially the Cogley view that would emerge as normative in church-state doctrine in Vatican II. The editors were actually quite careful about their orthodoxy. On one occasion, Paul Blanshard referred in one of his books to *The Commonweal* as "dancing on a tight rope over the gulf of excommunication," and the editors were quite upset. They felt it was libelous, hired a lawyer to line up the case, and wrote to the publisher. Jim O'Gara has recalled that they felt "that whatever the New York Chancery might think of us, if it came to a court case, they would at least say we were orthodox." The matter, however, never went to court as the editors agreed to settle for the publisher's promise to delete the comment in any further editions.[6]

The "Commonweal Catholic" tag, which George Shuster has reported goes back to Cardinal O'Connell and the early days of the magazine, was popular during this period in the 1950s. John Cogley has stated, however, that none of the editors considered themselves "Commonweal Catholics," and Jim O'Gara has added that the "Commonweal Catholic" tag which was sometimes put on the editors was "misleading" if the suggestion was that they were "less than devoted to the Church."[7]

Others seemed to feel that way too. One of the better-kept secrets of *The Commonweal* was that Thomas Molloy, the bishop of Brooklyn, whose diocese sponsored the *Brooklyn Tablet*, in many ways a leading adversary of *The Commonweal*, on a couple of occasions quietly made donations of $500 toward easing the financial stress of the magazine. Bishop John Wright contributed modestly to the magazine and wrote some articles for it, because he took an interest in the vigorous discussion touched off throughout American Catholicism by an essay on "American Catholics and the Intellectual Life" by Monsignor John Tracy Ellis which was published in *Thought* and partially reprinted in *The Commonweal*. The thrust of the article was similar to George Shuster's "Have We Any Scholars?" published in

1925, but thirty years of greater maturity for American Catholics assisted a more trenchant and at least somewhat less defensive reaction to it.[8]

Some of the largest financial contributions to the magazine came during the postwar and 1950s periods. Gregory and Gerard Smith, the latter of whom became rather well-known for his work at the Strategic Arms Limitation Talks in the 1970s, were prepschool friends of Philip Burnham and bought a modest amount of stock in the magazine after the war. Gregory, who worked briefly as a *Commonweal* editor, for several years contributed $10,000 worth of securities to the magazine. Mrs. George Craig, Jr., of Pittsburgh, also a friend of Philip Burnham, bought some stock in the magazine each year and on a couple of occasions donated $1,000. They have been the chief "angels" in the recent history of the magazine, which currently has two hundred contributors of $50 to $100 a year, but no large benefactors.[9]

Philip Burnham completely severed his relationship with the magazine in the late 1950s by selling his stock to Edward Skillin. Burnham spoke of himself not as pro-McCarthy, but as anti-anti-McCarthy, and worried about the things McCarthy brought up. John Cogley has recalled that Burnham was "very unhappy" about the magazine at that time, and "very critical" of it. "He felt much more at home with the *National Review*, but he was critical of them too. I think he always felt we were being somewhat hysterical in our anti-McCarthy position." "He felt so much at odds with our point of view," recalled Edward Skillin, "and we felt it too, because it meant that the stockholders meeting could be very difficult. In fact at one point James Burnham came around and made very critical remarks about how we ran the magazine, so we had the feeling—I guess it was sort of mutual—that this was sort of a disturbing element in the conduct of the magazine, and I guess he wanted to get out—didn't want to be identified as one of the principal stockholders."[10]

In 1959–60, Burnham contributed some essays to *Commonweal* offering a conservative point of view on various topics, but contributed nothing after that. His only recent writings have been a couple of essays in *Triumph*, the conservative Catholic monthly. In the 1970s, he has served as vice-president of Catholics United for the Faith, a conservative Catholic organization principally concerned with catechetical orthodoxy.

Throughout the 1950s, as has been the case with other decades, essays by conservative writers appeared. Erik von Kuehnelt-Leddihn,

Thomas Molnar, Frederick Wilhelmsen, William Buckley, and Russell Kirk were among the contributors. In their own writings, the editors were advocates, but the magazine was open to anything as long as it was good and pertinent writing.

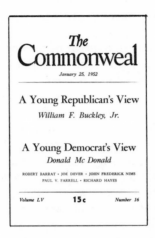

The
Commonweal
January 25, 1952

A Young Republican's View
William F. Buckley, Jr.

A Young Democrat's View
Donald Mc Donald

ROBERT BARRAT · JOE DEVER · JOHN FREDERICK NIMS
PAUL V. FARRELL · RICHARD HAYES

| *Volume LV* | **15c** | *Number 16* |

Regarding ecumenism too, the decade was a noteworthy one for *The Commonweal*. There were, as in previous decades, articles by Protestant and Jewish writers—Reinhold Niebuhr's and Will Herberg's essays on American Catholics, for example, were joined to a number of others on various facets of American Catholicism and published as *Catholicism in America*. But there was greater interpersonal rapport, too, among the editors of *Commonweal, Christian Century, Christianity and Crisis*, and *Commentary*. None of them was interested in the kind of phony American religiosity that many perceived and Will Herberg devastatingly described in *Protestant, Catholic and Jew*. Some of the closer relationships between the magazines began as a result of a trip to the Middle East of several weeks duration which John Cogley and Harold Fey of *Christian Century* went on in 1954. Cogley has stated that previous to that time, the *Christian Century* had been "crudely anti-Catholic." Rather rapidly, contacts expanded with Wayne Cowan, Robert McAfee Brown, Reinhold Niebuhr, and others. At times, day-long conferences of the "4 Cs" editors were held with various other individuals and groups in attendance too. Also, in a somewhat less structured way, a kind of "premature" ecumenism developed out of these social contacts, and was carried on in living rooms and bars. John Cogley has stated that "the White Horse Bar was the center of ecumenism for about five years." Cogley recalls these contacts and the writing and discussion engendered by them, to be the most important thing to "spin off" from *The Commonweal* during these years.[11]

If all of this, however, was "premature" ecumenism, it was not to be that way for long. Important changes were in store as the decade of the 1950s moved to a close.

At times, the history of a magazine may be significantly altered by developments within itself, such as serious financial problems or large-scale changes in editorial personnel. An example of this was the change which *The Commonweal* experienced in 1938 when Ed Skillin and Phil Burnham took over the magazine after the Michael Williams-George Shuster period which had lasted from 1924 to that time. On other occasions, however, it is events and developments outside a magazine's inner life that make for profound change, and it is this which happened to *The Commonweal* beginning in October, 1958, with an event which, while newsworthy, was rather routine. It concerned the first of three personalities whom we will discuss who profoundly changed the world and the American Catholicism in which *The Commonweal* was situated.

III. TO MATURITY AND IDENTITY CRISIS: THE COMMONWEAL, 1959–74

Three Personalities

On the eleventh ballot, Angelo Guiseppe Roncalli was chosen pope by fifty-one of his fellow cardinals. He was within one month of his seventy-seventh birthday and had spent about fifty years in the Vatican diplomatic bureaucracy before becoming the cardinal patriarch of Venice. There was much speculation in the secular press before, during, and after his election, on a supposed alternation in the papacy of "political" and "pastoral" popes, and on the election of a "compromise" pope, an aged, placid man who would live but a short while in his new position. *The Commonweal* criticized such speculation and classification of popes, pointing out that it had not been indulged in by writers in the Catholic press, as such calculations were "considered unseemly in Catholic publications." Two weeks before this, while the election which produced Pope John was in progress, the staff had editorialized against the Protestants and Other Americans United for Separation of Church and State, who had written Secretary of State John Foster Dulles to charge that Cardinals Spellman, Mooney, and McIntyre would violate American law by participating in the election of a new pope. The POAU cited the Immigration and Nationality Act of 1952 which stated that a citizen "shall lose his nationality by . . . voting in a political election in a foreign state or participating in an election or a plebiscite to determine sovereignty over foreign territory." Paul Blanshard made the same charges in an article in the *Christian Century*. According to Glenn Archer, the POAU's executive director, the American cardinals had no more right to vote for the new pope than other American citizens had to vote for Fanfani or Adenauer. The crucial question, he held, was "whether we will permit certain churchmen to perform acts of allegiance to a foreign state when we forbid such dual loyalty to other citizens." *The Commonweal* commented:

> If the question is one of selecting a new Pope, as in this instance, the
> P.O.A.U. stresses the fact that the man chosen as Pope will be head
> of a state. If the question is one of sending a U.S. ambassador to
> that state, the P.O.A.U. will dismiss the reality of the state and

emphasize the fact that the Pope is preeminently the head of the Roman Catholic Church. Either way, the heads of the P.O.A.U. must figure, they can't lose.

The editors dismissed such disingenuousness, and reminded Catholics that the POAU certainly did not speak for most American Protestants nor for what it called "other Americans" either.[1]

The new pope took the name John, and in a remarkably short time his humility and simplicity charmed the world. For example, he told newsmen that his own brother had made the best commentary on his election when the elderly Bergamo countryman wryly remarked: "So many men in our village have taken Holy Orders that according to the law of averages one of them had to become Pope." His sister, Assunta, on receiving news of the election, clapped her hands to her head and exclaimed, "My God, they've chosen little Angelo."[2]

Actually, part of the delight of the man was his great peasant bulk—his enormous ears, large nose, thick, stubby fingers, and his wide and generous smile. His whole genial appearance seemed the antithesis of the diplomat role he had filled for half a century. Further, his actions seemed to conform to his image. The morning after his election, John telephoned the editor of *L'Osservatore Romano*, Count Della Torre, waking him at 6:30, and asking that he come to see him. *L'Osservatore*, the conservative and semiofficial Vatican publication, had been much given to the baroque rhetoric of the nineteenth century, referring to the pope in the exalted and flattering language of courtly grandeur. Quotations from the pope were introduced with such phrases as: "We gather from the Holy Father's august lips," or "the illustrious and supreme Pontiff has said . . . " When Della Torre arrived, Pope John said, "We are living in the twentieth century. Let us have a style that suits the times and if you write simply 'the Pope has done this—the Pontiff has said that,' I would certainly prefer it." Then, perhaps to soften what would be taken as a reprimand, he smiled and corrected himself, "*We* would prefer it." In the interval between his election and his coronation, he took a tour of his tiny Vatican State. Poking his head into the carpentry shop, and seeing a number of men bent over their lathes and saws, he said, "This looks like thirsty work!" He then ordered wine for everyone and joined them in a toast. Visiting the wards in the Gesu Bambino Hospital, he stopped at one bed and bent over a small boy. "What's your name?" the pope asked. The child said that his name was a very long one with many saints in it, but that now everybody called him Guiseppe. "And what's your name?" the child asked innocently. "Oh, my name is Guiseppe too," the Pope told him, "but now everybody calls me John." And so they did.[3]

John Cogley remarked that after the genuine mourning for the great Pius XII, his successor had come on the scene "like a new sunburst," and had reminded the world that *joie de vivre* was a birthright that belonged to the children of God. Even Paul Blanshard, in his book on Vatican II, written in 1966, commented that though there were undoubtedly some legends circulating concerning the style of John, "probably most of the Johannine image-product was reasonably accurate."[4]

In his first Christmas message, in 1958, only a few weeks after his election, John spoke of "the vexing problem of the broken unity of the heritage of Christ" and of "our dear separated brothers." And he spoke not just to Catholics, nor just to Christendom, but to the world, of his concern for its unity and peace. E. E. Y. Hales has stated that "the novelty of his pontificate consisted in his concern not so much to preserve the faith, or to present it afresh (*aggiornamento*), or even to spread it, as to provide for and succour the whole of humanity; he seemed less preoccupied with the visible Church than with the world as a whole. Here, indeed, was a revolution."[5]

In January, 1959, he announced that he was calling an Ecumenical Council. It was the first since the Vatican Council of 1869–70, which had defined papal infallibility, and in the mind of some had done away with any further necessity for councils. It was the second since the sixteenth century Council of Trent and the days of the Protestant Reformation. *The Commonweal* commented that while Pope John had shown his concern for Christian unity from his first public address, "few people expected him to move so quickly to implement it." His reign, they predicted, would be "far more than the transitional one predicted by some when he was elected." He would "clearly make his own mark in history."[6]

Angelo Roncalli, eldest son in a family of thirteen children, was of a modest peasant background. He was distressed as pope when some with an exaggerated and sentimental hagiography would become excessive in describing the degree of his family's poverty. "We had the necessities of life," he would explain. He was the son of an able bodied tenant farmer who worked for a good master. In his short tenure as pope, a wholly new atmosphere was created toward Catholicism. Upon his death, he was able to leave each member of his family 10,000 *lire*, or about $17.50.[7]

As Pope John changed the international environment of Catholicism, so did John F. Kennedy, a Catholic of a much different background, change the national environment of Catholicism. His election in 1960 not only symbolized, but to some degree effected the cultural assimilation and acceptance of Catholics in America. He was not, however, the typical American Catholic. For one thing, his great wealth set him apart, but so did his educational background. He spent but one year, his thirteenth, at a Catholic school, Canterbury. He was then sent to Choate, and after prep school, to Harvard. He sensed his estrangement from the Catholic subculture, and once wrote to John Cogley: "It is hard for a Harvard man to answer questions in theology. I imagine my answers will cause heartburn at Fordham and B.C. [Boston College]." As Lawrence Fuchs has observed, "Unlike Al Smith, John Kennedy lived almost entirely apart from the world of Holy Name societies, Knights of Columbus, and Communion breakfasts." Rather than the usual deference of politicians toward Catholic clerics, Kennedy occasionally enjoyed quips at their expense. Once, while speaking at a dinner with an overweight monsignor, he called it an "inspiration . . . to be here with . . . one of those lean ascetic clerics who show the effect of constant fast and prayer, and bring the message to us in the flesh." Kennedy had no apologies about his Catholicism, but he didn't think that being a good Catholic meant that he had to be surrounded with Catholics or that he could not disagree with clerical authorities on public policy questions.[8]

In addition to Pope John and John F. Kennedy, another personality deserves introduction here for having profoundly altered the world political situation on which *The Commonweal* was to comment, namely, Nikita Khrushchev. Khrushchev's background was very different from Kennedy's, but very similar to that of Pope John's, and the similarity did not escape the Russian prime minister's attention. In the very interesting conversations which Norman Cousins held with Khrushchev in 1963, shortly after the Cuban missile crisis, the Russian commented on how helpful the pope's public statements had been at that time and added:

> He must be a most unusual man. I am not religious but I can tell you I have a great liking for Pope John. I think we could really understand each other. We both come from peasant families; we both have lived close to the land; we both enjoy a good laugh. There's something very moving to me about a man like him struggling despite his illness to accomplish such an important goal [world peace] before he dies.

Khrushchev spoke to Cousins also of de-Stalinization:

> . . . this was a real problem. Stalin had been worshipped by the
> Soviet people. Millions of people had gone off to war and died with
> the name Stalin on their lips. They had no idea how irresponsible
> and irrational he was. Did anyone have the right to disillusion those
> who had survived the war? Wouldn't there be a profound emotional
> shock if they were told that the man they had venerated for so long
> hadn't really known what he was doing. I wrestled with the problem,
> and then finally decided I had to tell the people the truth. At least
> twice I made long statements on the subject, telling the full story.
> You would suppose that by now people would know. Not so. Every
> day I meet otherwise intelligent people who still think Stalin was
> sane.
>
> There was a very important difference between Lenin and Stalin.
> Lenin forgave his enemies; Stalin killed his friends.[9]

It was, then, these three personalities, Pope John, JFK, and Khrushchev, and the events and developments associated with them, that
changed the world, and necessarily changed *The Commonweal* which
had to report and comment on them. We will discuss *The Commonweal* of these years principally by describing three issues and *The
Commonweal*'s response to them, namely, the presidential campaign
of John Kennedy, the Second Vatican Council, and world communism.

The Kennedy Campaign

In April, 1958, John Cogley wrote in his *Commonweal* column that
the way the Kennedy boom was booming, the questions which had
already been revived about whether a Catholic could ever reach the
White House were going to be heard more and more frequently.
Cogley said that what he found hard to take was some of the talk in
which what was a matter of prejudice was so often put forth as "a
grave intellectual quandary." He didn't doubt the sincerity of those
who professed to be tortured by the question, but commented:

> I do believe, though, they are working out a personal problem and
> have reached the stage where they feel a need to rationalize a posi-
> tion that is anything but rational. Anyone who has ever had to
> overcome a prejudice of his own, and most of us have, knows what
> they are going through.

If a Catholic couldn't be trusted with the presidential office because
of his religious commitments, could he be any more trustworthy as a

senator or as a Supreme Court justice? Cogley said he suspected that
the real reason why the presidency seemed to make such a difference
was that it was an office that was at least partly symbolic. "In his
person he represents the American people before the world. This
means for many that he should belong to the dominant ethnic and
religious group."

A year and half later, a few weeks before the election, the Reverend
Norman Vincent Peale, a prominent Republican clergyman, author,
and lecturer, then serving as spokesman for a new organization
called the National Conference of Citizens for Religious Freedom,
would be heard to comment: "Our American culture is at stake. I
don't say it won't survive [Kennedy's election], but it won't be what
it was." Upon hearing this Kennedy remarked, "I would like to think
he was complimenting me, but I'm not sure he was."[1]

For Cogley there were only two live questions: How many people
would vote against a candidate just because he was a Catholic? How
many people would vote for him for the same reason? Would they
cancel each other out, so the election could be determined by more
rational factors?[2]

In March, 1959, the publication in *Look* magazine of Kennedy's
views on church and state aroused controversy in Catholic circles,
and occasioned a critical editorial in *The Commonweal*. Among the
senator's more specific declarations in the interview were these:

> I believe as a Senator that the separation of church and state is
> fundamental to our American concept and heritage and should re-
> main so. . . . I am flatly opposed to the appointment of an ambassa-
> dor to the Vatican. . . . The First Amendment to the Constitution is
> an infinitely wise one. There can be no question of Federal funds
> being used for support of parochial or private schools. It's unconsti-
> tutional. . . .

The Commonweal's editors felt that Kennedy's remarks had been too
defensive and that by implication he was indicating that all Catholics
thought differently than he did on these points. They felt that he
should have made the basic point that there was no "Catholic position" on these matters—that they were not doctrinally religious
questions at all, merely points of constitutional interpretation and
practical judgment, on which Catholics were perfectly free to disagree
and on which they often did disagree.[3] The editors' point was to some
degree valid, but Kennedy simply did not think of the matters raised
in terms of Catholic positions, and to have done so probably would

have produced more confusion than clarity for the vast majority of the readers of the interview. His remarks were probably the most politically efficacious things he could have said, but he seems also to have believed them sincerely.

The Commonweal also took exception to Kennedy's remark that "Whatever one's religion in his private life might be, for the office-holder nothing takes precedence over his oath to uphold the Constitution." The notion that religion was personal and politics was public distressed the editors and they called his statement "an unnecessarily simple view of this most complex problem." The idea that there was a cleavage between one's religion and one's public life was the antithesis of what they and their magazine stood for. Some liberal Protestant circles reacted similarly. Robert McAfee Brown wrote in *Christianity and Crisis* that Kennedy's "effort to assure his possible constituency that he is just a regular American . . . has succeeded only in demonstrating that he is a rather irregular Christian." Martin Marty, associate editor of the *Christian Century*, observed that in the instance of Mr. Kennedy "we have a faithful Roman Catholic layman, regular at his worship, but one who is in many ways a son of his time: spiritually rootless and politically almost disturbingly secular." The Jesuit weekly *America* declared itself "taken aback" at Kennedy's statement, and other segments of the Catholic press criticized him even more harshly.[4]

The interview resulted in many letters to Kennedy, most of which were favorable. "I gave this interview of my own initiative," he responded in a form letter to those who favored his stand, "because I felt that the questions which were raised were matters which reflect honest doubts among many citizens." To his critics, he wrote that his remarks had not pretended to be "an exhaustive statement of Catholic thought . . . since I am trained neither in philosophy, theology nor church history," nor an exhaustive statement of

> my views on conscience, religion and public office. . . . I was simply stating candidly my firmly held belief that a Catholic can serve as President of the United States and fulfill his oath of office with complete fidelity and with no reservations. I see no cause to amend that statement now.[5]

It is clear that Kennedy viewed the questions he was asked in the *Look* interview in a less explicitly religious frame of reference than did his critics. It was, however, a frame of reference not notably different from Al Smith's in 1928, who as we have reported, found himself asking aides, "Will someone please tell me what the hell a papal encyclical is?" That Kennedy was "spiritually rootless" as Martin Marty claimed, is undemonstrated.

In April and May of 1960, there was another peaking of the religious issue in the campaign at the time of the Wisconsin and West Virginia primaries. In Wisconsin, Kennedy won the state with more votes than any candidate in the history of the state's primary, but he did not defeat Humphrey as decisively as some pollsters had finally predicted, and further, some attributed his win in the open primary to Catholic Republicans and his losses to farmers and Protestants. The result, wrote *Commonweal*, was that Kennedy's victory was impressive but not decisive, that Humphrey had run better than expected, and that the "religious issue" was more firmly a part of the campaign than ever. Much of the apprehension that *The Commonweal* and other observers felt, however, was relieved by Kennedy's stunning victory in West Virginia where he took 61 percent of the vote in a state where Catholics represented only 5 percent of the population. *The Commonweal* praised the statements opposing religious discrimination which were made by leading Protestant spokesmen during the campaign, and expressed hope for an issue-oriented voting pattern by both Catholics and Protestants.[6]

The statement by nationally prominent Protestant clergymen had been prepared at the request of Kennedy aides, though there was nothing partisan about it, and it was not released by the Kennedy office. Ted Sorensen, who worked on the project, encountered difficulty. Kennedy had suggested that he start with the Reverend Frederick Brown Harris, chaplain of the Senate, but Brown proved unwilling. Evangelist Billy Graham declined on the basis that his signing would help make religion an issue, but later in the year he combined negative comments on the Catholic church with the declaration that religion would definitely be a legitimate and major issue, "whether we like it or not," and participated in leading a Nixon rally in prayer. It was the Very Reverend Francis B. Sayre, Jr., dean of the Washington Episcopal Cathedral, and grandson of Woodrow Wilson, who helped get the project moving. His principal helper was Methodist bishop Bromley Oxnam, a leader of the POAU. Two years earlier, Senator Kennedy had joked at the Gridiron Dinner: "Should I be elected, I do hope that Bishop Bromley Oxnam of the P.O.A.U. will be my personal envoy to the Vatican—and he is instructed to open negotiations for that transatlantic tunnel immediately!" At the time of the primary, *Look* magazine was on the streets with an article by Bishop

Oxnam and Presbyterian leader Reverend Eugene Carson Blake, which *The Commonweal* felt unnecessarily raised questions concerning the ability of a Catholic president to participate in interfaith religious services. With Oxnam's signature and help, other Protestant leaders responded favorably, and one week before the primary an "open letter" to their "Fellow Pastors in Christ" was issued from Dean Sayre's office, signed by thirteen nationally known Protestant leaders. It was sent to every Protestant minister in West Virginia. "Quite apart from what our attitude toward the Roman Church may be," the letter said, religious lines should not be drawn. Protestant ministers should preach "charitable moderation and reasoned balance of judgment. . . . We are convinced that each of the candidates has presented himself before the American people with honesty and independence, and we would think it unjust to discount any one of them because of his chosen faith."[7]

West Virginia seemed to have settled the religious issue, and Kennedy went on to win the nomination on the first ballot at the Democratic Convention in July. Afterwards, however, it was decided to invite John Cogley to join the Kennedy staff as a campaign aide advising on relations with religious communities. Cogley was then with the Fund for the Republic, but had continued writing his *Commonweal* column after he had left his editor's post to go with the Robert Hutchins group. Cogley accepted the invitation to go with the Kennedy forces, but gave up writing his column during this period.

The religion issue peaked again in September with the formation of the National Conference of Citizens for Religious Freedom, mentioned briefly above. In addition to Norman Vincent Peale, the group of one hundred fifty was led by such notables as Dr. Daniel A. Poling, editor of the *Christian Herald*, and one-time Republican candidate for mayor of Philadelphia, Dr. L. M. Bell, an editor of *Christianity Today*, Dr. Glenn Archer of POAU, and the Reverend Donald Gill of the National Association of Evangelicals. The group's long statement which they released September 7, caused anger and dismay in many Americans. As Ted Sorensen has stated, many were shocked by the "transparent unfairness of three aspects of the meeting:

1. Men well known to be Republicans had pretended their opposition to Kennedy was for religious reasons.

2. Protestant clergymen opposed to the Catholic church's intervention in politics showed no compunction about openly intervening themselves.

> 3. The political position of the Catholic church had not only been inaccurately described but also inaccurately ascribed to Senator Kennedy, whose own views and legislative votes the group largely discounted."

The statement was met, however, by a chorus of Protestant respondents, the most effective of which were the eminent theologians Reinhold Niebuhr and John Bennett, who accused the group of loosing the "floodgates of bigotry clothed in the respectability of apparently rational argument." Reeling under the reaction, including the dropping of his spiritual advice column by several newspapers, Peale withdrew from the group, as the glare of publicity, mostly unfavorable, centered on him.[8]

On September 12, a group of one hundred churchmen and scholars—Protestant, Greek Orthodox, Roman Catholic, and Jewish —issued their statement calling for a truly open approach to the election. George Shuster and Ed Skillin were among twenty-nine Catholic signers, most of whom had written articles in *The Commonweal* at some time. The Protestants, numbering fifty-five, included Wayne Cowan, Bennett, Niebuhr, and others. Among the eight Jewish signers, Rabbi Arthur Hertzberg was probably the best known.[9] On the same day, John Kennedy made an important speech to the Greater Houston Ministerial Association, which had invited him to state his views on the religious question. The Peale publicity had helped set the stage for an especially tense meeting. The Kennedy group had prepared carefully for the meeting. The speech along with all possible questions that might come from the floor was reviewed by Kennedy with John Cogley and James Wine, who had joined Kennedy from the staff of the National Council of Churches. Sorensen had read the speech itself over the telephone to John Courtney Murray, SJ, the leading and liberal exponent of the Catholic position on church and state, to see if there was anything in its wording which might cause offense in the Catholic press, as had the *Look* interview. Kennedy had asked the staff to find out how many Catholics had died at the Alamo, and a Washington aide had been awakened at 4 A.M. to work on it. He reported back with a list of Irish-American names, but said that no religious affiliations were known. A line in the speech thus said, ". . . side by side with Bowie and Crockett died McCafferty and Bailey and Carey, but no one knows whether they were Catholics or not. For there was no religious test at the Alamo."

The speech was one of the most important in Kennedy's life. It was also one of his best. The question, he said, was not what kind of a church he believed in. What they should be concerned about was what kind of an America he believed in.

> I believe in an America where the separation of Church and state is absolute—where no Catholic prelate would tell the President (should he be Catholic) how to act, and no Protestant minister would tell his parishioners for whom to vote—where no church or church school is granted any public funds or political preference . . . an America that is officially neither Catholic, Protestant nor Jewish—where no public official either requests or accepts instructions on public policy from . . . any . . . ecclesiastical source . . . where there is no Catholic vote, no anti-Catholic vote, no bloc voting of any kind . . . and where religious liberty is so indivisible that an act against one church is treated as an act against all.

The speech continued to a powerful conclusion built around the oath of office which Kennedy had taken for fourteen years in the Congress. There were many questions, but he handled them satisfactorily and was enthusiastically applauded. Speaker Sam Rayburn who had at one point advised Lyndon Johnson against running as Kennedy's vice-president, saying he would be "ruined" by being on the ticket with "that Catholic," commented that "As we say in my part of Texas, he ate 'em blood raw."[10]

The speech was in great measure a triumph and turning point in the campaign. *The Commonweal* praised the performance as an example of how questions should be answered by other Catholics, namely, with simplicity and honesty. "He was as forthright as it is possible to be." (At one point he told a questioner, quite honestly but erroneously, that he thought the *Syllabus of Errors*, the infamous 1864 document of Pope Pius IX, was several centuries old.) Some were still unconvinced. Twenty-four hours after he spoke, a West Texas Baptist organization adopted a resolution saying Kennedy "is either denying the teachings of his church or is seeking to delude the American people." *Presbyterian Life* and *Christianity Today* wanted the Catholic church to announce its acceptance of Kennedy's views. The *Christian Heritage* continued its opposition and somehow revived the wild accusation that Rome had plotted the assassination of Lincoln. But the influential *Christian Century* switched from opposing Kennedy to neutrality, and *Christianity and Crisis* became even more sympathetic.[11]

As the election drew near, the religion issue seemed to have quieted, but then a final problem was raised by three American-born Roman Catholic bishops of Puerto Rico who two weeks before the election issued a pastoral letter "forbidding" the island's overwhelming Catholic population to vote for the Popular Democratic Party because it supported public health clinics which encouraged artificial birth control. American Catholics were stunned. Cardinal Spellman was quoted as saying that Puerto Rican voters would not commit a sin if they disregarded the directive. On the other hand, Bishop McManus of Ponce, formerly of Brooklyn, who was thought to have inspired the letter, said that "those who knowingly violate the injunction commit sin—the sin of disobedience." The pastoral's unprecedented strictures on voting and its timing, so unfortuitous to Kennedy, have no completely satisfactory explanation that would eliminate the possibility of an anti-Kennedy motivation, though it does not seem probable. The incident caused more controversy in the election here than in Puerto Rico, where it was ignored with Catholic Puerto Ricans voting overwhelmingly to the contrary of its instructions. Kennedy knew the affair had hurt him. It had been widely reported in the press, often under the heading, "They Said It Couldn't Happen in America." He commented to Ted Sorensen that if enough voters realize that Puerto Rico is American soil, "this election is lost." Kennedy had suspected earlier that the Catholic hierarchy was basically opposed to him. In 1959, there had been a controversy when the American Catholic bishops had issued a formal statement on population pressures calling the term "population explosion" (a term frequently used by Kennedy in speeches on the developing nations) a "recently coined terror technique phrase." Kennedy was angry that so sensitive and divisive an issue had been raised on the eve of his official campaign, and according to Sorensen, he felt that they "had either deliberately issued this statement at that critical time or else were thoughtlessly unaware of the damage it would do to his chances." On another occasion, while driving with Sorensen, Kennedy commented of bishops: "Naturally most of the hierarchy are extreme conservatives. They are accustomed to everyone bowing down to them, to associating with the wealthiest men in the community. They like things as they are—they aren't going to be reformers." Still later, as president, he quipped to a Catholic Youth Convention: "In my experience monsignors and bishops are all Republicans while sisters are all Democrats." Of the Puerto Rican affair, *The Commonweal* commented that it was at least clear that there was no plot by the hierarchy to promote Kennedy.[12]

The Commonweal did not officially endorse Kennedy as it had done with Stevenson in 1952, nor did it endorse Richard Nixon. At times during the period of televised debates, it criticized both candidates. Associate editor James Finn wrote an article on why he preferred Kennedy, citing Kennedy's factual approach as opposed to Nixon's emotional and irrelevant style of responding during the campaign. The editors' position collectively was to hope that the factors which normally counted in elections—"the significant, the trivial and the foolish"—would play their due part and would outweigh if not eliminate religious prejudice.[13]

In considerable measure, their hope was achieved. Religion did play a significant role in the decisions that many voters made, but not a decisive role in the election. Theodore White has stated, "There is no doubt that millions of Americans, Protestant and Catholic, voted in 1960 primarily out of instinct, kinship and past." American Catholics voted preponderantly for Kennedy, but estimates vary as to how preponderantly. George Gallup held that 78 percent of all Catholics voted for Kennedy, in social breaks ranging from 65 percent for college-educated prosperous Catholics to 83 percent for poorer grade-school-educated Catholics. The IBM data computers held that only 61 percent of all Catholics voted for Kennedy. All agree that there was a significant return to the Democratic party by Catholics. Gallup had estimated the Catholic vote as 56 percent Democratic in 1952, and 51 percent in 1956, but 78 percent in 1960. American Catholics had been heavily Democratic for a century, though many had voted for Eisenhower in 1952 and 1956. Were they voting in 1960 by faith, by political conviction, or by resumption of interrupted habit? In analysis of the returns from New York, Illinois, Pennsylvania, and New England, it appears clear that many Catholics voted for Kennedy because he was a Catholic. Similarly, an analysis of returns from Oklahoma, Tennessee, Utah, Florida, Kentucky, Oregon, Indiana, Ohio, and Wisconsin shows that many Protestants voted against Kennedy because he was a Catholic. The significant thing, however, is that these kinds of votes were not typical of the electorate. Kennedy was not elected by his religion, nor was he defeated by it. He was not elected by the Catholic vote, nor by a federation of American minorities, though many blacks, Jews, and others saw him as responsive to their needs. Kennedy had cast his appeal above all to the overwhelmingly Protestant majority of Americans and it was ultimately they who elected him. The total number of Protestants who voted for him outweighed the number of Catholics and Jews combined. His triumph was then a triumph of American tolerance.[14] It was, said *The Commonweal*, "a momentous thing, in our still developing, still unfinished, pluralistic society . . . a tribute to . . . the men of good will who spoke up . . . a bright omen for the working out . . . of the religious and racial suspicions and animosities that still divide us."[15]

The election was especially momentous for the self-awareness of American Catholicism. Previous to it, it was easy to find justification for an inward turning, defensive relationship on the part of American Catholics toward American society and culture. Afterwards, it was not nearly so easy. Further, it was greatly encouraging to the already existing forces within American Catholicism that had been working for years to promote a greater engagement with American society by Catholics. Significant among these existing forces was, of course, *The Commonweal*. If Carlton Hayes's series of articles in 1925, "Obligations to America," could be called the platform of *The Commonweal*, the election of John Kennedy in 1960 would have to be called the point at which it began to be adopted by significantly large numbers of American Catholics.

The Second Vatican Council

The excitement generated by the election of Kennedy was carried forward by the positive reaction of nearly everyone to Pope John and the prospect of the Ecumenical Council. In 1959, in a private conversation with Bishop John Wright of Pittsburgh, Pope John, who had begun at age seventy-seven to try to learn English, asked Wright of Kennedy's chances in the election. "Very good," Bishop Wright replied, and the Pope, fully aware of the 1928 stories that the pope would soon be governing America, jokingly added, "Do not expect me to run a country with a language as difficult as yours."[1] The story circulated quickly, especially after the election. Catholics were loosening up, were joking more about themselves, were more self-confident. They began to think critically about themselves and their Church, about how things might be improved, about how the *aggiornamento*, the "updating," that Pope John spoke of might be achieved. Meanwhile, the elderly Pope John himself kept up a remarkable amount of activity. In 1960, he established a permanent Secretariat for Christian Unity, with Augustin Cardinal Bea as its director; he then reversed the Church's stand of aloofness toward the World Council of Churches by sending a team of theologians as official observers to its assembly in New Delhi; he held an unprecedented meeting with the archbishop of Canterbury. In 1961, he issued a major social encyclical *Mater et Magistra,* the contents of which were front page news in most parts of the world. It was, however, the little things he did that seemed at times even more significant. For example, he restored the old practice of papal visits to prisoners ("since you could not come to see me, I came to you").[2]

The swirl of activity and preparation for the Second Vatican Council prompted considerable soul searching on the part of laity and clergy alike concerning the role of the laity in the Church. In some dioceses the laity were invited to make known to the hierarchy their hopes and desires for the contemporary Church. Cardinal Koenig of Vienna, speaking at a meeting of Catholic newsmen, stated: "Do not wait for the Bishop or for a report from Rome, if you have something to say about the Council. Sound a warning whenever you feel you ought to. Urge, when you feel urging is necessary. . . . Report everything that the people and the Catholics expect concerning the Council." *The Commonweal* cited the statement approvingly, and invited a number of American Catholics to write of their understanding of the layman, and their hopes and expectations for the Council and the Church.

Father Robert Hovda began the series by pointing out that in regard to the theology of the layman in the Church, Catholics were emerging from a period of "intense and unbalanced reaction." While the lay people's part, office, functions, or ministry in the Church had never been denied in principle, it had rarely been affirmed. The Church was not only a priestly and institutional reality, but a prophetical one as well. However, emphasis on the prophetical was so lacking, especially since the time of the Protestant Reformation, that "we have tended in practice to reduce the Church to the priestly and institutional." This was in practice, not in doctrine, but practice could teach too, and "sometimes more powerfully." Thus, freedom of thought and speech and criticism, public opinion, the responsibility of laity and clergy to express their ideas—outside the Church these were "almost universally thought to be alien to Catholicism." Further, there was within the Church "a marked hesitancy to be open

. . . forthright . . . critical." As a result of this, he said, a caricature of the Church was almost everywhere accepted as its authentic portrait. "It sees the Church as a mother whose smothering embrace crushes breath and life out of her children, reducing them to a kind of dazed and inert half-human existence." This reluctance to speak one's mind on issues, this irrational kind of "obedience," this assumption that a constructive kind of contribution was an act of disloyalty—this was "treason to the Church, to our sacramental initiation, to our bishops and Pope who deserve this contribution, and to the Holy Spirit." Hovda called for the establishment of structures at all levels of Church life at which the needed dialogue could be promoted. He suggested some kind of revival of the early Church practice of the participation of the laity in the election of bishops, and hailed the re-publication of Cardinal Newman's essay, "On Consulting the Faithful in Matters of Doctrine," which emphasized the part played by the laity in the development of doctrine. Newman, he said, showed the relationship between the magisterium and the faithful, not in terms of an active and passive element, but a much more complicated relationship—"as between a husband and wife in marriage."[3]

Philip Scharper, who had served briefly as a *Commonweal* editor in the late 1950s and was at the time of writing chief editor of Sheed and Ward publishers, contributed the second article in the series. He emphasized the importance of recapturing the priestly role of the laity. He pointed out that the priesthood of the laity, a fundamental tenet of the Protestant Reformation, had been spoken of by Pope Pius XII who had declared that the laity should be informed of the priesthood that is theirs by virtue of baptism, and that the fact of their priesthood "should neither be minimized nor denied." Yet in spite of this strong papal directive, Scharper reported that in the years since it had been given he had never heard a single sermon on the topic, nor was it a subject of discussion in general Catholic periodical or newspaper literature. In addition to pursuing this question, he hoped the Council would address itself to questions of religious liberty and church-state relations. Most of the world's Catholics, he observed, had long accepted the "liberal" view and were convinced that the Church was most free to be herself when she was as free from privilege as she was from persecution. Finally, he called for the creation of a climate of urgency in which theologians would work to discover the "practical corollaries of the Church's teachings." For example, there had been recovered after centuries of virtual ignorance, an awareness of the Church as the Mystical Body of

Christ. But there seemed to be an inadequate exposition of the practical consequences of the doctrine for those problems which pressed most heavily upon modern man.

> Why, for example, were so many Catholic churches in our South segregated so completely for so long a time? What cast of mind accounted for the fact that the Supreme Court decision of 1954 opened the doors of Catholic colleges to more Negroes than had the fact that the Catholic Negro was a member of Christ's Body?

An exploration towards understanding the meaning of work in a complex, industrialized society was similarly needed, and so was an awareness of the Christian's responsibility toward the peoples of the world who were struggling upward toward a condition of authentic humanity. The peril of seeming irrelevance, said Scharper, confronted not only Roman Catholicism but all Christian churches, and this was one of the strongest arguments for Christian unity. No matter how remote unity in creed might seem, unity in charity and concern could suffer no delay. This, observed Scharper, was what he felt was prominently in the mind of Pope John when, in speaking of the Council, he said: "We do not intend to conduct a trial of the past; we do not want to prove who was right or who was wrong. The blame is on both sides. All we want is to say: 'Let us come together. Let us make an end of our divisions.' "[4]

Joseph Cunneen, managing editor of the lay edited theological quarterly *Cross Currents*, then entering its second decade, wrote on "The Realities of Parish Life." He emphasized just how difficult the problems of communication in the Church were.

> . . . what response outside of downright hilarity would greet any wide-eyed "Catholic Action-ist" who told the local Holy Name Society—to say nothing of that more representative group, the men who do not attend the meetings—that their views on the coming Council were being solicited? "I can't get through to my pastor," one might say, "on why I object to using envelopes in the collection, or why I want to keep my family together, and not ship the kids off to a separate children's Mass; how can I have anything to say to theologians and cardinals?"

Despite the genuine nature of the appeal for dialogue by a few like Cardinal Koenig, said Cunneen, in the day-to-day life of the local church one could easily get the impression that the "age of the layman" was merely a new slogan for "the inevitable Catholic organizations, summoned into being to suggest the outlines of vast popular support." A change to genuine communication was possible, but it would take a dramatic effort to achieve it. It would be necessary to reflect on those patterns of Catholic life that contributed towards prolonging indefinitely a state of adolescence among the laity. For example, said Cunneen, "Catholic schools that pride themselves on their discipline rarely provide the most exemplary models of student self-government." Similarly, did the nature of the Church really call for "a clerical Sherman Adams, shielding bishops or the Pope from disturbing facts, especially if they [were] not couched in the terms of seminary rhetoric?" Cunneen was cheered by reports that the Council would give emphasis to the importance of the office of bishop, especially since the notion of papal infallibility was "usually seen in hopelessly unbalanced perspective." In summation, he asked for a Council that would not just be a public relations success, but one that would result in a "deeper understanding that the spirit in which the entire Church is called into Council is not for a certain number of days over in Rome, but something to be continued in human contacts and open communication every day in every parish.[5]

The other articles in the series were similarly incisive. Historian John Tracy Ellis quoted the 1889 remark of the bishop of Peoria, John Lancaster Spalding, that it was time for the Church to change from its practice of pretending it wanted real lay participation, when in truth it did not. There had been some improvement since that time, said Ellis, but it would be "less than honest" to describe the channels of lay participation as "fully open." John B. Mannion, of the Liturgical Conference, called for a vernacular liturgy, and the principle of adaptation of the liturgy to accommodate local customs and cultures. Scientist Charles M. Herzfeld spoke of the foolish and unnecessarily defensive position of many churchmen that so limited dialogue between them and Catholic lay intellectuals—scholars, teachers, scientists, administrators, writers. Justus George Lawler hoped the Council might result in a stripping away of some of the "vestigial protocol and panoply" that encumbered the bishop's office, and that these prelates might come to a new appreciation of their role as teachers and witnesses and be relieved of their characteristic muteness that had resulted in a "church of silence" that was not located behind the Iron Curtain. William Nagle scored the failures of laymen and clerics alike in their work of bringing Christ into the world. It was necessary for both to do a substantial amount of study-ing if they were to appreciate what was happening in the Church, and it was necessary that they talk openly to one another. The lack of communication was painfully evident regarding rhythm and birth control. Statistics indicated that Catholic married couples used contraceptive methods of birth control "about as often as non-Catholics." The majority of Catholic married couples who did not practice contraception, Nagle estimated, were "simply following the direction of the Church rather than any strong conviction about the validity of the natural law argument." There was little evidence that bishops and priests realized the seriousness of the perplexity of Catholic couples on this matter. A "head-in-the-sand posture of Catholic moralists" was evident. Some Catholic universities had even turned down foundation grants for study on rhythm and population control on the ground that the subject was "too controversial." Birth control was the most glaring example of a communications gap between clergy and laity. A second problem that Nagle saw was the growth in the United States of "a new anti-clericalism." It did not have the secular roots of the anticlericalism of the Continent. Its source was rather in the frustration, the disenchantment, the disillusionment of many lay Catholics who had "somewhere caught a glimpse of what the Church should be and of what they should be in the Church," and who were "now painfully aware of the gap between the ideal and the reality." The situation resulted in the "deinstitutionalized Catholic" who had, according to Nagle, become "quite common" among educated laymen. Such Catholics went to Mass and the sacraments, but retreated from "involvement" in the institutional Church. This increase in "deinstitutionalized Catholics" among the very laymen who should be leaders, presented one of the most serious problems the Church faced, said Nagle, and he saw "little evidence that our ecclesiastical leaders are even aware that it exists."[6]

How well would the Council meet this formidable agenda of problems, which were, to be sure, not the express agenda of the Council, but were an informed and articulate appraisal of Church needs? It is now a familiar story that the Council for the most part was a remarkable achievement. What some feared would be a conservative Council rubber-stamping decisions controlled by the Roman Curia, showed a mind of its own. Its first order of business was the election of members to the all-important working committees. Then, as Gary MacEoin has reported:

> Cardinal Lienart of France challenged the official [Curial] list of candidates. Cardinal Frings of Germany backed him. There was scattered applause. The Fathers looked at one another. The applause spread. It was agreed by acclamation to adjourn for informal discussions leading to more representative lists. "Bishops in Revolt"

screamed the forgivably inaccurate headlines. The world was shocked, then elated. Everyone wanted more information. The Council had ceased to be an internal Catholic affair.[7]

Over the next four years, from 1962 to 1965, the Council progressed as perhaps the most abundantly reported religious event of modern times. Gunnar Kumlein, a journalist residing in Rome, had for some years filed reports on events there for *The Commonweal*. In addition to him, John Cogley and Jim O'Gara attended sessions of the Council. Michael Novak, a frequent contributor on a number of topics, attended the Council, wrote a book about it, and was a source of information for the magazine. But, perhaps most helpful were the contributions of Hans Küng and Gregory Baum. Küng, celebrated for his *Council, Reunion and Reform*, an influential book written before the Council charting avenues of approach for it, attended the Council as a theological expert and advisor to the German bishops.

THE

Commonweal

The Aims of
Christian Democracy   *Eduardo Frei*

The Council:
A Good Beginning   *Gregory Baum*

Protestantism and
Authority   *Robert McAfee Brown*

VOLUME LXXXI, NO. 2   OCTOBER 9, 1964   TWENTY-FIVE CENTS

Baum, a Canadian priest, attended in the same role of theological expert and advisor to Cardinal Leger of Montreal. He filed many reports for *The Commonweal*, and like Küng, his reports had the benefit of being written by persons who were participants as well as reporters of the affair. In truth, however, Cogley and O'Gara were to some degree participants as well as reporters. For example, on October 21, 1964, Cogley was invited by the African bishops to address their weekly meeting, and with about a hundred bishops and priests in the audience, Cogley spoke to them of the need for dialogue *within* the Church, and gave them as an analogy for authority in the

Church, not a political model, but the family. O'Gara and Cogley, along with Martin Work of the National Council of Catholic Men, and Michael Novak, were invited to brief two of the Council's "lay auditors" on the state of the Catholic laity in the United States. It would be erroneous, however, to regard these and a few similar expressions of some kind of lay participation in the Council as very significant or influential. As John Cogley wrote:

> As a layman you are on the outside looking in. . . . That elusive fellow, "the Catholic layman" has received a great deal of attention within the aula of Saint Peter's: the Fathers have talked about him; his theological status has been beautifully defined in that most important decree, On the Church; and there are constant assurances that he has important significance, usually called a "role" in the concerns of the Council. But his part in the actual day to day business has been more that of a Hollywood extra than of a supporting actor.

True, there were lay auditors at the daily congregations, and three or four laymen actually addressed the Council, but as Cogley said, ". . . you do not kid yourself: this is a clerical affair—the great gulf remains fixed . . . in some ways the Protestant clergyman in Rome is more 'in,' more one of the boys, than the Catholic layman. Not only is he likely to be playing a more intimate part in the affairs of the Council; his 'professional' credentials are in order—or almost."[8]

Still, Cogley was hopeful for the Council, and was convinced the Holy Spirit was present in it. On the conclusion of the Council, Jim O'Gara wrote that for his part he hated to see it end. The Church needed dialogue, and the Council had been the greatest promoter of it. Also, its achievements had been considerable: some real dialogue with the modern world, liturgical reform, biblical renewal, religious liberty, collegiality, ecumenism, an enriched relationship with Jews and other religious traditions too, and a whole new understanding of what the Church was, based much more on the doctrine of the Mystical Body of Christ, and much less on a juridical, hierarchical, organizational structure.[9] It was virtually a complete vindication of the positions for which *The Commonweal* had argued for years, though they at no point allowed themselves the pleasure of any "We told you so" writing on its achievement.

Gregory Baum, in his measure of the Council, wrote that "taking into account the historical reality of the Catholic Church and measured by what the Council started with," its achievements were "nothing short of miraculous." Structural reform and doctrinal renewal had been initiated, and an orientation toward the future had become visible, but much would now depend on "the sensitivity of the Christian people to the Holy Spirit." Hans Küng wrote a lengthy catalogue of the achievements of the Council, and spoke of it as "the fulfillment of a great hope," but his concern, like Baum's, was oriented to the future and the challenge the Council proposed. Misunderstandings could be avoided, he suggested, by clear and thorough explanations of changes *before* they were put into effect. Post-Vatican Catholicism must continue in the task of "listening anew to the Gospel of Jesus and of reading the signs of the times." He listed particular questions not solved by the Council and awaiting positive solution:

> . . . birth control seen from the point of view of personal responsibility; solving the problems connected with mixed marriages (validity and the education of children); priestly celibacy in the Latin Church; reform of the Roman Curia in personnel and structure; the formal abrogation of the Index and censorship; reform of penitential practice: confession, indulgences, fast and abstinence; reform of dress and titles of clerical dignitaries; effective participation of the involved parties in the appointment of bishops; transferring the papal election from the college of cardinals to the Bishops' Council, a body more representative of the Church.[10]

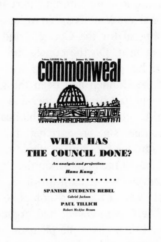

There was still much to be done, but the mood was one of excitement and expectation. The Council was in great measure a blueprint. What would be built, what would emerge from it? Whatever, there were real grounds for hope in the principles of the Council, particularly that of collegiality. It called for openness, dialogue, and discernment of the Spirit by and from all. Michael Novak has recalled his "feeling of exhilaration" the night of the climactic vote on collegiality. "The moon over St. Peter's Square was brilliant and full and those who walked there while the waters of the fountain peaked and fell knew that Roman Catholicism had taken an enormously important turn."[11]

We will return to what was around that "turn," but let us turn our attention now to *The Commonweal* and its analysis of communism during these years.

The Commonweal and Communism

The de-Stalinization move by Nikita Khrushchev at the Twentieth Party Congress in 1956 was in no way interpreted by *The Commonweal* as the signal for a new relationship with communism. It was, wrote Michael Harrington, one of its chief contributors on matters in this area, a "new line." To be sure, there had been significant changes in Stalinism since his death, but they had not altered the fundamental nature of Russian society or the nature of the various Communist parties. In political terms, cooperation with Communists remained "as impossible as ever." The various national Communist parties were "agents of international Stalinism." A few months later, however, following the spectacle of Russian tanks in the streets of Budapest, Harrington reported many Communists as shaken to the very depth of their being by the revelations of Khrushchev and the murder of Hungarian freedom, and urged that during this period of honest groping that dialogue had "become possible for the first time in years." This did not mean, however, "diminishing one whit our opposition to Communism." In May, 1959, *The Commonweal* editorialized in support of a papal decree of Pope John warning Catholics they could no longer receive the sacraments not only if they voted for Communist candidates but even if they voted for non-Communist candidates who formed coalitions with Communists. The decree, they said, simply clarified what should have needed no clarification: "collaboration with Communists by Catholics is impossible." In 1961, the editors expressed their reservations on Mr. Khrushchev's frequently used term, "peaceful coexistence." It seemed to mean economic, ideological, and political conflict rather than military confrontation, and yet, "under this Khrushchev formula there is a place for Soviet pressure on Berlin, and substantial intervention in the Congo, Laos and wherever opportunity beckons." On Khrushchev's visit to the UN a year before, they had commented that his performance "dramatized the dimensions of the Communist challenge."[1]

While *The Commonweal* was strongly and firmly anticommunist, it was in no way attracted by a variety of anticommunism such as the John Birch Society posed, and of the group founded in late 1958 by Robert Welch, they hoped in a 1961 editorial that it might "yet decline into the unlamented demise it so richly merits." James O'Gara wrote that one could understand how a call to the radical right might sound attractive to some Americans because of the rapidity of social and cultural change.

> To the old-line American of the rural and small-town West and South, the face of our culture must seem almost unrecognizable. Negroes and other minorities fight for their place in the American sun, and priests and ministers encourage them. Jews refuse to stay behind the ghetto wall; symbolically enough, they sit on the Supreme Court and in the President's Cabinet. Conservative Protestants fear that the power of Rome is growing; Catholics are "getting in everywhere" and one of them even occupies the White House. Conservative Catholics feel no better; the first Catholic President is a Harvard man and a liberal, and all this talk from Rome about ecumenicism and liturgical reform makes them nervous.

While O'Gara could understand how some might find comfort in the thought that the clock of history could be turned back, "perhaps even to those halcyon days before there was an income tax," aid or comfort for the John Birchers was not in order. Its mad cries of "Communist" against Eisenhower and Warren were a false anticommunism. The real thing, he said, "is or should be a serious business."[2]

In 1963, relations between Catholicism and communism underwent change. Pope John's "bombshell," as *The Commonweal*'s Gunnar Kumlein called it, was his reception of Khrushchev's daughter and son-in-law, Aleksei Adzhubei, in a private audience, which, to the consternation of some, was held only a few weeks before the Italian elections. It seems quite clear, however, that John did this not out of any desire to influence the Italian scene, but out of his profound grasp of the fact that he was the head of the Church all over the world and not just in Italy. He knew he was in failing health, that his days were numbered, and he knew that a dynamism was increasingly evident in the communist world that he wanted to reach out to. A year before, at the opening of the Second Vatican Council, he had made it clear that he wanted the Council to speak positively and that he didn't want the familiar list of condemnations, not even another condemnation of communism. One result of Pope John's new diplomacy, including his appeals for peace during the Cuban missile crisis, appeals that were given prominent attention inside the Soviet Union, had been the release of Archbishop Joseph Slipyi who had been imprisoned in Siberia for eighteen years. The conversation between Norman Cousins and Khrushchev was substantially concerned with achieving this end, and the then *Saturday Review* editor had been requested by the Vatican to undertake the diplomatic mission for them. An interesting aspect of the story is that following the release of Slipyi a papal medallion was bestowed on Khrushchev through Cousins, and it seems to have been highly prized by the wry Russian prime minister. When Cousins visited Khrushchev a year later, Khrushchev began their conversation by thanking him for Pope John's medallion, which he said he kept on his desk at all times. He added:

> When Party functionaries come to see me, I play with it rather ostentatiously. If they don't ask me what it is right away, I continue to let it get in the way of the conversation, even allowing it to slip through my fingers and to fall on the floor, so that they have to watch out for their toes. Inevitably I am asked to explain this large engraved disc. "Oh," I say, "it's only a medal from the Pope. . . ."[3]

Nineteen sixty-three was also the year of Pope John's famous encyclical *Pacem in Terris*, which in one of its significant passages indicated the rationale of some of his moves, as he drew a sharp distinction between "false philosophical teachings regarding the nature, origin, and destiny of the universe and man" and "historical movements that have economic, social, cultural or political ends." Such movements, the encyclical said, "cannot avoid . . . being subject to change, even of a profound nature." The pope had seen realism and value in a more flexible response to a communism which clearly was no longer monolithic. He did not, however, countenance its ideology. *The Commonweal* praised John's refusal to attempt "to solve the problems of the present generation with the solutions of the past," and said that he had "made an important, perhaps historical, attempt to change the direction and tenor of the Cold War."[4]

In 1961, *The Commonweal* had made it clear that their notion of a serious anticommunism did not mean a return to the foreign policy of John Foster Dulles. They were uneasy when John Kennedy, following the Cuban invasion fiasco, appeared to speak "as if the world were now polarized by the two great powers of the U.S.S.R. and the United States." They felt that the world was not completely divided into two warring camps, but was becoming increasingly pluralized. In such a welcome situation, they felt we should not let our opposition to communism stand in the way of the advancement of our national interests.

> Is it, for example, in our national interests to force new nations to choose between the two great powers? Or is it not possible that nations uncommitted to either side will provide a stability the world badly needs? Only when these questions with all their implications are answered can we go to the more particular questions of where we should commit ourselves with money, men and arms. But to answer these questions properly demands that we be willing to reconsider the direction we are taking. A polarized foreign policy is inadequate to a plural world.[5]

The Commonweal was quite correct in recognizing that the convulsions that were taking place on various continents were not the result of attractions to either communism or Western democracy. Other nations and peoples had their own aspirations, and were frequently more concerned with the basic necessities of life than with ideology. *The Commonweal* also began from that time to give a cautious recognition to the fact that even with avowedly communist countries a certain diversity or pluriformity was emerging and that the beginnings of this could be traced to the Khrushchev speech at the Twentieth Party Congress in 1956. This was not, of course, what Nikita Khrushchev intended by the speech, which may have been motivated simply by his desire to consolidate his domestic political position, but that is how it developed.[6]

Vietnam

We have framed our discussion of the early 1960s around Pope John, John Kennedy, and Nikita Khrushchev, and the issues which they raised either directly or indirectly for *The Commonweal*. We will handle the latter portion of the decade in terms of two basic issues. The first is the Vietnamese War, which managed to subsume a number of concerns foreign and domestic. In discussing it, we will also include as a separate but related topic, the presidential elections of

1968 and 1972. Our second basic issue will be postconciliar Catholicism and *The Commonweal*'s evaluation of it and relationship to it. A final consideration will be to report on the internal changes in *The Commonweal* during this time, in terms of personnel and ideology.

The deficiencies of an ideologically oriented foreign policy have by now been epitomized by Vietnam in the minds of many observers.[1] As we have seen, *The Commonweal* in 1961 expressed its opposition to a foreign policy based on rigid ideological considerations. How one will apply a principle like this, however, is difficult to predict, and for *The Commonweal* of 1961, Vietnam constituted "one auspicious place for the free world to make a stand." True, bureaucratic failings offset the "personal integrity of the intrepid if authoritarian President Ngo [Diem]," but with the help of American aid, South Vietnam had "survived and made appreciable progress." It was not, however, strong enough to repel "a full-scale assault from without." If possible, UN forces should be dispatched, but if quick and effective UN action proved impossible, "then the regional defense pact should be brought into action and mobile American units sent as a constituent part." South Vietnam was "a nation eager to defend itself, inviting and wholeheartedly welcoming outside aid."[2]

In January, 1947, in an editorial entitled "White Man's Burden," *The Commonweal* had supported French military action in Indochina against Ho Chi Minh, "because you cannot suddenly let go of colonies when finally they become a real burden, for then is the time when moral responsibility is put to the test." They felt Ho was a false "George Washington" who had been carefully trained in Moscow, and that the French were there militarily "to prevent the Indo-Chinese from breaking out of a system, which with all its faults still desires freedom, and entering another system which denies it. If you forget all about the white man part of it, the French are carrying the burden that civilization still must assume in order to save itself." George Sheldon, a graduate student at the University of Chicago, who had recently returned from a tour of duty with the OSS in the Far East, responded with a vigorous letter against the "superficial" editorial, and was invited to develop his ideas further in an article. The result was an ably drawn brief for Vietnamese independence and freedom, which *The Commonweal* published while rejecting its argumentation, the editors holding that "the future of their freedom lies with the future of our own; all our freedoms must be recreated and guaranteed by the concert of powers." Sheldon wrote a rejoinder pointing out that the editors' comment was fine, but that Vietnamese appeals to the Security Council of the UN had brought no response. He added:

> Is there something sacred about a tyranny because it happens to be a French tyranny? The Vietnamese are familiar with this notion and they are dumbfounded. They are at a loss—and so am I—to understand how genuine oppression can be less evil than a hypothetical sort.

The editors remained convinced, however, "that irresponsible withdrawal before colonial revolutionary action" would not "insure viable freedom to those who revolt."[3]

In the spring of 1954, with Dien Bien Phu under siege, and the ears of *The Commonweal's* editors still ringing with cries of their "softness" on communism, for their vigorous anti-McCarthy stands, the editors were ready to go to "the brink" with John Foster Dulles, and over the brink if necessary in a commitment of American air and sea support, and the intervention through the United Nations, of American and UN ground troops. They recognized that this ran the chance of World War III, but the alternative to this "frightful risk" was "a Communist-dominated Asia." What had the editors most upset was that the United States was so unprepared militarily. They slashed away at the "more bang for a buck" policy that substituted threats of atomic retaliation for "flexible military power at the scene of danger," and argued that it was not possible to "win the cold war at a cut rate." From this time on *The Commonweal* argued strongly for the preparation of counterinsurgency forces and the preparation of multiple military responses. Much would change between 1954 and 1961, but *The Commonweal's* support for this position remained, and the position gained widespread support in the late 1950s and was a tenet of Maxwell Taylor and the Kennedy administration. This was the background out of which *The Commonweal* came to see Vietnam in 1961, as "the one auspicious place for the free world to make a stand."[4]

In 1962 they praised the establishment of the Military Assistance Command in Vietnam, but pointed out that since victory depended "primarily on the will of the people to resist," economic aid by the United States and political reform by the "authoritarian" but "courageous" President Ngo Dinh Diem was needed. At this time *The Commonweal* envisioned the presence of "a few thousand men." Later that year they expressed reservations on the character of the leadership of Diem based on his lack of initiative toward social and political reform:

> The official U.S. position seems to be that we have no choice except to support President Diem, who is at least a sincere anti-Communist and a determined leader, strictly on his terms, with or without reforms. Maybe so, but we can't help remembering that previous Administrations gave just these arguments for supporting other leaders who were strong and dedicated anti-Communists in countries which are today an embarrassment and danger.[5]

In early 1963 as criticism of our Vietnamese involvement was beginning to manifest itself, *The Commonweal* published an article which argued that the war was really for our own self interest. It was not a chivalrous compact, but a worthwhile *quid pro quo* "with the absolute minimum of cost and risk for dividends paid." Also, throughout 1963, the editors' criticism of Diem grew stronger as they described the situation in Vietnam as changing "from a bad dream into something approaching a nightmare." It was American money, they argued, that had kept his regime in power, and it should not be used to subsidize a dictatorship. "If it is not already too late, President Diem should be left with no doubt on this point." They were especially troubled by what they described as the "folly" of the Catholic Diem's anti-Buddhist policies, and were gratified when the archbishop of Saigon issued a pastoral letter quoting *Pacem in Terris* on the rights of conscience of citizens. A few weeks later, after they had read Marguerite Higgins's reports in the *Herald Tribune* arguing that the Buddhist cause was hollow and opportunistic, they stated that the situation was complicated and controverted, and illustrated "how uncertain our knowledge of Vietnam really is."[6]

On August 21, 1963, Diem made what proved to be a fatal mistake, by having some police and special troops raid the principal pagodas in Saigon and elsewhere throughout the country and set them on fire, while declaring martial law. Diem seems to have felt, perhaps correctly, that the Buddhists, who had achieved a momentum against him, were determined to push demands on him so far as to make his fall inevitable, and that strong action like this was the way to reassert his initiative and authority. Henry Cabot Lodge arrived as the new U. S. ambassador the next day and found a widespread and intense dissatisfaction with Diem's regime. After the pagoda raid, *The Commonweal* held that the only question was "how to ease Diem out." U. S. policy was initially to try to retain Diem and get him to conciliate the Buddhists while agreeing to the ousting and removal of the Nhus, his brother and sister-in-law, who were special objects of disaffection. Ngo Dinh Nhu, however, was in control of the combat forces in Saigon, and because of this Lodge wired Washington, which had proposed a military coup with U. S. support to achieve these ends if necessary:

> Believe that chances of Diem's meeting our demands are virtually nil. At same time, by making them we give Nhu chance to forestall or block action by military. Risk, we believe, is not worth taking, with Nhu in control combat forces Saigon. Therefore, propose we go straight to Generals with our demands without informing Diem. Would tell them we prepared to have Diem without Nhus but it is in effect up to them whether to keep him.[7]

American policy seems to have feared that if the Ngo family survived the coup and came out on top, they would "sharply reduce American presence in Vietnam." Secretary of State Rusk at this time even speculated that the possible conversation with Diem on the ousting of the Nhus might lead to his taking "some quite fantastic action such as calling on North Vietnam for assistance in expelling the Americans." (In April, 1963, Diem had requested a *reduction* in the number of American advisers, who then numbered twelve thousand.) The coup, which seemed imminent in August, did not materialize. Lodge favored the coup, which he felt would be successful, as he saw in it the only way of gaining a more popular government and winning the war. He thought the coup should be a "truly Vietnamese movement" even if it put him "rather in the position of pushing a piece of spaghetti." It was to be two more months before the coup was initiated. During that time, Washington quietly cut off import aid (about $150 million) in an effort to force reforms on the Diem regime, but Nhu himself announced the aid cut and asserted that the Vietnamese were prepared to carry on without American help. Washington communicated to the coup group that it would not thwart a change in government, nor deny economic and military assistance to a new regime, but it was anxious to evaluate their plans two days in advance, so that the probability of success could be known. McGeorge Bundy and others were particularly concerned about the hazard of an unsuccessful coup being "laid at our door." Paul Harkins, the U. S. military commander in Vietnam, had grave doubts on the plot to oust Diem. He felt that the political and military situation was not as bad as Lodge had evaluated, that Diem would change direction, and that it was wrong "to change horses too quickly."[8]

After all, rightly or wrongly, we have backed Diem for eight long hard years. To me it seems incongruous now to get him down, kick him around and get rid of him. The U. S. has been his mother superior and father confessor since he's been in office and he has leaned on us heavily.

Leaders of other under-developed countries will take a dim view of our assistance if they too were led to believe the same fate lies in store for them.

In the end, however, it was Lodge's view that prevailed. On November 1, Diem called Lodge, told him that some military units had rebelled, and asked what the attitude of the United States was. Lodge said he was not "enough informed" to be able to tell him. Diem pressed him:

Diem: But you must have some general ideas. After all, I am a Chief of State. I have tried to do my duty. I want to do now what duty and good sense require. I believe in duty above all.

Lodge: You have certainly done your duty. As I told you only this morning, I admire your courage and your great contributions to your country. No one can take away from you the credit for all you've done. Now I am worried about your physical safety. I have a report that those in charge of the current activity offer you and your brother safe conduct out of the country if you resign. Had you heard this?

Diem: No. (And then after a pause) You have my telephone number.

Lodge: Yes. If I can do anything for your physical safety, please call me.

Diem: I am trying to re-establish order.[9]

Diem and Nhu refused to surrender to the attack on the palace, but after several hours, when it was clear that the troops they had counted on had either been neutralized or had gone over to the side of the plotters, they escaped through a secret tunnel to a jeep that took them to a place of hiding in the Chinese sector of the city. There they hid for several hours. They surrendered themselves the next day and were shot while being taken to the generals' headquarters.[10]

The Commonweal stated that there was a widespread consensus, which they shared, that the Diem regime needed to be replaced, but that Diem "deserved a far better fate, even if in the end he did not deserve the Presidency." They were skeptical of the junta for the killings and for their attempt to cover them with a suicide story that no one accepted. *The Commonweal* awaited the next development and commented:

The war in Vietnam must be won, but it remains to be seen whether that goal can be achieved in a way which is just, humane and sensitive to human rights.[11]

What followed was a rapid succession of coups and countercoups with some seven governments emerging in Vietnam during 1964 alone. Meanwhile, as the generals played politics and kept their attention on Saigon, the military situation deteriorated. At home, Lyndon Johnson, who had taken over following the Kennedy assassination, was busy putting his own stamp on his administration, which meant primary attention to social and economic legislation—the ill-fated "War on Poverty." In August, 1964, however, he announced a "limited and fitting" air raid on North Vietnam in response to attacks by North Vietnamese PT boats in the Gulf of Tonkin. *The Commonweal* supported the response, but wondered if Johnson's show of force would have been as great if Senator Goldwater, "the principal exponent of 'firm will' in foreign policy" had not been turned to by the Republicans. Also they found the language of the congressional resolution on the affair unnecessarily broad in granting advance approval of "all necessary measures . . . to repel any armed attack."[12]

As the 1964 election came and went, *The Commonweal* showed little wholehearted enthusiasm for either candidate, though it regarded the election of Hubert Humphrey as a "bright spot," and predicted that the use Johnson made of Humphrey would "tell us much about the character of the administration." By this time, *The Commonweal* saw a negotiated settlement in Vietnam as the only way out, though it suspected that a "massive military build-up by the United States, and perhaps a token raid or two on North Vietnam" would be necessary to get the Communists to the negotiating table. At the time, U. S. troop strength was at about twenty-two thousand.[13]

A buildup more massive than *The Commonweal* could have dreamed of began in 1965, as did much more than "a token raid or two" on North Vietnam. By July, 1965, Jim O'Gara wrote that he was firmly convinced that escalation of the war was wrong, but he was just as convinced that unconditional withdrawal from it was wrong. He quoted with approval Senator Fulbright's call for "resolute but restrained" action until the Communists saw they couldn't win a complete victory.[14]

By the fall of 1965, *The Commonweal*'s editorial position was giving measured praise to those demonstrating against the war, though they regretted that the demonstrations seemed only to solidify support for the administration. The demonstrators, they said, had pointed out very real moral issues: napalm bombing, administration deceits, steady escalation of the war, and the abysmal nature of the regime which ruled South Vietnam (Ky had become premier, with Thieu as chief of state at this time).[15]

In December, 1965, *The Commonweal* called for cessation of the bombing which it had in February supported as a short-term gamble toward negotiations. It also proposed a temporary unilateral cease-fire, initiative on negotiations by the appointment of U. S. negotiators and a negotiation site, and a U. S. withdrawal in slow stages in exchange for UN supervised protection of pro-Saigon Vietnamese and elections. It was time, the editors said, to explore every avenue to end "this brutal, degrading war."[16]

A consistently critical line on the continuation and extension of the destruction in Vietnam followed during the ensuing years in *The Commonweal*. While it admired the vision of an independent South Vietnam bristling with democratic politics and social reform, it recognized that its chances of attainment were infinitesimal, and the costs of its pursuit enormous. The war was producing more evil than good, and was diverting resources desperately needed for positive social uses at home and abroad.[17]

The same kind of shift in editorial viewpoint on the war that had occurred in *The Commonweal* occurred also in *Christianity and Crisis* and the *Christian Century*, both of which had supported early U. S. involvement in Southeast Asia to prevent it from falling to communism. The neo-evangelical *Christianity Today* and the Jesuits' *America* continued to support the war. In the fall of 1967 while *America* was supporting the war "to prevent 17 million Vietnamese from being swallowed up by a voracious and aggressive communism," *Commonweal* was supporting the escalation of dissent to the level of civil disobedience "in the tradition of Thoreau."

> This might take the form of withholding of taxes, counseling, aiding or abetting young men on avoidance of the draft . . . or disruption tactics of various sorts. Such conduct might sound extreme to some, but . . . the war is so wrong, and ways of registering concern about it have become so limited, that civil disobedience is the only course left.[18]

The Commonweal's editorial was written in support of a statement by a group of Catholic intellectuals on the illegality and immorality of the war, and of the necessity to develop forms of resistance to it. The statement had been drawn up by Peter Steinfels and Wilfrid Sheed, both editors of *Commonweal*, and Alice Mayhew, an editor at Random House and head of the Catholic Peace Fellowship in New York. The signers included John Cogley, Maisie Ward, J. F. Powers, Anne Fremantle, and others. *The Commonweal* expressed its support, "both with regard to objectives and means."

The Presidential Elections of 1968 and 1972

In early November, 1967, Senator Eugene McCarthy announced that he was seriously weighing the possibility of running against Lyndon Johnson in some selected primaries, and *The Commonweal* responded with an enthusiastic "first hurrah" in a lead editorial. It indicated the strength of the "dump LBJ" forces, the editors said, that a senator as respected as McCarthy had emerged as a serious contender. His record was distinguished and he had been "consistently the voice of sober reflection, coolness and integrity." What he offered was "not only the possibility of a way out of Vietnam, but the chance for a remaking of a system where obfuscation and deceit have become the daily ration of a government to its people." How much of a chance he had was a matter of debate. A few weeks later, he formally declared his candidacy, and CBS reporter Mike Wallace called the confrontation "a David and Goliath contest," but Allard K. Lowenstein commented: "Who the hell do you think won that one?" Lowenstein, a national vice-chairman of the ADA, was enthusiastic about the possibilities of a Democratic challenge to Johnson, and had sought a candidate since the spring, but had been turned down by Robert Kennedy, George McGovern, James Gavin, Frank Church, and others. McCarthy had agreed with Lowenstein that someone should run, but had said he felt that Kennedy had a much broader base. In August, however, he was particularly angered when Nicholas Katzenbach had come before the Senate Foreign Relations Committee of which he was a member, and said that the president had the authority even without the Tonkin Gulf Resolution to do everything he had done or might want to do in Vietnam, without conferring with the Congress at all. McCarthy denounced it as "the wildest testimony I have ever heard." According to Katzenbach there was no limit to what the president could do. "There is only one thing to do," said McCarthy, "take it to the country."[1] From this time on, the momentum towards his candidacy was set.

For *The Commonweal*, the McCarthy candidacy was almost too good to be true. He had been a long-time contributor of articles to the magazine on such topics as "The Christian in Politics," and "The State and Human Freedom." In 1952, with his own election coming up, he had confronted Joe McCarthy in a radio debate, the first member of either the House or Senate to oppose him face to face. Aides had begged him not to do it, but he came out of it looking better than anyone had anticipated. Born in a small, mostly German Catholic community in Minnesota, McCarthy at age sixteen entered St. John's University, thirty miles away at Collegeville. At the time, the famous Father Virgil Michel was there preaching and teaching liturgical renewal and the necessity of Catholic involvement in social action. McCarthy graduated in three years *summa cum laude*, and also made a name for himself as a fair athlete playing baseball and hockey. He then did graduate work in sociology and economics at the University of Minnesota, taught high school for several years and at twenty-five studied for the priesthood for a year, but decided against it. He was a civilian and employee in the War Department during the war years, where he worked on breaking the Japanese code. He married in 1945 and took a $2,750-a-year job teaching economics at the College of St. Thomas in St. Paul. After reading the papal Christmas Allocution of 1946 on democracy and the need for Christian involvement, he got into politics in 1947 and was elected to the House in 1948 and the Senate in 1958. He came by a sense of humility naturally. When McCarthy tried for the Senate, his father Michael was asked what he thought. "Yes, Gene is doing all right," he said, "but you should ask me about my son Austin. *He's* a doctor."[2]

McCarthy's background and attitudes were quite similar to those of some of *The Commonweal*'s editors. Could it be that Eugene McCarthy, a person to whom the tag "Commonweal Catholic" might suitably be applied, could be elected president? *The Commonweal* would clearly have been delighted by such a development, and not simply because of his affiliation with the magazine. But such was not to be. When McCarthy failed to receive the nomination, *The Commonweal* felt that the great hope for meaningful change was lost. What had promised, after the Johnson withdrawal, to be a new spring in American politics was proving instead to be "a continuation of the bleak winter into which the nation drifted under Johnson." Humphrey, whom the staff had regarded so highly four years earlier, was now a personification of "machine politics," clearly "not his own man," whose nomination dramatized "the impoverishment of the national political state." Except for the race issue, he represented nothing different from Nixon or Wallace.

> Thus the supreme irony: the rout of Lyndon Johnson, so complete that he could not even put in an appearance at the national convention of the party he leads, results in a situation in which all his potential successors are Sir Echoes of the very policies that led to his repudiation.[3]

They granted that Hubert Humphrey would "probably be a better president than Richard Nixon," but stated that the *New York Times* was "somewhat ridiculous" with its hailing of Humphrey as "an internationalist with a broad and imaginative outlook." What was important, they urged, was "that liberal and left candidates for Congress be supported" (their examples were Democrat Allard Lowenstein and Republican James Farmer), and that a responsible and politically relevant movement begin "the arduous process of forming its own political party on a long-range basis." The McCarthy and Robert Kennedy campaigns had shown how "exhilarating a political movement can become—if it speaks to the needs of the people, who themselves feel an intimate tie with the final results of their labors." What was necessary was to build on this toward posing "a humanistic, responsive alternative to the politics of racism and militarism." The editors commented that it would be "a long haul."[4]

The Commonweal had previously avoided third party notions, with John Cort being particularly strong against them, but the editors were now quite negative on both candidates. Managing editor John Deedy even spoke of Humphrey's election as something that would "chill you." Newspaper columnist Murray Kempton, on the other hand, could write:

> We are two nations of equal size. . . . Richard Nixon's nation is white, Protestant, breathes clean air and advances toward middle age. Hubert Humphrey's nation is everything else, whatever is black, most of which breathes polluted air, pretty much what is young. . . .

Kempton's remark was perhaps as simplistic in its way as was Deedy's in another way, but one can understand Humphrey in 1968 on the Vietnam issue—and that was *the* issue—as simply recognizing that one could not tell the truth on Vietnam and win, that it was necessary, as Senator George Aiken suggested, to declare victory and withdraw. The national self-righteousness was what was "chilling." But, politically, could thousands of American dead young men, to say nothing of even more dead Vietnamese, be openly branded a mistake? Was it self-righteous on the part of those, mainly though not exclusively the intellectual community, who seemed to demand this? On the other hand, from the frame of reference of *The Commonweal*, does Christian humility and honesty demand such an admission of wrongdoing, however well-intentioned (and this is not necessarily to grant that even all the intentions were defensible)? In an imperfect world, how much should one compromise in making the best of a bad situation?[5]

Meanwhile, Richard Nixon, whom James O'Gara and many others

saw making his political exit in 1962, whom Allard Lowenstein regarded in the mid-1960s as incapable of beating Arthur Goldberg for mayor of Cairo, emerged as president of the United States, on the basis of a "Southern strategy," the possibility of which Theodore White had described in 1960. Nixon's narrow victory was achieved to some degree on the basis of the disaffection of Catholics with the Democratic party and candidate. Hubert Humphrey attracted the support of only 59 percent of Catholics, whereas Lyndon Johnson in 1964 had matched John Kennedy by attracting 76 percent of the Catholic vote.[6]

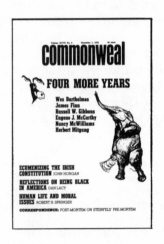

The movement of Catholics away from the Democratic standard-bearer continued in the 1972 election, with only some 30-40 percent of Catholics voting for McGovern. Some political strategists spoke of 1972 as the year of the Republican "Catholic strategy," but others thought religion was the weakest of handles on the overall category of defecting blue and white collar Democrats. None the less, a supposedly private Nixon letter to New York's Cardinal Cooke expressing opposition to abortion was leaked to the press, and the president made one of his rare campaign appearances at a Knights of Columbus banquet to speak in promising terms of support for parochial schools. John Cardinal Krol, president of the U.S. Catholic Conference, the most powerful Catholic churchman in the nation, visited the Nixon yacht, *Sequoia*, during the campaign, and stood side by side with the candidate while giving the benediction at the Republican National Convention before a television audience of millions.

Discussing his association with the president, the Cardinal said simply: ". . . we share a common concern over the depletion . . . of the religious and moral convictions which govern human behavior."[7]

The Commonweal evaluated the president's moral sensitivities somewhat differently. Richard Nixon, they stated, promised in 1968 to bring us together, secure our streets, and quickly end the longest, costliest war in our history. Instead, he has impugned the patriotism of those who questioned him, manipulated Americans suffering the anxiety of social change, and expanded into Laos and Cambodia the war he pledged to end. "He has rained countless tons of bombs daily on the now bomb-cratered surface of North Vietnam because, in his value system, life is above all a ruthless struggle to be 'first'—for a nation as for an individual—no matter what the cost in truth or human lives." For the second time in the history of the magazine, it endorsed a presidential candidate, supporting McGovern "because the overriding issues are moral ones." The staff spoke of moral issues "not in the narrowly religious sense," but as members of a tradition shared by their Jewish and Protestant brothers, that holds that God has given man freedom and responsibility to work for a just society on earth. Concretely, they felt this called for a more equitable distribution of wealth, the full integration of black people into American society, the right of every young person to a full education, decent housing and guaranteed health care, crime control, and prison reform. They stated that McGovern and Shriver came from this tradition and were dedicated to these goals.[8]

There were some *Commonweal* relationships in the campaign, both historical and contemporary. R. Sargent Shriver was the son of parents who were among Michael Williams's group of Calvert Associates. Shriver's father was a convert to Catholicism who became an avid reader in the faith and hosted prominent European Catholics like Hilaire Belloc and Paul Claudel. On his mother's side, he was a descendant of a three-hundred-year-old Maryland Catholic family that had come over with the first Lord Baltimore to settle Maryland. His godfather was James Cardinal Gibbons, a close friend of his maternal grandfather. The family fortune was largely lost in the Crash of 1929, and Shriver worked his way through Yale University and Law School, developing wide-ranging intellectual concerns. The contemporary tie to *The Commonweal* was in the presence of Michael Novak as a Shriver speechwriter during the campaign. Novak, a highly respected writer and theologian, was a regular *Commonweal* columnist.[9]

Viewing the election results, the editors did not see the massive defeat of McGovern as any great outpouring of love for President Nixon. They pointed out that 45 percent of the eligible voters had stayed home, and that while the president had the active support of about one-third of the people, the rest were still waiting for someone who would understand their needs and embody their hopes. They felt that McGovern had not run such a bad campaign; he faced the people and answered their questions. Compare this, they asked, to Nixon, "Who as Pete Hamill said, 'spent the election in hiding, the Howard Hughes of Presidential candidates; he let advertising agents and wiretappers and burglars do his work for him.'" The editors were most distressed, however, that the election seemed to bespeak a lack of comprehension of the war: "It was clear all along that to elect him [McGovern] might mean a public acknowledgement that America had been collectively morally wrong in its longest war, that had cost over 55,000 American lives and millions of Vietnamese military and civilian casualties." They felt that McGovern had addressed the best instincts of the people, even when they could not see their better selves in him.[10]

Postconciliar Catholicism

The early 1960s had been years of great hope, with John Kennedy, Pope John XXIII, and even Nikita Khrushchev. By 1964, however, they were all gone—Kennedy was assassinated, Pope John died of cancer, and Nikita Khrushchev was replaced in office. On the domestic scene there was progress on civil rights around the charismatic Martin Luther King, and talk of seriously changing the face of poverty for many Americans, but too soon an assassin's bullet would take King, and the "war" on poverty would not really be fought, because of the all-too-real war which was going on in Southeast Asia. As to the state of postconciliar Catholicism (i.e., from 1965 on), one would have to say that its unhappy course followed a timetable similar to that of the depressing descent of events in Vietnam, though there was of course no cause and effect relationship.

In one sense, however, the Church did have a "Vietnam," and this was the issue of birth control. The teaching that no artificial means, i.e., reliable means, of birth regulation were permitted for Catholics had not been uniformly accepted by Catholics at least since the Depression of the 1930s, when the birth rate dropped for Catholics and all Americans. There was some, but little, public grumbling, as we have discussed earlier, but how widespread the disagreement was is difficult to gauge. Most of those couples who resorted to contraception probably did so in stress-filled situations and with some guilt feelings afterwards, but with puzzlement as to the reason for the birth control strictures.

The "natural law" explanation of the teaching was a puzzle to the average Catholic, who followed the rule much as one would run the number of laps prescribed by a coach, without question. Even those who grasped the natural law explanation, mostly the college-educated, found the explanation worked better in a classroom than elsewhere. But on the whole, the doctrine was held by a majority of Catholics whatever their level of education. They considered their priests to be intelligent and honest, and they were. If a layman couldn't understand this thing called "natural law," at least "Father" could, and he wouldn't mislead you. Besides, what were you? . . . some kind of Protestant? As Catholic sociologists would comment in the 1960s, the doctrine was so identified with Catholicity, identified in such an unbalanced way, that the Catholic subculture was virtually preoccupied with avoiding contraception as the realization of marital virtue.[1]

In the 1960s, all of this came undone. With the election of Kennedy, the defensive Catholic posture no longer was appropriate and a more self-questioning and critical attitude emerged which was doctrinally supported by a renewed theology of the laity, which seemed at least to mean that laymen might have some sound thoughts as a result of their "temporal" experience, and that they should communicate their insights. These were the chief factors in bringing the changed atmosphere, though talk of the "population explosion" and the availability of "the pill," were also factors. Contraceptives were strange and awkward devices with a kind of built-in psychological barrier. But pills presented no such hang-up psychologically, as people already took pills for all kinds of things, and there seemed to be nothing unnatural about them.

Of course, *The Commonweal*, which did something of an about-face on the issue of birth control, did so in a more reasoned fashion than is indicated in the above remarks which are describing the general change among the Catholic populace. The framework out of which *The Commonweal* operated on this and other questions, however, was one common to the magazine and to a whole emergent group of increasingly well-educated Catholic Americans. First, there was the development of an historical consciousness, not only an evolutionary world view, but a realization that what had been in the Church too, was a process of change, and that not all the developments were necessarily good. This was coupled with a biblical renewal and an understanding of the Church as "the people of God" that necessarily had ramifications in the way in which offices in the Church and their exercise would be understood. Secondly, there was a stress on communication, dialogue, honesty, truthfulness, that correctly caught the necessary and appropriate spirit of the times. Implicit in this emphasis was an understanding that one did not merely appeal to the authority of office to settle questions, for if so, why should one "dialogue" to begin with. No—questions should be settled on a rational basis, with the submission of evidence as the crucial factor.

This was *The Commonweal*'s frame of reference in the 1960s. Birth control was simply the issue which most grossly violated these norms. It was not that the editors did not begin with strong commitments that realized the importance and centrality of the question among Catholics. John Cogley, for example, upbraided Reinhold Niebuhr for dismissing the question of contraception as a triviality. Niebuhr, he said, was making a sectarian judgment: ". . . with Dr. Niebuhr's theological prepossessions, it is easy to dismiss, say, contraception as a trifle, though it is anything but that for a Catholic."[2] A fundamental difficulty was the lack of open discussion of the question of birth control among Catholics. Curiously, it was priests who were looked to as experts on the matter, so theologically abstruse was it considered. Their knowledge of the experiential aspects of it, of course, was abstract, and therefore more congenial to the abstractions of the natural law explanation. Further, in case any priest was disposed to revisionist views, he knew the firm hand of Church authority would soon be on him for such views, and few ventured forth publicly on the matter. Father Louis Janssens of the theological faculty at Louvain was one who did, and his article arguing the moral acceptability of the pill was front page news in many newspapers. Most Catholic theologians said they disagreed with Janssens. *The Commonweal*, however, questioned the "apparent unanimity" with which the Janssens position was rejected, and commented that "in the normal course of debate on a relatively new moral problem one would expect that at least a few theologians would take a position different from that of their colleagues. *The Commonweal* wondered where the real consensus of Catholics was on the issue of birth control, though in that period of reticence one could not say.[3]

Gradually more candor and experience were brought to the question. In the pages of *The Commonweal* and elsewhere, Daniel Callahan and Michael Novak wrote on it, and in June, 1964, a whole issue of the magazine was given to the topic, with a number of contributors, mostly priests. Michael Novak then edited a volume of essays entitled *The Experience of Marriage*, written by some fifteen Catholic married couples. Gradually other books appeared, and in the third session of the Vatican Council in the fall of 1964, the question was really blown open by challenging speeches from Cardinal Leger, Cardinal Suenens, and Patriarch Maximos. After that theologians could with relative impunity write openly, and discussion on the matter in which a good number of lay people had now also joined showed rather clearly that a Catholic consensus on the matter was not located where it was once thought to be. In April, 1965, *The Commonweal* editorialized for change. It pointed out that where "a few years" ago, no questions were thought to exist, Rome having spoken on the matter, a number of "realities" had now intruded. One was the "desperate need for world population control."

> For a time there were confident assertions that a better distribution of the world's resources, liberalized immigration policies, exploitation of the sea, perfection of the rhythm method, even human settlements in outer space, would take care of the expanding population. Some of this whistling in the dark can still be heard, but the sound becomes fainter all the time.

Furthermore, whereas it had been said that by relying on the sacraments and living a life of self-control, periodic abstinence could be eminently satisfactory and effective for those couples forced to limit their families, the testimony of the laity, "which only recently was allowed to surface, reported just the opposite." The natural law argument that it was said could be established by reason alone, was shown to be unreasonable or unintelligible to many.

> . . . the more the Church has wrestled with its conscience, the more it has examined its old arguments, the more it has allowed all sides to have a say, the clearer it has become that the unanimity of belief necessary to declare a doctrine to be part of the Catholic faith, does not exist. That in itself ought to still any self-righteous voices— whether on the side of those who advocate a rigid adherence to the status quo or those who advocate a radical change.

For their part, they favored change. "We hope that eventually the magisterium will declare in favor of the right of couples to employ whatever means of family limitation they find to be spiritually, psychologically and scientifically most effective." They said they expected an imminent statement on the matter from Pope Paul whom they congratulated for his courage in soliciting a wide range of opinions by expanding a papal study commission on the matter, and said that it was necessary to wait "not just for the Pope, but with him."[4]

Those who were waiting, would, however, have a long wait. The papal encyclical *Humanae Vitae* would come in August, 1968, with its hard-line reaffirmation of old norms. By that time, *The Commonweal* had to point out that for millions of lay people, the birth control question had been confronted, prayed over, and settled—"and not in the direction of the Pope's encyclical." It said that to call the encyclical a bitter disappointment would be an understatement. It expressed sympathy for the pope in trying to relate to the dynamic currents in the Church, but found his attempts at striking a balance of things poorly weighed. Father Bernard Haring wrote that he was convinced Pope Paul wrote the encyclical out of love for the Church, but out of that same motivation, it was necessary to contradict him. Within two months, some six hundred American Catholic theologians had done that, by endorsing a statement that held that though some positive values concerning marriage were expressed in the encyclical,

> . . . we take exception to the ecclesiology implied and the methodology used by Paul VI in the writing and promulgation of the document: They are incompatible with the Church's authentic self-

awareness as expressed in and suggested by the acts of the Second Vatican Council itself. The encyclical consistently assumes that the Church is identical with the hierarchical office. No real importance is afforded the witness of the life of the Church in its totality; the special witness of many Catholic couples is neglected; it fails to acknowledge the witness of the separated Christian churches and ecclesial communities. . . . Furthermore, the encyclical betrays a narrow and positivistic notion of papal authority, as illustrated by the rejection of the majority view presented by the commission established to consider the question. . . .

The statement went on to score "unfounded assumptions" about the alleged evil consequences of methods of artificial birth control, and to affirm that the encyclical's "mere repetition of past teaching" was inadequate. The fact that Pope Paul had rejected the overwhelming majority opinion of his own study commission was especially distressing. The evidence had been gathered, and the conclusions were that change was needed. Now, however, that change was being rejected, and not on the basis of more convincing evidence. Rather, the reason for the rejection of the commission's report, as Paul himself stated in the encyclical, was *"above all* because certain criteria of solutions had emerged which departed from the moral teaching on marriage proposed with constant firmness by the teaching authority of the Church" (par. 6, italics mine). Paul had agreed with the minority position paper of the papal commission: it was impossible to conclude that the Church could have made such a big mistake; God was on our side, not the Anglicans and others who had changed their position on this. As Father John Courtney Murray had commented, however, "the Church reached for too much certainty, too soon, and went too far." Murray held that the birth control issue was an illustration of the Church caught in transition from classicism to historical consciousness.[5]

It was essentially that, but it was more. As *The Commonweal* commented at the time of the leaked publication of the papal commission reports in 1967, it was "for better or for worse," a focal point, a symbol, for "all manner of issues far more basic than the morality of contraception." Among these, they said, were the nature of marriage, the man-woman relationship, the role and value of the Church's teaching authority, the place of the free conscience in the Church, the validity of "natural law," the nature of morality, and the Church's witness to the world. Also, there was the relationship of faith and reason, man's biological and social development, the population explosion, and the distribution of wealth and resources in the world. If one considered all this, there was, the editors said, every reason to see the birth control issue as "*the* great symbol of the Church's attempt to come to terms with its own history and with its attempt to show the contemporary pertinence of Catholicism to human life."[6]

The Commonweal's Daniel Callahan, perhaps the most influential Catholic layman of the 1960s, had stated early in the decade that the basic problem for the Church was honesty. Pope Paul had not lied in the encyclical—no one really felt that. But somehow many felt that what was honest or authentic for the Church was that people came first, not institutional considerations or questions of authority. In this sense, honesty was a casualty of the affair.

Birth control was the unique issue of the decade, but unfortunately, only in degree, for it was in many ways the paradigm of failure for a number of other issues. Authoritarian solutions not based on evidence emerged at the level of statements and actions by the American Catholic bishops collectively, by statements and actions by individual bishops in their dioceses, and so on by many pastors, parish priests, and religious superiors. The problems ranged from priestly celibacy to the appropriate age for first confession, from the necessity for religious dress for nuns and sisters to the adequacy of Catholicism's response to the emergent black identity, from liturgical renewal to a more adult centered catechesis, from Daniel Berrigan's imposed exile by Cardinal Spellman to new uniforms for the parish basketball team.

The Commonweal did not equivocate when it came to taking stands on some of the more important of these issues, but it did urge on all a careful self-scrutiny and moderation, which it said did not mean simply holding one's tongue, for silence was not really the way to show one's concern for the Church. It urged moderation especially for superiors and bishops: "If the Church is facing a crisis of authority, it is because authority has too often outreached itself."

> These are indeed troubled times for the Church. No doubt we all share in the blame for this to some extent, but it still must be said that a major part of the blame rests squarely on the shoulders of those in authority, from the Pope on down. The present troubles in the Church are not taking place because reform is going too fast; they are happening because the pace of reform in the Church is all too slow—so slow in fact that some of the best people are beginning to question whether reform inside the Church is possible at all. The bright visions envoked by the Second Vatican Council have been dimmed; the eager hopes have been all dashed . . .

What would it take, they asked, to make men like Cardinal O'Boyle (who had indulged in a vendetta against a large number of priests in Washington for their temerity in speaking their convictions on the birth control issue) accept the spirit of the Council, "to make them embrace collegiality and turn it into a living reality?"

> What, for that matter, will it take to make the Pope treat his fellow-bishops in the spirit of collegiality? What will it take to achieve a real sharing of authority in the Church, from the Pope with a synod of bishops to the local pastor with the parishioner?

It was necessary that reform, they said, become "a fact instead of an unobserved catchword."[7]

The Commonweal in a New Era

Who was *The Commonweal*, and to what degree can it be criticized for having achieved or failed to achieve its function during these years?

The 1960s brought some new editorial faces and to some degree a new style to *The Commonweal*. One of the most significant of these personalities was Daniel Callahan, who unlike any previous *Commonweal* editor, had had it as his conscious goal to become a lay theologian. The son of an upper-middle-class Catholic family from the area of the nation's capitol, Callahan in 1948 had decided to attend Yale, where as a senior in 1952, he studied under Father John Courtney Murray who was a visiting professor. Callahan confided to Murray his desire to be a theologian, and asked the priest for help in planning his studies toward his career. Since at that time virtually no one studied Catholic theology who was not in a seminary, Murray could offer no suggestion of a Catholic university to the young man. Callahan thus turned to philosophy and, since he also had the desire to bridge the Catholic and secular world, decided he would attend Georgetown for a master's degree and then go on for his doctorate at Harvard. First, however, came a stint as an enlisted man in the Army, and his marriage to Sidney de Shazo in June, 1954. Then he received his quota of Thomism at Georgetown and continued his studies at Harvard in 1957 where he served as a teaching fellow in Roman Catholic studies, and assistant to the renowned Christopher Dawson. He had completed all but his dissertation in 1961 (he received his degree in 1965) and was interested in teaching the philosophy of religion in a secular university, but found that in 1961 there were no jobs for Catholics in his field of concentration. There were some possibilities teaching straight philosophy, but another opportunity opened for Callahan. *The Commonweal*, for whom he had started writing articles in 1958, offered him a job. He accepted with the idea of biding his time till an attractive teaching position was available, but as he has stated, "once I got there, I found I really liked it, and was reluctant to go back to full-time teaching."[1] Within a few years, some prestigious teaching positions were offered him, but he decided to stay at *Commonweal*, as he was "kind of turned off by the academic life." The staff when Callahan joined *Commonweal* was Ed Skillin as editor, Jim O'Gara, managing editor, and Dick Horchler and Dan Callahan as associate editors. The spot for Callahan had opened when Jim Finn left to become education director of the Council on Religion and International Affairs, and later editor of its publication, *Worldview*.

A year later, Horchler left to go to Cowles magazines and later to a position as program director for the National Conference of Christians and Jews. He was replaced by Walter Arnold, a Harvard graduate who stayed but a year and was replaced by John Leo, a graduate of St. Michael's College, University of Toronto, who had been one of the editors of the *Catholic Messenger* of Davenport, Iowa. Then in 1964, the staff was expanded by the addition of Peter Steinfels, a graduate of Loyola University in Chicago, and a doctoral candidate at Columbia. The staff was thus Skillin, O'Gara, Callahan, Leo, and Steinfels. Wilfrid Sheed had joined the magazine in a part-time capacity as drama critic. Philip Hartung was a quiet presence, continuing in his part-time role of turning out first-rate movie reviews, as he had done since the late 1930s.

Callahan, Leo, Steinfels, and Sheed represented something of a new breed, or at least a new generation. Steinfels, for example, was the first *Commonweal* editor whose parents had been readers of the magazine. All of them were the children of rather prosperous and sophisticated parents. This was one notable distinction between them and such *Commonweal* figures as Jim O'Gara, John Cogley, and William Clancy who had dominated the magazine in the 1950s. Cogley, Clancy, and O'Gara were of humbler origins. There were other differences too. Cogley, Clancy, and O'Gara were all Irish, had all gone to Catholic colleges, and had all at some point studied at least briefly for the priesthood (as had Philip Scharper). Callahan, Leo, Steinfels, and Sheed were of a more diverse ethnic background, a more diverse educational background (Sheed attended Oxford), and none of them had ever been seminarians.

Daniel Callahan has expressed the view that he and his confreres represented the emergence of a post-Kennedy Catholicism, out of the ghetto, having no sense of being in tension with society, successful in bridging the Catholic and non-Catholic group. Assimilated, liberated from a defensive Catholicism, they were among other things ready to take a more critical look at Catholicism, and especially in the case of Callahan, to get into doing some serious theology.

This led to some tensions between on the one hand Skillin and O'Gara, and on the other, Callahan, Leo, and Steinfels. The protagonists became O'Gara and Callahan. Skillin was not without conviction, but his personality and strong influence of Benedictine spirituality made contention antithetical to his character. He thus more or less withdrew. O'Gara was a quiet sort too, but remained an Irishman. So did Callahan despite all his "assimilation" and his most natural retiring qualities. He was the senior member of the younger group, both in his staff position and age, being five years older than Leo and ten years older than Steinfels.

The O'Gara-Callahan differences would eventually build to something of a confrontation over the direction the magazine should take in the latter 1960s, but it wasn't simply a 1950s person, O'Gara, versus a 1960s person, Callahan. To be sure, the *Commonweal* of the 1950s was heavy on politics and lighter on theology, had a more self-conscious notion of Catholic orthodoxy, and was not inclined to be openly critical of encyclicals or bishops—and these things changed somewhat in the 1960s; but all the editors from Skillin on down supported the change—some feeling perhaps more apprehension and regret than others that a more criticizing role relative to the Church was needed.

Thus in 1965, they strongly criticized the encyclical *Mysterium Fidei* on the Eucharist, saying that Pope Paul had compounded confusion with unclarity "by employing a whole host of quotations which clearly refer to the doctrine of the real presence as if they had equal relevance to the question of transubstantiation."

A year before, in 1964, they published well-documented reports on institutional racism and indifference to it in the Roman Catholic church in Philadelphia and Los Angeles, but called them stories that were not easy to tell. Toward the close of the Council, they pointed out the problem of undue pomp in the Church. They praised such gestures as Pope Paul's giving away his gold and silver tiara for the poor (it was purchased by Cardinal Spellman as an artifact for the New York archdiocese), the elimination of ostrich feathers from the papal train, and the trimming of the long trailing cloaks of the cardinals. They felt, however, that much more was needed.

> Reform here is long overdue. Vatican ceremony still apes the manners of a suddenly-rich petty baroque court, sustained by an overblown complacency and an Italianate love of a good show. As understandable as all this may be historically, it has nothing to say to the Church universal, much less to the disinherited outside the Church whom we declare it our purpose to serve.

They caustically commented that "starving people do not identify quickly with men who wear gold hats."[2]

On clerical celibacy, they saw two main questions: Would a body of married priests be able to render to the Church and its people some significant services? Would such a body assist the Church in making its witness more efficacious in the world? They felt the answer to both questions was yes. While the celibate priesthood was a good and long-standing tradition, it was not the only tradition the Church had had, and there was no need for it to be the only tradition today.[3]

In addition to such forthright editorial stands as those indicated above, which all the editors endorsed, Daniel Callahan and John Leo contributed numerous articles of a searching nature in the areas of theology and church affairs. Leo's swinging and irreverent writing style was particularly irksome to some readers. Gradually, however, after having given a more intense interest and attention to matters theological and ecclesiastical than any previous *Commonweal* editors, Callahan and Leo cooled with the affair. John Leo left the magazine in March, 1967, to join the *New York Times* where he expressly did not wish to write about religious affairs. He later took a post working on air pollution for Mayor John Lindsay. Callahan remained, and in a major editorial change became executive editor. Ed Skillin moved from the editor's to the publisher's chair, to concentrate on the business aspects of the magazine, and Jim O'Gara became editor. Michael Novak, then teaching religion at Stanford, was named associate editor at large. Robert McAfee Brown and Harvey Cox had become regular Protestant contributors with periodic columns beginning early in the 1960s. The most major change made at the time, however, was the employment of John Deedy as managing editor. Deedy had been the editor of the *Pittsburgh Catholic*, had a strong background as a Catholic newspaperman, had edited *Eyes on the Modern World*, and coauthored *The Religious Press in America*.

In hiring Deedy, however, O'Gara did not consult Callahan (who would rank above Deedy) or the other members of the staff, as had been customary with new appointments. Callahan, who admires and respects Deedy and is on quite friendly terms with him, confesses that if he had been asked he would have suggested trying to get "someone from the *New Republic* or in the secular world." By this time, Callahan, in his words, "had thrown over the old conservative theology and didn't care for the new stuff." He did not find the more radical Catholic theologians such as Rosemary Ruether and Leslie Dewart attractive, as "their radical stuff was as religion-obsessed as the old." He felt that the appropriate future for the magazine was more secular, that it should model itself on something like *Commentary* and concern itself with questions of meaning and value and religion, but religion in a less denominational and more ecumenical way. He felt they should be competing more with the *New York Review of Books* and the *New Republic*. He had big aspirations for the magazine and felt they should have been more venturesome financially in their promotion. Callahan has commented:

> They [Skillin and O'Gara] had no big aspirations for the magazine. They felt they were already at the top. Peter [Steinfels] and I came in from the larger secular world. O'Gara felt we were at the top and we were, in the only league he knew. If you looked in terms of the Catholic league we were at the top; in terms of the other league we were at the bottom.

By September, 1968, though he had planned to make a lifetime career of work with *The Commonweal*, Dan Callahan resigned. He had received a grant to write a book on abortion and shortly formed an Institute for Society, Ethics and the Life Sciences, which would make some excellent contributions to the difficult ethical questions raised by developments in the life sciences. He was joined at the Institute in 1972 by Peter Steinfels, who retained his *Commonweal* column, however.[4]

Skillin and O'Gara both felt that *The Commonweal* really only made sense as a Catholic journal of opinion. There were secular journals of opinion that were very good and were more liberally endowed financially than was *Commonweal*. They could pay more and could at least at times do some of the secular things in a more thoroughgoing way than could *Commonweal.* What *The Commonweal* had that made it distinctive was that it spoke out of a religious tradition.[5]

Skillin and O'Gara really seemed to have the correct insight into the situation. It was its speaking out of a religious tradition that made *The Commonweal* unique. Further, magazines are not abstractions. Where one can go with them is in great measure determined by the readership. *The Commonweal's* readership, I would estimate, looked to it to speak at least on some issues, out of its religious tradition. *The Commonweal* to some degree was a movement, in a way that the *Nation* or the *New Republic* simply was not. Thirdly, Callahan in his conception of a liberated secularity may have been himself a victim of a ghetto mentality no less real than that of some Catholics—the ghetto mentality of the New York intellectual community, which at times seems to conceive the world as a cocktail party with four corners occupied respectively by the *New York Review of Books, Commentary,* the *New Republic,* and the *Nation.*

Skillin and O'Gara, who in the end held ultimate power, won the debate, but still had plenty of problems. Money was the biggest of these. Circulation had increased dramatically during the high interest and hopes of the Council years, doubling from twenty-three thousand to forty-six thousand between 1962 and 1966 and reaching a high of fifty thousand in 1968, but in the postconciliar fallout that hit other Catholic journals such as *America* too, it dropped back to about thirty thousand by the 1970s. This created a revenue decrease, as did the great cutback in Catholic book publishing and hence, advertising. At the same time, production costs, mailing, and salaries were increasing, due in part to inflation. Contributions of $50, $100, or more by a group of interested persons known as Commonweal Associates had helped greatly during the 1960s when the magazine had no large contributors such as had helped in the 1950s, but by January, 1970, the staff made a general appeal to all subscribers to assure continuation of the magazine. Forty-six thousand dollars was the goal set. Almost that amount was raised in a significant vote of confidence by the readership in a magazine which to some degree was still searching anew for its identity, and at times coming across as a "poor man's new left," as John Cogley characterized it.[6] Gradually, however, a new and strong identity began to manifest itself in *The Commonweal* of the postconciliar era.

Did <u>The Commonweal</u> Fail <u>Aggiornamento?</u>

Andrew Greeley in an essay on American Catholicism from 1950 to 1980 has described the "failure" of the "so-called Catholic intelligentsia" in meeting the challenge of *aggiornamento*. He writes that an intelligentsia has two functions: to criticize the old and to hypothesize about the new; and while the American Catholic intelligentsia has effectively criticized the old, it "has resolutely refused to prophesy about the new" and "does not permit itself to have any hopes for the new to emerge."

> We need only read through the two principal organs of the so-called Catholic intelligentsia of the United States—the *National Catholic Reporter* and *Commonweal*—to discover that they are waspish, strident, shrill and negative. There is precious little vision of hope in either of them. Given the immense influence that these journals have on the elite groups within the American Church, their failure to elaborate a vision toward which one might strive, and to discover developments that seem to be pointing in the direction of such a vision, must be considered as a major failure.[1]

Greeley's basic questions for *The Commonweal* are two: Did it hypothesize adequately about the new? and, Was it as hopeful as it should have been?

Concerning the first question, it should be observed that it is not the *Commonweal*'s function to produce detailed blueprints for Church renewal. The Canon Law Society has produced such blueprints, and they have been welcomed by *The Commonweal*. (If *The Commonweal* had produced such documents, they would no doubt have run the risk of being criticized by Greeley and others as presumptuous and arrogant usurpers.) There was, however, no lack of hypothesizing in its pages about the new. Actually it moved rather quickly to positive and constructive efforts for the renewal of the Church, and to the contrary of Greeley's assertion, spent an adequate but relatively short time pointing out inadequacies in what had gone before. The editors correctly perceived that *Commonweal* readers were not interested in a morose delectation with the inadequate areas of previous Church practice. *The Commonweal* abounded with creative ideas on Church renewal by John Tracy Ellis, Mary Perkins Ryan, Arlene Swidler, Thomas Merton, Gordon Zahn, and a host of others, and their ideas were subjected to careful scrutiny and debate in correspondence columns. The *Commonweal*'s series of articles on the future of the parish, for example, was a first-rate contribution by distinguished writers toward dealing with a fundamental question the Council had dealt with only obliquely.[2]

Some readers were no doubt offended by occasional lapses in tone, taste, or intellectual rigor in the magazine, but there were not a great number of these, and they were not substantive in their effect. *The Commonweal* abounded in good, constructive ideas, and it was not the only source of such ideas. *Aggiornamento* did not live up to expectations, not because it lacked ideas, but because such ideas were not implemented—and blame for this can not be laid at *The Commonweal*'s door.

Greeley's second question concerns whether *The Commonweal* was as hopeful as it should have been during the postconciliar years. If anything, *The Commonweal* may have entered the postconciliar period with too much hope. Having approached the Council cautiously, the staff emerged from it with an excitement, exhilaration, and hope that was well expressed by the thoughts quoted from Michael Novak earlier, which he felt in Rome the night of the decisive vote on collegiality. Their hope was basically simple. It was merely a hope that honesty, dialogue, and collegial decisions based on evidence might emerge at all levels of the Church. For a while they tried to whistle a happy tune, but the music just became too inappropriate. As a journal of opinion, they could not merely become cheerleaders in a power of positive thinking exercise, seeking to effect change through a moderately liberal soft sell of the clerical and hierarchical decision-making mechanisms. Besides, *America* was already doing essentially that. Rather, *The Commonweal* spoke realistically and honestly with no purpose other than to describe the truth as it saw it—which is what a journal of opinion is supposed to do.

Continuing On

The Commonweal continued in an authentic Catholic-catholic identity, speaking out on issues in the world and in the Church, in continuity with the role it had served for almost half a century. American Catholicism in the 1960s had neglected to encourage and enlist the aid of many reform-minded laymen, religious, and clergy who in the enthusiasm of those days were more than willing to work on her inner renewal. One is tempted to think that later historians will speak of this missed opportunity much as it is now customary to speak of the Church's failure to relate to the needs of black people at the end of the Civil War. As Archbishop Spalding said in 1865, it was ". . . a golden opportunity . . . which neglected, may not return."[1]

Though institutional renewal did not really emerge, many American Catholics retained a sense of Catholic identity and became more involved than ever before in their community, nation, and world. *The Commonweal*'s platform of "Obligations to America" as written by Carlton J. Hayes in 1925 was being more fully realized than ever. But the critics of the "Americanism" of Al Smith were being proved

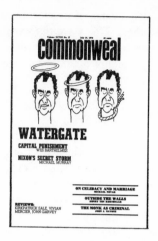

curiously right in one sense too. The religious dimension of Catholic existence had always had an internationalist thrust and imagery to it, and this put at least some Catholics in a position more psychologically ready to criticize the United States when this would be the necessity of an authentic citizenship. Defensiveness was going away rapidly and criticism and creativity were replacing it. An historic Catholic people in America were becoming aware of the positive values of its ethnic diversity and its position as the swing vote between progress and reaction. How would these forces develop? What direction would they take? What would happen in terms of human renewal and church renewal?

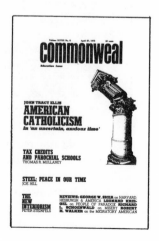

Whatever, as long as financially possible, *The Commonweal* would continue. Ed Skillin has expressed his concern, however, that a new generation of Catholic readers will not sufficiently emerge. Many young Catholics still equate the Church with the institution, and their disdain for the latter is so great that it is questionable whether they will be able to retain a sufficient Catholic identity or concern to care to read *The Commonweal*. Skillin and O'Gara are sure, however, that the Church needs *The Commonweal* and intend to do all in their power to meet that need. Skillin, who owns controlling interest in the magazine, and has brought it his quiet, dedicated, and devout concern through the years, has arranged to have the magazine continue beyond his lifetime. Jim O'Gara has stated:

> I find it hard to believe that there is not a need for an independent, intellectual voice in the Church. I think the Church would be considerably poorer if it didn't have this. If not the *Commonweal*, then somebody else would have to do the same job.[2]

Like many Americans and many Catholics, the staff of *The Commonweal* is not as sure of the exact dimensions of its function and its future as it was ten years ago. It is sure, however, that it has a future and a function in the Church. It even has hope for that future.

IV. CONCLUSIONS: A GOOD RECORD

Conclusions

1. *The Commonweal* recapitulates American Catholic history.

The first conclusion which we might draw from our study of the history of *The Commonweal* is that the magazine recapitulates in its history the broad outline of the history of American Catholicism itself. American Catholicism contains an early Anglo-American period, somewhat aristocratic in nature, with its members socially and culturally assimilated in the American environment. The personification of the period was the first American Catholic bishop, John Carroll, a member of the Carroll clan of Maryland, and cousin of Charles Carroll, who had been a signer of the Declaration of Independence, an ally of George Washington, a member of the U.S. Congress—almost president of the United States—who was reputedly the wealthiest man in the country. John Carroll's brother Daniel had also signed the Declaration of Independence and served in public life, and John himself served on a diplomatic mission with Ben Franklin at the request of the Continental Congress. The Catholics of the period, which lasted till about 1820, were a small minority, but were, especially in their elite leadership, clearly members of the establishment.

This was true also of *The Commonweal* of the first period in our study. The whole symbolism of the Calvert Associates and the elaborate rituals that Michael Williams conceived for the annual Calvert Day, the celebration of the 1634 arrival of the *Ark* and the *Dove* in Maryland, were an attempt to recall the period, and were also ways of relating to the wealth and talent needed to launch and sustain the magazine. Lawrason Riggs, the descendant of the Washington banking family who attended Yale with Cole Porter (collaborating with him in a musical which failed on Broadway), and later returned to his alma mater as Catholic chaplain, was, as we have seen, a generous donor to the magazine, wrote for it, and was a member of its editorial council. Riggs symbolized the Anglo-Catholic period of *The Commonweal* just as John Carroll symbolized the Anglo-Catholic period of American Catholicism. This is not to say that Riggs himself was that influential on the magazine, however. Rather, he symbolized its style: well-to-do, Ivy league, literary, Catholic, of broad interests. The magazine's early ecumenical, intellectual, and literary quality was largely the expression of Catholic Ivy league writers and intellectuals, well-removed from immigrant origins. The early editorial council was clearly of this character, and the magazine's early battle over the barring of a Catholic from appointment as a fellow of Harvard University was indicative of an issue close to home. The magazine was highbrow and at times high church. Its letters column could debate for some weeks, for example, what the correct translation of *reverendior* was. It was, however, genuinely intellectual, though unduly deferential to Chesterton and Belloc as was the style of those days, and promoted a rather vigorous critique of Catholic intellectual life. In Michael Williams and George Shuster it had men of broad experience, dynamism, and talent. To the former should go praise for having the imagination, courage, and pragmatism that launched *The Commonweal*; to the latter must go much of the credit for making the magazine develop in a more responsive and creative way to the environment of world and church in which it operated.

Edward Skillin and Philip Burnham were transitional persons in the Shuster tradition. Deeply religious, and primarily concerned with the social and political meaning of their faith in the midst of the Depression, they brought the magazine much closer to a grass roots Catholicism of a radical and renewal-minded mode of thought. That John Cogley and James O'Gara, both graduates of the Chicago Catholic Worker movement should have emerged as key figures in this period of *The Commonweal*'s history was rather natural. Here was *The Commonweal*'s second stage of history, a stage corresponding to the long immigrant period of American Catholicism under Irish hegemony. *The Commonweal*'s likeness, however, was not to the defensive and fiercely polemical Bishop John Hughes of New York, who unfortunately seemed to set the style for many a later bishop, but to such creative and open Catholic leaders of the nineteenth century as Bishop John England, Orestes Brownson, Issac Hecker, John Ireland, and others known as Americanizers. *The Commonweal* of this second period would fight against unfair or unfounded criticisms of American Catholics, but would mostly urge Catholics to a more vigorous participation in American life, a theme common to the whole history of the magazine.

The third period of the magazine coincided roughly with the third period of American Catholicism, and was the period of cultural acceptance and assimilation symbolized and to some degree effected by the election of John Kennedy. The problem for Catholicism in this era has been twofold: first, to come to grips with the world of the twentieth century, and this is what has been attempted in Vatican II and its aftermath; second, to express a positive relationship and contribution to American society after the tumbling of the ghetto walls since 1960. The true value and role of the institutional Church in meeting the challenge of this more secular period has been and is a matter of considerable debate, and the differences between James O'Gara and Daniel Callahan as to the direction of the magazine are a mirror of an important facet of the contemporary history of American Catholicism. The decision of John Cogley, on September 26, 1973, to enter the Episcopal church seems to occur in this context too, though there is a rather poignant note of personal weariness in Cogley's statement on his surprise move: "I have . . . recognized that I am not getting any younger and that I have my own life to live, whatever is left of it. The day finally came when I decided that I could no longer remain in an ecumenical twilight zone."[1]

2. *The Commonweal* has been an independent intellectual voice in American Catholicism.

Our second conclusion is that *The Commonweal* has been an independent intellectual voice in American Catholicism. That it has been an intellectual voice is clear enough, but has it been completely independent through the years? Concerning its independence of Church authority and control, the only question seems to be the Spanish Civil War controversy, particularly at the time of the Madison Square Garden rally in 1937. At the time, Edward Skillin, then a junior staff member, wrote Abbot Alcuin at St. John's Abbey:

> The thing [rally] of course has the hearty approval of the hierarchy not to mention the Apostolic Delegate, and may succeed in raising from well-fed Catholics—not this well-fed one—a considerable sum to build up the morale of our saintly champion [Franco] and his patriotic foreigners.[2]

Shortly after this, Skillin wrote Alcuin that *The Commonweal's* reporting of the Spanish tragedy was "essentially untruthful" and that it and the American Catholic press generally had failed in its first duty to its readers: "to give them the facts, the truth."[3] There seems to be a genuine question as to whether *The Commonweal* handled the truth pragmatically at the time, though it is quite possible that Michael Williams was sincere. Since that time, and throughout the

Skillin regime, there seems to be no question concerning the magazine's honesty and integrity with the truth.

It might be asked, however, if the magazine was not liberal in a
doctrinaire fashion and thus not really independent. It is true that
from 1938 on the magazine was more characterized by advocacy
rather than forum style journalism, but any intelligent point of view
could get an airing in its pages. Indeed, some of the more vigorous
criticisms of the Catholic left, for example, have been made in *The
Commonweal.* Some might even call them iconoclastic. Hence John
Cort would write of Peter Maurin, the revered founder with Dorothy
Day of the *Catholic Worker:*

> In private conversation he could be very agreeable. He would listen
> to your ideas and comment on them in a quiet, kindly way. But as
> soon as somebody else joined you, Peter's whole aspect and style of
> speech changed. His voice grew louder and he began to talk in "Easy
> Essays," those blank-verse declamations which he delivered in a
> heavy French accent and with appropriate arm-waving. He was, it
> seemed, simply not capable of adapting his ideas to ordinary give
> and take discussion. He thought in memorized patterns and anybody
> who tried to break up the pattern just had to be shouted down.[4]

Similarly, Philip Berrigan has received both praise and criticism in
Commonweal. John L. McKenzie, his fellow priest and confrere in
the Catholic Peace Fellowship, wrote of the discussion on race in
Berrigan's book, *A Punishment for Peace*:

> I have become accustomed to the guilt-jags and self-flagellation of
> the white liberal; I still do not enjoy it. Guilt by association, as far as
> we honkies are concerned, has become a way of life with them; none
> of us can do anything right or think good thoughts. Thinking be-
> comes a bit fuzzy in such an atmosphere of emotion.[5]

James Finn has done the same kind of thing with a recent book by
Thomas and Marjorie Melville, former Maryknoll missionaries in
Guatemala. Of the Melvilles' reflections on their experiences and the
conclusions they have drawn, Finn writes:

> They have perceived real injustices and they are angered into making
> severe judgments. What becomes gradually clear is that the Melvilles
> have changed the pattern of their lives, but not their mindset. They
> have adopted a new political catechism next to which the Old Balti-
> more catechism is a model of subtlety, discrimination and intellec-
> tual refinement. But they are still missionaries eager to convert . . .
> they now bring to social matters the same moral arrogance and
> simple-mindedness they initially brought to matters religious.[6]

One may agree or disagree with comments like these as did readers of the magazine, but it cannot be called a doctrinaire liberal line. *The Commonweal* has been an independent intellectual voice.

3. *The Commonweal* has been correct in its analysis of most of the big issues it has faced.

Our third conclusion is that *The Commonweal* has been correct in its analysis of most of the big issues it has faced. To say this is to offer the highest praise to a journal of opinion. Its big issues have been the Spanish Civil War, the Isolationist-Interventionist controversy, the Joseph McCarthy hysteria of the 1950s, Catholic renewal and Vatican II, and the Vietnam War. A retrospective view would give it high ratings on all but the second of these.

On the Spanish Civil War issue, it is sufficient to note the poignant resolution made in September, 1971, by an assembly of two hundred fifty Spanish bishops and priests for the role played by the Spanish church between 1936–39. "We humbly recognize," stated the resolution, "and ask forgiveness for this, that we failed at the proper moment to be ministers of reconciliation in the midst of our people then divided by a fratricidal war."[7]

In regard to the isolationist-interventionist controversy, it is interesting to note *The Commonweal*'s editorial praising *Christianity and Crisis* on the twenty-fifth anniversary of that journal launched under the leadership of Reinhold Niebuhr in 1941. The editors praised the way in which *Christianity and Crisis* made its first contribution by opposing "the utopian pacifism and isolationism which marked much American religious thought at the outbreak of World War II."[8] Our analysis has shown that *The Commonweal* exhibited some of that isolationism. But its lack of dogmatism helped it since the magazine at that time published analyses from all points of view, and the pages of the magazine in those days crackled with debate.

The McCarthy period was an era of great challenge for the magazine and for American Catholicism. There was the attempt by McCarthy to smear the magazine itself, and for American Catholics there was the temptation to enter American life through the door of self-righteousness rather than service. The magazine met each of these challenges admirably. It showed that the Catholic press was not monolithic, and that one could be anticommunist without being hysterical.

Vatican II was a great vindication for the magazine and the program of Catholic renewal that was associated with its pages. John

Cogley reported from Rome in 1963, for example, that he had learned that *The Commonweal* over the years had been read carefully by at least some ranking prelates in the Vatican, one of whom congratulated him on the magazine's having sensed the mood of the universal Church long before it found expression at the Vatican Council. "It must be a great satisfaction to know that stands which were misunderstood at the time are being so frequently vindicated," the official stated. Cogley was so surprised that his words did not come freely and he could only mumble something, while remembering "some old letters-to-the-editors and hostile editorials that used to talk indignantly about the Mind of the Church, often identifying it with a set of political prejudices and unquestioning acceptance of the status quo."[9]

On Vietnam, *The Commonweal* initially supported the action there as did many other liberals who had reacted against Dulles's brinkmanship by supporting a multiple response and counterinsurgency military posture. But on closer scrutiny the editors changed their minds and by 1965 opposed the war. Further, they opposed it cogently, vigorously, and consistently. It was November, 1972, before the American Catholic bishops opposed the war, and then their opposition to it barely received a mention in most Catholic dioceses and parishes throughout the land.

One could mention any number of issues in addition to the above that have been identified as major. The 1936 Olympics, Father Charles Coughlin, Dresden, Hiroshima, and others are noteworthy. The magazine's "track record" is remarkably good. One would think that simply on the basis of its record it would be accorded a special hearing in Catholic circles at least. On the contrary, however, it is still in an outcast position there, and is banned from the magazine racks of many Catholic churches. In the McCarthy era, the House Un-American Activities Committee was fond of speaking of people as being "prematurely antifascist," which they equated with communist. Apparently one was permitted to be antifascist as long as one waited until this position was officially permitted and recognized. Similarly, even though almost all the major stands of *The Commonweal* have been vindicated, it seems to be resented rather than admired in official Catholic circles. Hence, the editors seem to be regarded as having been "premature" in their opposition to Vietnam, "premature" in their espousal of religious liberty, etc. Clearly they are considered "premature" in their positions on contraception, celibacy, and genuine collegiality, but most polls indicate that the magazine's positions on these issues represent majority thinking among Catholics.[10]

4. *The Commonweal* has been a nonmovement movement in American Catholicism.

Our fourth conclusion is that *The Commonweal* has been a non-movement movement in American Catholicism. Jim O'Gara has said that "for better or for worse," the magazine has never tried to be a movement. It has obviously had a lot of followers, but in the opinion of O'Gara, it has been a detached intellectual force rather than a popular movement. "The typical *Commonweal* editor," says O'Gara, "is very questioning even of his own affirmations, and that's not the kind of stuff out of which movements are made."[11]

What O'Gara says is true, but I believe *The Commonweal* has been a nonmovement movement, very real yet not very visible. The magazine's tentative and searching quality may have had its intellectual making of distinctions, but there was no obfuscation, nor was there any lack of candor, and this was attractive to a significant and concerned group of readers. The magazine's renewal rate through much of its history was a very high 80 percent, and many of the readers were great letter writers. In many ways, a genuine community was formed, and in Troeltschian terms we might say that *The Commonweal* achieved certain dimensions of a sect quality precisely in its relationship to the Roman Catholic church. It never intended this however.

One of the unspoken bonds of unity in this group was its dissatisfaction with a simply clerical and mechanical Catholicism. In 1965, Thomas Merton wrote that the renewal of the Church depended on the difficult and sacrificial task of "changing a clerical Church back into a lay Church."[12] This was not a new insight at that time, nor was it one that bespoke an anticlerical attitude as that term is generally understood. Rather, it was an anticlerical*ism*. It was something that many priests and religious perceived better than many lay people did. It was something that Father John J. Burke had perceived at the time after World War I when he was exercising leadership in setting up the National Catholic Welfare Council. In the conflict which followed, however, as George Shuster has remarked, "Burke began to be shoved more and more aside, and what remained of all these Burkean insights was incorporated in *The Commonweal*. . . . *The Commonweal* was probably the only thing that survived."[13] But the spirit of a genuinely free, responsible, and creative lay Christianity survived with it, one that was not simply the bottom of the ecclesiastical pyramid, awaiting instructions from the chain of command. The term "lay Christianity" for this, however, is perhaps a misnomer, as it clearly included many priests and religious, such as H. A. Reinhold, Virgil Michel, and others. It was more than anything a vision of a genuinely communal church, one such as has been perhaps best articulated by Gabriel Moran, among contemporary writers. It still included a very genuine role for church authority, but stressed the importance of grass roots initiatives and efforts. It was therefore natural that the Catholic Worker movement should have in one sense spun off from *The Commonweal* in 1933, and that the magazine took such an avid interest in it and any number of other renewing efforts. Also the magazine's long interest in the liturgy and its close association with *Worship* magazine and the monks of St. John's Abbey, was natural, as the liturgy was understood as the center and vivification of the community. All of this, of course, was an anticipation of Vatican II.

Another unifying element in this nonmovement movement was the humble charisma of some of its leaders, though they never laid claim to any such title as "leader." John Cort, for example, was a very authentic kind of person to whose writings people were drawn with respect. A young Harvard graduate in the mid-1930s, he had become, to the consternation of his family, a Catholic convert, and was then attracted to the Catholic Worker where his service earned him a TB condition that resulted in the loss of a lung. He differed, however, with Peter Maurin's "Strikes don't strike me" labor philosophy, and organized the Association of Catholic Trade Unionists, which worked to get the church "on the side of the poor at a time when union members were still poor." The father of eight children, he spent twelve years working in organized labor, and in 1958 ran for the Massachusetts legislature and lost. In 1960, he and his family went to the Philippines with the Peace Corps. In 1964, he was invited by the governor of Massachusetts to head a multipurpose anti-poverty agency for the state. The 1970s found Cort and his family living in Roxbury, Boston's ghetto, and working to improve the lot of people there. Cort was unusual, of course, but he was the kind of person readers liked to identify with, as he seemed to exemplify many of the nobler instincts of man and did so out of a Catholic identity. To be sure, John Cort was much more of an activist than the typical *Commonweal* editor, but there was a quiet charisma about a good number of them. George Shuster, C. G. Paulding, John

Cogley, and Daniel Callahan come to mind, and Michael Williams and a good number of others should not be omitted. It was not so much intellectual rigor, though they did not lack this, but a simple and honest writing style by men who had their feet in their community, that marked them as authentic, and their writing as distinguished. Perhaps one of the best pieces of writing John Cogley ever produced, for example, was an essay on Christmas built around his recollections of a Christmas class play from his third grade days.[14] This was written by one who has been dubbed the dean of intellectual Catholic journalists, and perhaps appropriately so. The non-movement movement that has been *The Commonweal* has been a strange but fascinating phenomenon. In its fifty years it has ranged from Michael Williams's line up of the wealthy to get the venture going to the line up of down and outers who have learned to await the quiet Edward Skillin as he emerges from *The Commonweal's* office in the 1970s.

5. *The Commonweal* has been perhaps the most significant achievement of the American Catholic layman.

Our final conclusion is that *The Commonweal* has been perhaps the most significant achievement of the American Catholic layman. The American Catholic layman, at least from the time of the crushing of lay trusteeism in the nineteenth century, has been kept in an extremely subservient position. Opportunities for the layman to exercise initiative in the Church were restricted out of an alleged love of good churchly order and a rather jaundiced view of the layman in American Catholic history. The only posttrusteeism stirring among laymen in the nineteenth century was the prophetic voice of Orestes Brownson and an abortive lay congress movement in the 1880s. The American Federation of Catholic Societies was formed in 1901, and in theory was a lay organization, but it was disorganized, clericalized, and underfunded and was absorbed into the National Catholic Welfare Council shortly after World War I. We have already mentioned that Father John Burke's hopes for a free and creative role for the laity in the NCWC were dashed (the National Council of Catholic Men was developed simply as the appearance of an organization, with a shell that was safe and servile) and what was left of his insight was achieved in *The Commonweal*. Some years subsequent to *The Commonweal's* founding in 1924, other independent Catholic publications such as *Cross Currents, Jubilee,* and the *National Catholic Reporter* emerged, as did lay movements of social impact such as the

Catholic Worker and the Catholic Interracial movement, but at this point in history one would have to consider carefully the claim that *The Commonweal* has been perhaps the most important symbol and achievement of the American Catholic laity. It has not worked consciously toward that claim, and has no hang-up of lay triumphalism. It has had fraternal clerical cooperators from the beginning and now has its first clerical staff member in Raymond Schroth, SJ, but its historical significance is that of an independent lay achievement.

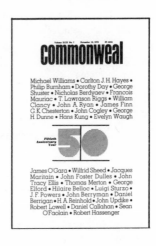

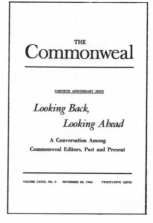

NOTES

PART I

The Background

1. Martin E. Marty, *Righteous Empire: The Protestant Experience in America* (New York: The Dial Press, 1970), p. 211.
2. Michael Williams, *The Book of the High Romance* (New York: Macmillan, 1928), p. 218.
3. Interview with Edward Skillin by Robert Clements, summer, 1969.
4. For a sketch of the life of Michael Williams, see George N. Shuster, "Michael Williams," *Catholic Press Annual* (1964), pp. 19–22. Also, Robert Clements at Notre Dame University is preparing a doctoral dissertation on certain aspects of *The Commonweal* which will contain a full chapter on Williams.

The Idea

1. Michael Williams, *The Present Position of Catholics in the United States* (New York: Calvert Publishing Co., 1928), p. 17. This also contains basic documentation on the founding of *The Commonweal*.
2. R. Dana Skinner, "The Two Years Before," *The Commonweal*, 3 Nov. 1939, p. 37. *The Commonweal* is hereafter cited as *Com.*
3. John F. McCormick, "Fifteen Years," *Com.*, 8 Dec. 1939, p. 161.
4. *Ibid.* A list of fifty-three "founders" of the Calvert Associates is recorded in Williams, *The Present Position of Catholics*, p. 31.
5. George N. Shuster, "Fortieth Anniversary Symposium," *Com.*, 20 Nov. 1964, p. 263.
6. Skinner, "The Two Years Before," p. 38.
7. Shuster, "Fortieth Anniversary Symposium," p. 263.

The First Issue and an Early Platform

1. "An Introduction," *Com.*, 12 Nov. 1924, p. 12.
2. *Ibid.*
3. *New York Times*, 21 Nov. 1924; *America*, 22 Nov. 1924, p. 140; "How Contemporaries View The Commonweal," in Michael Williams, *The Present Position of Catholics in the United States* (New York: Calvert Publishing Co., 1928), p. 17.
4. "An Ancient Typography," *Com.*, 26 Nov. 1924, p. 59; Williams, *The Present Position of Catholics*, p. 17.

Early Controversies

1. "Week by Week," *Com.*, 26 Nov. 1924, p. 57; John Jay Chapman, "Mr. Chapman Replies to Mr. Cram," *Com.*, 10 Dec. 1924, p. 116; "Week by Week," *Com.*, 10 Dec. 1924, p. 113.

2. "The Roman Church and Taxation," *Christian Century*, 22 Jan. 1925, pp. 114–15.
3. "Are Catholics Christians?" *Com.*, 4 Feb. 1925, p. 334; cf. the response in "Are Catholics Christians?" *Christian Century*, 5 Mar. 1925, pp. 306–8.
4. "Lanterns and Torches," *Com.*, 16 Sept. 1925, p. 434.
5. George N. Shuster, "Memoir on the Father Burns Era," an unpublished manuscript made available by the author.
6. George N. Shuster, "Have We Any Scholars?" *America*, 15 Aug. 1925, pp. 418–19; George N. Shuster, "Insulated Catholics," *Com.*, 19 Aug. 1925, pp. 337–38.
7. Shuster, "Memoir on the Father Burns Era."
8. "Catholic Colleges," *Com.*, 23 Sept. 1925, pp. 481–82. Discussion followed in the correspondence sections of each of the next several issues.
9. John Tracy Ellis, *American Catholics and the Intellectual Life* (Chicago: Heritage Foundation, 1956), p. 45.

Evolution and Theology, Protestants and Catholics

1. "World Problems of 1925," *Com.*, 7 Jan. 1925, p. 226.
2. "On Teaching Evolution," *Com.*, 22 Apr. 1925, pp. 647–49.
3. "Concerning Evolution," *Com.*, 10 June 1925, pp. 119–20.
4. Frank R. Kent, "What Dayton Thinks," *Com.*, 29 July 1925, p. 289.
5. Michael Williams, "Sunday in Dayton," 29 July 1925, p. 287.
6. Michael Williams, "Summing-Up at Dayton," *Com.*, 5 Aug. 1925, p. 305.
7. T. Lawrason Riggs, "Fundamentalism and the Faith," *Com.*, 19 Aug. 1925, pp. 344–46.
8. George N. Shuster, "Fortieth Anniversary Symposium," *Com.*, 20 Nov. 1964, p. 262.
9. *Ibid.*
10. *Com.*, 6 July 1927, p. ii.
11. Quoted in Michael Williams, *The Present Position of Catholics in the United States* (New York: Calvert Publishing Co., 1928), p. 25.
12. Williams, *The Present Position of Catholics*, pp. 19–20.

The Candidacy of Al Smith

1. "Pulpits and Politics," *Com.*, 28 Jan. 1925, pp. 85–86.
2. "Barring Sacramental Wine," *Com.*, 28 Jan. 1925, p. 310; "Commencement Oratory," *Com.*, 24 June 1925, p. 174; "The Prohibition Issue," *Com.*, 8 Feb. 1928, p. 1024.
3. "Should a Catholic Be President?: An Open Letter to Mr. Charles Marshall," *Com.*, 13 Apr. 1927, p. 623.
4. "A Voice from the Grave," *Com.*, 20 Apr. 1927, p. 646.
5. John A. Ryan, "Church, State and Constitution," *Com.*, 27 Apr. 1927, pp. 680–82.
6. Alfred E. Smith, "Catholic and Patriot: Governor Smith Replies," *Atlantic Monthly* 139 (May 1927): 722.

7. Michael Williams, *The Shadow of the Pope* (New York: McGraw-Hill, 1932).
8. Interview with George N. Shuster by Robert Clements, 10 June 1969, generously supplied to this writer.
9. Calvert Associates, *Calvert Handbook of Catholic Facts* (New York: Calvert Publishing Co., 1928).
10. Interview with Carlton Hayes by J. David Valaik, 9 Aug. 1961, and reported in his article, "American Catholic Dissenters and the Spanish Civil War," *Catholic Historical Review* 53 (Jan. 1968): 540.
11. "A Word about the Press," *Com.*, 13 Feb. 1929, p. 415.

TURNING THE DECADE

1. "Weighing the Big Invisibles," *Com.*, 14 Sept. 1927, p. 428.
2. "Comfort on Credit," *Com.*, 30 Nov. 1927, p. 749.
3. "The Good Time Coming," *Com.*, 29 May 1929, p. 86.
4. "Money Talks," *Com.*, 26 Oct. 1927, p. 596; "The American Goose-Step," *Com.*, 2 Oct. 1929, p. 543.
5. "Urbi et Orbi," *Com.*, 20 Feb. 1929, p. 442.
6. "Mussolini Again," *Com.*, 11 Apr. 1928, p. 1280.
7. From the editorial comment introducing the articles; Walter Lippmann, "Autocracy Versus Catholicism," and Dino Bigongiari, "Mussolini: Servant of Italy," *Com.*, 13 Apr. 1927, pp. 627–28.
8. Interview with George N. Shuster by Robert Clements, 10 June 1969; cf. "The World and Its Conduct," *Com.*, 25 Nov. 1925, p. 57; "The Shenandoah," *Com.*, 16 Sept. 1925, p. 439, and "Week by Week," *Com.*, 25 Nov. 1925, p. 61; "The Death Penalty," *Com.*, 27 Apr. 1927, p. 678; "Justice at Midnight," *Com.*, 24 Aug. 1927, p. 372, and elsewhere throughout the issues of 1927 and 1928.
9. "Mainly about Ourselves," *Com.*, 26 Mar. 1930, p. 575.
10. "The Revival of Christian Economics," *Com.*, 6 May 1932, p. 1.
11. Quoted by Reinhold Niebuhr in "Catholics and the State," *New Republic*, 17 Oct. 1960, p. 15, as cited in David O'Brien, *American Catholics and Social Reform* (New York: Oxford University Press, 1968), p. 45.
12. "Rome Answers Lambeth," *Com.*, 14 Jan. 1931, p. 283; "Rome Has Spoken," *Com.*, 21 Jan. 1931, p. 310.
13. "The Birth Control Revolution," *Com.*, 1 Apr. 1931, p. 589.
14. See, for example, Edward Roberts Moore, "The Malice of Contraception," *Com.*, 20 May 1931, pp. 68–71.
15. Frank A. Smothers, "New Light on Birth Control," *Com.*, 8 Mar. 1933, p. 511.
16. Ernest Dimnet, "New Light on Birth Control," *Com.*, 12 Apr. 1933, p. 663.
17. Wilfrid Parsons, SJ, "Is This 'Catholic' Birth Control?" *America*, 25 Feb. 1933, p. 497.
18. "The Roots of Life," *Com.*, 14 July 1933, p. 276.
19. Cf. Edwin V. O'Hara, *The Church and the Country Community* (New York: Macmillan, 1927), pp. 7–9.

20. "The Problem of Problems," *Com.*, 25 Nov. 1931, p. 86.
21. James J. Walsh, "Are We Due to Disappear?" *Com.*, 1 Oct. 1930, p. 549; "Falling Birth Rate," *America*, 12 Aug. 1933, p. 434.
22. "Annals of the Poor," *Com.*, 23 Nov. 1932, p. 90.
23. *New York Times*, 14 Nov. 1932; *Com.*, 23 Nov. 1932.
24. "Rats," *Com.*, 4 Jan. 1933, p. 256.

THE COMMONWEAL, THE 1932 ELECTION, AND FDR

1. "Mr. Roosevelt's Candidacy," *Com.*, 4 May 1932, p. 3; Foster Stearns, "Political," *Com.*, 9 Nov. 1932, p. 47; Charles Willis Thompson, "Will Catholics Vote for Thomas?" *Com.*, 31 Aug. 1932, pp. 422–44; "Socialism and Catholic Action," *Com.*, 7 Sept. 1932, p. 437.
2. Both letters in "Communications," *Com.*, 5 Oct. 1932, p. 536.
3. For general Catholic reaction to Roosevelt cf. David O'Brien, *American Catholics and Social Reform* (New York: Oxford University Press, 1968), pp. 47–70; Karl Alter, *Toledo Blade*, 13 Mar. 1933, as quoted in O'Brien, p. 52; Skinner to Marvin McIntyre, 13 June 1933, Roosevelt Papers, in O'Brien, p. 52; Williams to Ryan, 8 Oct. 1930, Ryan Papers, Catholic University Library, Washington, D.C.; Ryan to Williams, 18 Apr. 1938, Ryan Papers; on Woodlock, interview with George N. Shuster, 3 June 1970.
4. "Watching the New Deal," *Com.*, 7 July 1933, p. 259; "Recovery and Reformation," *Com.*, 17 Nov. 1933, p. 58; "Sabotaging the New Deal," *Com.*, 4 May 1934, p. 2.
5. Wilfrid Parsons, "An Open Letter to Ambassador Daniels," *America*, 1 Apr. 1933, p. 619. The open letter was also carried nationally in the NCWC news service.
6. "The New Deal and Mexico," *Com.*, 26 Oct. 1937, p. 600.
7. "President Roosevelt and Mexico," *Com.*, 29 Nov. 1935, p. 115; William Franklin Sands, "Our Diplomacy and Mexico," *Com.*, 10 May 1935, pp. 33–35; George Q. Flynn, *American Catholics and the Roosevelt Presidency, 1932–1936* (Lexington: University of Kentucky Press, 1968), p. 150.
8. "Russian Recognition," *Com.*, 3 Nov. 1933, pp. 3–4.
9. "The Recognition of Russia," *Com.*, 1 Dec. 1933, p. 115.
10. Ryan Papers, Catholic University Library, Washington, D.C.
11. Cf. "Maryland Day," *Com.*, 6 Apr. 1932, p. 619. Information on the affair at the Waldorf has been derived from the program for the event, a copy of which was given the writer by Edward Skillin.
12. George N. Shuster, *The Ground I Walked On* (New York: Farrar, Strauss, Cuddahy, 1961), pp. 41–42.
13. "We Appeal to Our Readers," *Com.*, 4 May 1932, p. 1; "Our Readers Respond," *Com.*, 11 May 1932, p. 29; G. K. Chesterton, *Com.*, 2 Nov. 1932, p. 3; John Tracy Ellis, *Com.*, 30 Nov. 1932, p. 113; "Personal to Our Readers," *Com.*, 14 July 1933, p. 277.
14. George N. Shuster to John A. Ryan, 20 Apr. 1933, and John McCormick to John A. Ryan, 22 June 1933, Ryan Papers.
15. "Land of the Free," *Com.*, 22 Mar. 1933, p. 561; Michael Williams, "Message from Rome," *Com.*, 26 Apr. 1933, p. 707.

16. Amleto Cicognani, *Com.*, 23 Nov. 1934; Arthur J. Conway, "The Permanent Things," *Com.*, 15 Sept. 1933, p. 468; Charles B. Hedder, "Criticizing the Commonweal," *Com.*, 3 Nov. 1933, p. 21; "Defending The Commonweal," *Com.*, 24 Nov. 1933, pp. 104–5.
17. All these developments were discussed by George N. Shuster in an interview with this writer, 3 June 1970.

THE 1936 OLYMPICS, NAZI GERMANY, AND FATHER CHARLES COUGHLIN

1. "The Olympic Games," *Com.*, 9 Aug. 1935, p. 355.
2. "Boycott the Olympics!" *Nation*, 21 Aug. 1935, p. 201; "Move the Olympics!" *Christian Century*, 7 Aug. 1935, p. 1007; AFL and Runyon in Richard D. Mandell, *The Nazi Olympics* (New York: Macmillan, 1971), pp. 77–78.
3. Mandell, *The Nazi Olympics*, pp. 71–76.
4. George N. Shuster, "General Sherrill and the Olympics," *Com.*, 8 Nov. 1935, p. 41.
5. George N. Shuster in his review of Richard Mandell's *The Nazi Olympics*, *Com.*, 28 May 1971, pp. 291–92. To my inquiry about documentation for the repentance of Bishop McIntyre, George Shuster has written: "There is no documentary evidence concerning Bishop McIntyre's all out 'repentance.' My principal *Commonweal* supporter in the effort to frustrate Hitler was John McCormick, who was also an adviser to Macmillan on Catholic books. . . . After the War, he went to see the Bishop because a censor had ruled that Catholic bookstores were not to sell the books of C. S. Lewis, one of the company's authors. It was on this occasion that there was talk about the *Commonweal*. McIntyre said that he did not regret many of his attitudes toward the magazine, but said that he wished he had not done what he did about the Berlin Olympics." George N. Shuster to the author, 28 June 1971.
6. "German Olympics," *Catholic World* 142 (Jan. 1936): 393–95; "Nazis and Olympics," *Sign* 15 (Oct. 1935): 132; George N. Shuster, "General Sherrill and the Olympics," *Catholic World* 142 (Jan. 1936): 393–95.
7. Interview with George N. Shuster, 3 June 1970.
8. Charles J. Tull, *Father Coughlin and the New Deal* (Syracuse: Syracuse University Press, 1965).
9. "Dangers of Demagogy," *Com.*, 8 Dec. 1933, p. 144; George N. Shuster, "Is Liberty a Lost Cause?" *Com.*, 11 May 1934, p. 39; "The Clergy in Politics," *Com.*, 22 Mar. 1935, pp. 579–80; "Putting the Church in Her Place," *Com.*, 5 Apr. 1935, pp. 635–36.
10. Michael Williams to John A. Ryan, 10 Apr. 1935, Ryan Papers, Catholic University Library, Washington, D.C.; John A. Ryan, "Quack Remedies for the Depression Malady," *Catholic Charities Review* 19 (Apr. 1935): 107; T. Lawrason Riggs, *Com.*, 5 Apr. 1935, p. 656; "Father Coughlin Again," *Com.*, 7 Aug. 1936, p. 355.
11. "The Main Issue," *Com.*, 2 Oct. 1936, pp. 513–14; on Ryan-Coughlin

cf. Tull, *Father Coughlin*, p. 151; "The Ryan-Coughlin Controversy," *Com.*, 23 Oct. 1936, p. 598.

12. "Father Coughlin and the Jews," *Com.*, 9 Dec. 1938, p. 169; John A. Ryan, "Anti-Semitism in the Air," and George N. Shuster, "The Jew and Two Revolutions," *Com.*, 30 Dec. 1938, pp. 260–64.

THE COMMONWEAL AND THE CATHOLIC LAYMAN

1. Interview with George N. Shuster, 3 June 1970. It was logical that Burke should think in this way. The original organization, the War Council, had grown out of the concern of the Knights of Columbus, Father Burke, and an interested group of priests and laymen from various dioceses, to meet the spiritual needs of Catholics in military service. It is interesting that the NCWC (later the USCC), as the national organization of the hierarchy, was dependent upon the original initiative for organization of a group of laity and priests. Cf. T. T. McAvoy, *A History of the Catholic Church in the United States* (Notre Dame: University of Notre Dame, 1969), pp. 363–70.

2. "What Shall the Layman Do?" *Com.*, 23 Sept. 1925, p. 462.

3. Mark O. Shriver, "Catholic Lay Organization," *Com.*, 4 Nov. 1925, pp. 642–43.

4. Peter Moran, CSP, "Lo! The Poor Layman," *Com.*, 24 Feb. 1926, p. 440; Rev. Edward Hawks, "On the Layman," *Com.*, 10 Mar. 1926, p. 496; "Nineteen Thirty-Three," *Com.*, 4 Jan. 1933, p. 254; "Who Is to Blame?" *Com.*, 18 Jan. 1933, p. 310.

5. "Dilemmas of the Rank and File," *Com.*, 26 July 1935, pp. 313–14.

6. Sermons, cf. "A Layman's Plaint," in the correspondence section through much of 1932; e.g. Virgil Michel, "The Layman in the Church," *Com.*, 4 June 1930, pp. 123–25; J. Elliot Ross, "Who Are the Laity?" *Com.*, 20 Nov. 1936, pp. 97–99.

THE SPANISH CIVIL WAR

1. H. Stuart Hughes, *Contemporary Europe: A History*, 2nd edition (Englewood Cliffs, N.J.: Prentice-Hall, 1966), p. 296.

2. *Public Opinion, 1935–1946*, ed. Hadley Cantril (Princeton: Princeton University Press, 1951), p. 808.

3. Cf. Hugh Thomas, *The Spanish Civil War* (New York: Harper & Bros., 1961), pp. 161, 175.

4. For information on this I am grateful to George N. Shuster who has made available to me a revised copy of the speech he gave covering *The Commonweal* and the Spanish Civil War at MIT on May 24, 1969, hereafter cited as "MIT Speech." See also, J. David Valaik, "American Catholic Dissenters and the Spanish Civil War," *Catholic Historical Review* 53 (Jan. 1968).

5. "Perils of a Communist Victory in Spain," *America*, 8 Aug. 1936, p. 420.

6. "Spain," *Com.*, 31 July 1936, p. 336; "Murder in Madrid," *Com.*, 28 Aug. 1936, p. 414; reaction, p. 488.

7. "Communications," *Com.*, 19 Mar. 1937, p. 585.
8. Shuster, "MIT Speech."
9. *Ibid.*
10. The *Catholic Worker* and the *Chicago New World* were not in the rabid pro-Franco group. Whether they were "minor sheets" is debatable.
11. Shuster, "MIT Speech."
12. George N. Shuster, "Some Further Reflections," *Com.*, 23 Apr. 1937, pp. 716–17.
13. Shuster, "MIT Speech."

THE COMMONWEAL IN TRANSITION

1. "Religion and Liberty," *Com.*, 16 Apr. 1937, p. 680.
2. Interview with George N. Shuster, 3 June 1970.
3. E. R. Pineda, "Is Spain with the Loyalists?" *Com.*, 21 May 1937; p. 90.
4. "For Spanish Relief," *Com.*, 28 May 1937, p. 129; interview with Edward Skillin by the author, 2 Feb. 1970; H. A. Rienhold, *H. A. R., the Autobiography of Father Reinhold* (New York: Herder and Herder, 1968), p. 111.
5. Hayes to Williams, 29 June 1937, a copy of which was sent to Msgr. John A. Ryan and is found in the Ryan Papers, Catholic University Library, Washington, D.C.
6. Williams circular letter, 23 June 1937, to those attending the June 11 meeting. It contains an uncontested summary of events. In Ryan Papers.
7. Hayes to Williams, 29 June 1937, Ryan Papers.
8. Cf. Dana Skinner to John A. Ryan, 18 June 1937, Ryan Papers.
9. Hayes to Williams, 23 June 1937, Ryan Papers.
10. Cf. Dana Skinner to John A. Ryan, 18 June 1937, Ryan Papers.
11. *Ibid.*

PART II

THE NEW COMMONWEAL

1. Thomas T. McAvoy, CSC, "The Formation of the Catholic Minority," in *Catholicism in America*, ed. Philip Gleason (1948; reprint ed., New York: Harper and Row, 1970), p. 13.
2. Interview with Edward Skillin, 22 Feb. 1971.
3. Riggs Papers, Box 24, Library of Congress. Ross Hoffman, however, has recalled the situation somewhat differently. According to him, Hayes, with whom he was quite friendly as he was with Riggs, extended "a sounding not an offer" concerning the editorship of *The Commonweal*. Hoffman did meet with John McCormick, whom he said gave him "an impression that he did not much like the idea of me in that position." According to Hoffman, no official offer was ever

made or declined, and salary considerations had nothing to do with the dissolution of the idea. Hoffman has commented that while he was flattered at the overture, he was thankful afterwards that it fell through, as he was too young and inexperienced for the job. Ross J. S. Hoffman to the author, 19 June 1971. Hoffman was 35 at the time.

4. Hayes to Riggs, 23 Nov. 1937, Riggs Papers. "Ross Hoffman has just written me that McCormick is again a bit optimistic [about the financial difficulties] and promises a final decision by the end of the week." It is clear that no final affirmative decision was given.

5. Interview with Edward Skillin, 22 Feb. 1971.

6. *Ibid.*

7. "Contributing Editors," *Com.*, 3 June 1938, p. 141. The others were William Agar, Donald Attwater, Herbert C. F. Bell, John Gilland Brunini, Barry Byrne, Ruth Katherine Byrns, John C. Cort, Mary Kolars, Maurice Lavanoux, Elizabeth Lynskey, John F. McCormick, Harry McNeill, John J. O'Connor, William O'Meara, R. Dana Skinner, Daniel Sullivan, James Vaughan, Daniel C. Walsh, James J. Walsh.

8. George N. Shuster, "Terror in Vienna," *Com.*, 15 Apr. 1938, pp. 678–80.

9. Interview with Edward Skillin, 22 Feb. 1971; "Civil War in Spain and the United States," *Com.*, 24 June 1938, pp. 229–30.

10. "The Commonweal and the Spanish War," *America*, 2 July 1938, pp. 292–93, and 23 July 1938, p. 364; *Public Opinion 1935–1946*, ed. Hadley Cantril (Princeton: Princeton University Press, 1951), p. 808.

11. "Cardinal Spellman," *Com.*, 15 Dec. 1967, p. 348.

LITURGY AND LIFE, CAPITALISM AND LABOR

1. Cf. Paul Marx, OSB, *The Life and Work of Virgil Michel* (Washington: Catholic University Press, 1957), p. 100.

2. "Catholic Action Again," *Com.*, 13 Feb. 1929, p. 419; for the letters, cf. Marx, *Virgil Michel*, pp. 140 and 174.

3. "Liturgical Briefs," *Orate Fratres*, 19 Apr. 1942, p. 280.

4. They decided not to publish it, however, and asked him instead if they might receive editorial support in *Orate Fratres* (Skillin to Michel, 1 July 1938). Skillin remarked that they were grateful for some support they had received from the *Chicago New World* and from Cardinal Verdier, and that in summing up the many hostile reactions, they intended "to exemplify a Benedictine calm and firmness."

5. Virgil Michel, "What is Capitalism?" *Com.*, 29 Apr. 1938, pp. 5–9; Arthur Stanley Riggs, "American Breakdown?" *Catholic World* 146 (Feb. 1938): 551.

6. Cf. Neil Betten, "Catholic Periodicals in Response to Two Divergent Decades," *Journalism Quarterly* 47 (1970): 303–8; *America*, 28 Jan. 1933, p. 4; Felix Kelly, "The Key to Success," *Catholic World* 115 (Aug. 1922): 674.

7. Cf. Martin Marty, *Righteous Empire: The Protestant Experience in America* (New York: The Dial Press, 1970), p. 240.

8. John C. Cort, "Catholics in Trade Unions," *Com.*, 5 May 1939, pp. 34–36.

ISOLATIONISM-INTERVENTIONISM AND WORLD WAR II

1. George N. Shuster, "Mr. Chamberlain's Dove," *Com.*, 21 Oct. 1938, p. 666; Donald Attwater, "In England Recently," *Com.*, 21 Oct. 1938, p. 666; "Pause after Munich," *Com.*, 14 Oct. 1938, p. 625; "The Stop Hitler Drive," *Com.*, 31 Mar. 1939, p. 617; "Easter Express," *Com.*, 24 Mar. 1939, p. 589; "Neutrality Formal or Genuine," *Com.*, 15 Sept. 1939, p. 465; "The Neutrality Law," "Neutrality Our Only Course," "Australian vs. Gallup Poll," *Com.*, 29 Sept. 1939, pp. 505–7.
2. "For Sharp Analysis and Debate," *Com.*, 21 June 1940, p. 177; also, interview with Edward Skillin, 22 Feb. 1971.
3. "Conscription for Total Defense," *Com.*, 5 July 1940, p. 219; see polls in Dexter Perkins, *The New Age of Franklin Roosevelt, 1932–45* (Chicago: University of Chicago Press, 1957), p. 113.
4. William Agar, "The War," *Com.*, 28 June 1940, p. 211; Philip Burnham, "Obstacles to War," *Com.*, 5 July 1940, p. 227.
5. "Our Choice for 1940," *Com.*, 8 Mar. 1940, p. 423; John Cort, "Campaign for President," *Com.*, 22 Mar. 1940, p. 475, and "Campaign for President," *Com.*, 17 May 1940, p. 81; "Roosevelt—Willkie—The Fence," *Com.*, 23 Aug. 1940, pp. 360–63; Edward Skillin, "The Catholic Press and the Election," *Com.*, 1 Nov. 1940, pp. 50–52, and Michael Williams, *Com.*, 1 Nov. 1940, p. 53.
6. Cf. *Public Opinion 1935–1946*, ed. Hadley Cantril (Princeton: Princeton University Press, 1951), pp. 618–21.
7. "Action and More Action," *Com.*, 11 Apr. 1941, p. 611; William Agar, "Forum," *Com.*, 21 Mar. 1941, pp. 532–33.
8. "Forum," *Com.*, 13 June 1941, pp. 173–74.
9. "Russia and the War," *Com.*, 18 July 1941, p. 292; interview with Edward Skillin, 22 Feb. 1971.
10. "Clergy Poll," *Com.*, 31 Oct. 1941, p. 37.
11. "Spring Crisis," *Com.*, 3 Feb. 1939, p. 393; "The War," *Com.*, 19 Dec. 1941, p. 211.
12. "War Aims Taking Form," *Com.*, 12 June 1942, p. 171; "Conditions of Peace," *Com.*, 17 Sept. 1943, p. 527; "Area Bombing," *Com.*, 17 Mar. 1944, p. 531; reactions, cf. "Revolt Against Bombs," *Newsweek*, 20 Mar. 1944, p. 86; William Shirer, *Herald Tribune* (New York), 12 Oct. 1944; Rudolph M. Morris, "Bombing," *Com.*, 7 Apr. 1944, p. 622.
13. Eliot proposal, *Herald Tribune* (New York), 6 June 1945; C. G. Paulding, "Poison Gas," *Com.*, 22 June 1945, pp. 229–30.
14. "Horror and Shame," *Com.*, 24 Aug. 1945, p. 443.
15. "American Moral Standards," *Sign* 25 (Oct. 1945): 3; "Atomic Bomb," *Catholic World* 161 (Sept. 1945): 449–52; "Spires or Bombs," *America*, 18 Aug. 1945, p. 394; Daniel Berrigan, "Christian Witness," address to College Theology Society at Rosemont College, fall, 1964, unpublished; "Our Fearful Responsibility," *Tablet*, 11

Aug. 1945; "And Now . . . Peace," *Catholic Standard and Times*
(Philadelphia), 17 Aug. 1945; "The Atomic Bomb," *Catholic Tran-
script* (Hartford), 9 Aug. 1945; Hanson W. Baldwin, "The Atomic
Weapon," *New York Times*, 6 Aug. 1945, p. 12.

SOME ISSUES DURING THE 1940S

1. "Native Born," *Com.*, 17 Apr. 1942, p. 635; "Motes and Beams,"
   Com., 6 Feb. 1942, p. 379; "A Tip for Baseball Magnates," *Com.*,
   28 Aug. 1942, p. 437.
2. Alice Renard, "A Negro Looks At the Church," *Com.*, 13 June 1947,
   p. 211; letter of reaction, p. 261; on Chicago, see St. Clair Drake
   and Horace R. Cayton, *Black Metropolis* (New York: Harper Torch-
   books, 1962) 2: 413, note on 415, as quoted by Edward Wakin and
   Joseph Scheuer in *The De-Romanization of the American Catholic
   Church* (New York: The American Library, 1970), pp. 249–50.
3. George H. Dunne, SJ, "The Sin of Segregation," *Com.*, 21 Sept.
   1945, pp. 542–45; "St. Louis University," *Com.*, 4 May 1945, p. 60.
4. Harry Binsse, *Com.*, 1 Aug. 1941, p. 355; John Cort, *Com.*, 29 Aug.
   1941; Harry Sylvester, *Com.*, 12 Sept. 1941, p. 496; Katherine Burton, *Com.*, 3 Oct. 1941, p. 566.
5. Cf. Cogley's comments in *Generation of the Third Eye*, ed. Daniel
   Callahan (New York: Sheed and Ward, 1965), p. 248.
6. Interview with Edward Skillin, 22 Feb. 1971.
7. Rev. William Boyd, "Communications," *Com.*, 2 Mar. 1945, p. 494;
   "Where It's Always Open Season," *Com.*, 2 Nov. 1945, p. 61; "Pilot
   on Pravda on Commonweal," *Com.*, 27 July 1945, p. 349.
8. Michael Williams, "Letter from Michael Williams," *Com.*, 3 Nov.
   1944, pp. 58–59.
9. Michael Williams, "An Open Letter to the Editors of The Commonweal," *Com.*, 17 Aug. 1945, pp. 428–30.
10. Interview with John Cogley, 9 Nov. 1970.
11. *Com.*, 17 Aug. 1945, pp. 430–31; interview with Edward Skillin, 22
    Feb. 1971.
12. Interview with Edward Skillin, 22 Feb. 1971; liturgy articles, e.g.
    H. A. Reinhold's "The Spirit of the Roman Liturgy," *Com.*, 1 Jan.
    1943, pp. 270–72; "Hallowing All of Life," *Com.*, 8 Oct. 1943, pp.
    607–610; "Our Lenten Liturgy," *Com.*, 25 Mar. 1949, p. 582; cf.
    H. A. Reinhold, *H.A.R., the Autobiography of Father Reinhold*
    (New York: Herder and Herder, 1968), pp. 105–114.
13. Cf. Paul Marx, *The Life and Works of Virgil Michel* (Washington:
    Catholic University Press, 1957), pp. 57–58; Herbert McEvoy, "Com-
    munications," *Com.*, 28 Apr. 1939, p. 19; John C. Cort, "Communi-
    cations," *Com.*, 9 June 1939, p. 183; *America*, 11 Sept. 1937, p. 531;
    H. A. Reinhold, "About English in Our Liturgy," *Com.*, 16 Mar.
    1945, p. 540.
14. O'Donnell in *New York Times*, 9 Nov. 1943; R. B. Perry and *Com-
    monweal*, *Com.*, 7 Jan. 1944, p. 304.
15. John Broderick, "The Taft-Hartley Bill," *Com.*, 20 June 1947, pp.
    235–37; Benjamin L. Masse, "Why Taft-Hartley Must Be Repealed,"

America, 11 Dec. 1948, pp. 258–261; John B. Sheerin, "Union Leaders and Taft-Hartley," *Catholic World* 166 (Nov. 1947): 144; "Give a Thing a Name," *Com.*, 3 Oct. 1947, p. 588.

16. John C. Cort, "Labor and the Elections," *Com.*, 13 Aug. 1948, p. 418, and "The First Reaction," *Com.*, 11 July 1947, p. 312; "The Dewey-Warren Ticket," *Com.*, 9 July 1948, p. 295.
17. "Straight from the Horse's Mouth," *Com.*, 19 Nov. 1948, p. 132; "The New Mandate," *Com.*, 19 Nov. 1948, p. 131.
18. Interview with Edward Skillin, 22 Feb. 1971 and 3 Nov. 1971. Philip Burnham has been given an opportunity to comment on this interpretation, and has neither confirmed nor denied it.
19. Interview with James O'Gara, 3 Nov. 1971, and with John Cogley, 9 Nov. 1970.

THE COMMONWEAL AND McCARTHYISM

1. Cf. Samuel Eliot Morison and Henry Steele Commager, *The Growth of the American Republic*, 5th ed. (New York: Oxford University Press ,1962), 2:865 ff.; Eric F. Goldman, *The Crucial Decade and After* (New York: Vintage Books, 1961).
2. Goldman, *The Crucial Decade*, pp. 139–40, for the account of the meeting.
3. "And I'll Tell You No Lies," *Com.*, 31 Mar. 1950, pp. 646–47; Christopher Emmet, "The McCarthy Muddle," *Com.*, 21 Apr. 1950, pp. 673–75; James O'Gara, "These Gentle Traitors," *Com.*, 21 Apr. 1950, pp. 48–50; "A Case of Overreaching?" *Com.*, 28 Apr. 1950, pp. 140–41; letter, 9 June 1950, p. 219.
4. "The Long Road," *Com.*, 2 June 1950, pp. 187–88; "Prose and Poetry," *Com.*, 9 June 1950, pp. 212–13.
5. "Senator McCarthy's Charges," *America*, 1 Apr. 1950, p. 737; Vincent P. DeSantis, "American Catholics and McCarthyism," *Catholic Historical Review* 51 (Apr. 1965): 1–30, has been helpful throughout this section; "McCarthy, MacArthur, and McCarranism," *Sign* 31 (Oct. 1951): 6; "McCarthyism!" *Ave Maria*, 1 Sept. 1951, p. 259; "The Methods," *Ave Maria*, 16 Jan. 1954, p. 6.
6. *Brooklyn Tablet*, 30 Aug. 1952.
7. Interview with John Cogley, 9 Nov. 1970. Later Cogley received more money, and today Jim O'Gara reports that salaries at *Commonweal* are respectable.
8. Cf. "Draw Your Own Conclusions," *Com.*, 16 Oct. 1953, pp. 29–301; "Senator McCarthy Replies," 27 Nov. 1953, p. 190.
9. Sheil's speech as quoted in DeSantis, "American Catholics and McCarthyism," pp. 8–9.
10. "A Bishop Speaks Out," *Com.*, 23 Apr. 1954, p. 57.
11. Cf. DeSantis, "American Catholics and McCarthyism," p. 11.
12. *Ibid.*, pp. 23–24; polls in Morison and Commager, *The Growth of the American Republic*, p. 986.
13. Interview with James O'Gara, 3 Nov. 1971.
14. *Ibid.*

THE LIBERAL CATHOLIC AND CULTURAL FREEDOM

1. William P. Clancy, "The 'Liberal Catholic,' " *Com.*, 11 July 1952, pp. 335–37; quote is from first page of the *Wanderer*, Catholic weekly of St. Paul, Minn., and quoted in John Cogley, "Anathema Sit," *Com.*, 26 Feb. 1954, p. 516; "The 'Liberal Catholic,' " *America*, 26 July 1952, p. 410; *Catholic Mind* 50 (Sept. 1952): 554–59.
2. Cf. William P. Clancy, "The Catholic as Philistine," *Com.*, 16 Mar. 1951, pp. 567–69; "*The Miracle* and Related Matters," *Com.*, 2 Mar. 1951, pp. 507–8.
3. *Ibid.*
4. Walter Kerr, "Catholics and Hollywood," *Com.*, 19 Dec. 1952, pp. 275–77.
5. John Cogley, "Catholic Eggheads," *Com.*, 19 Dec. 1952, p. 274.

KOREA, PRESIDENTIAL POLITICS, THEOLOGY, AND COMMONWEAL

1. "Taking a Stand," *Com.*, 7 July 1950, p. 307; "In the Public Interest," *Com.*, 20 Apr. 1951, p. 27; "Blood, Sweat and Tears," *Com.*, 15 Dec. 1950, p. 243.
2. "Our Choice for President," *Com.*, 26 Sept. 1952, pp. 595–98.
3. "The President's Personal Victory," *Com.*, 23 Nov. 1956, p. 195.
4. Interview with John Cogley, 9 Nov. 1970.
5. "The Church-State Problem," *Com.*, 7 Aug. 1953, pp. 431–32; interview with John Cogley, 9 Nov. 1970.
6. Interview with James O'Gara, 3 Nov. 1971; Paul Blanshard, *The Irish Catholic Power* (Boston: Beacon Press, 1953), p. 324.
7. Interview with John Cogley, 9 Nov. 1970; interview with James O'Gara, 3 Nov. 1971.
8. Interview with James O'Gara, 3 Nov. 1971; "Of Note," *Com.*, 11 Nov. 1955, pp. 143–44.
9. Interview with Edward Skillin, 22 Feb. 1971.
10. Interview with John Cogley, 9 Nov. 1970, and Edward Skillin, 3 Nov. 1971.
11. *Catholicism in America:* A series of articles from *The Commonweal* (New York: Harcourt, Brace and Co., 1954); Will Herberg, *Protestant, Catholic and Jew* (Garden City: Doubleday, 1955); interview with John Cogley, 9 Nov. 1970.

PART III

THREE PERSONALITIES

1. "Election of the Pope," *Com.*, 14 Nov. 1958, p. 163; "The P.O.A.U. on the Papal Election," *Com.*, 31 Oct. 1958, pp. 115–16; Paul Blanshard, "The Papal Election and American Law," *Christian Century*, 19 Nov. 1958, pp. 1331–33, response by John Cogley, "Yankee Go Home," *Com.*, 12 Dec. 1958, p. 291.

2. Louis Michaels, *The Humor and Warmth of Pope John* (New York: Templegate Publishers, 1965), pp. 10–11.
3. *Ibid.*, pp. 11–13.
4. John Cogley, "The New Pope," *Com.*, 28 Nov. 1958, p. 228; Paul Blanshard, *Paul Blanshard on Vatican II* (Boston: Beacon Press, 1966), pp. 18–19.
5. E. E. Y. Hales, *Pope John and His Revolution* (New York: Doubleday, 1965), p. 82.
6. "The Pope Calls a Council," *Com.*, 6 Feb. 1959, p. 484.
7. Hales, *Pope John*, p. 9.
8. Lawrence H. Fuchs, *John F. Kennedy and American Catholicism* (New York: Meredith Press, 1967), pp. 204–7.
9. Quoted in Norman Cousins, "The Improbable Triumvirate," *Saturday Review*, 30 Oct. 1971, pp. 29–30.

THE KENNEDY CAMPAIGN

1. Theodore C. Sorensen, *Kennedy* (New York: Harper and Row, 1965), p. 188.
2. John Cogley, "Those Other Americans," *Com.*, 18 Apr. 1958, p. 74.
3. "A Catholic for President," *Com.*, 6 Mar. 1959, pp. 587–88.
4. Robert McAfee Brown, "Senator Kennedy's Statement," *Christianity and Crisis*, 16 Mar. 1959, p. 25; Martin E. Marty, "Politics to Decide Election, Protestant Editor Says," Religious News Service, 27 Oct. 1960, as quoted in Patricia Barrett, *Religious Liberty and the American Presidency* (New York: Herder & Herder, 1963), pp. 9–10; "On Questioning Catholic Candidates," *America*, 16 Mar. 1959, p. 25; Sorensen, *Kennedy*, p. 109.
5. Sorensen, *Kennedy*, p. 110.
6. "The Religious Issue," *Com.*, 22 Apr. 1960, p. 79, and "A Fading Political Issue," 27 May 1960, p. 219.
7. "Who Is the Bigot?" *Com.*, 13 May 1960, pp. 164–65, and Eugene C. Blake and G. B. Oxnam, "A Protestant View of a Catholic for President," *Look*, 10 May 1960, pp. 31–34; Sorensen, *Kennedy*, p. 144.
8. Sorensen, *Kennedy*, p. 189; Peale group's statement in Barrett, *Religious Liberty*, pp. 149–152; for Niebuhr and Bennett, see the *New York Times*, 16 Sept. 1960, p. 18.
9. Text of the statement and a complete list of signers in Barrett, *Religious Liberty*, pp. 152–60. The American Jewish Committee and most Jewish organizations were "fearless and forthright in demanding that candidates for public office be judged on their individual merit and not as members of religious, racial, or ethnic groups." Barrett, p. 26.
10. Sorensen, *Kennedy*, pp. 190–91; text of speech in Barrett, *Religious Liberty*, pp. 160–64; Rayburn, Pierre Salinger, *With Kennedy* (New York: Doubleday, 1966), p. 377, and Sorensen, p. 193.
11. "Catholic Opposition to Bigotry," *Com.*, 30 Sept. 1960, p. 5; Lawrence H. Fuchs, *John F. Kennedy and American Catholicism* (New York: Meredith Press, 1967), pp. 181–82.

12. "Puerto Rican Pastoral," *Com.*, 4 Nov. 1960, pp. 139–40; Sorensen, *Kennedy*, p. 209.
13. "Heating Up the Campaign," *Com.*, 4 Nov. 1960, pp. 140–41; James Finn, "The Difference to Me," *Com.*, 4 Nov. 1960, pp. 143–45; "Before the Election," *Com.*, 11 Nov. 1960, p. 164.
14. Theodore H. White, *The Making of the President 1960* (New York: Atheneum, 1961), pp. 355–57.
15. "Tallying the Results," *Com.*, 25 Nov. 1960, p. 219.

The Second Vatican Council

1. Theodore C. Sorensen, *Kennedy* (New York: Harper and Row, 1965), p. 194.
2. Quoted in "The New Encyclical," *Com.*, 28 July 1961, p. 412.
3. Robert Hovda, "The Layman: Victim of Reaction?" *Com.*, 1 June 1962, pp. 249–52.
4. Philip Scharper, "Renewal of the Church," *Com.*, 8 June 1962, pp. 276–78.
5. Joseph E. Cunneen, "Realities of Parish Life," *Com.*, 15 June 1962, pp. 298–300.
6. John Tracy Ellis, "The Catholic Layman in America Today," *Com.*, 22 June 1962, pp. 319–22; John B. Mannion, "First, the Liturgy," *Com.*, 29 June 1962, pp. 346–48; Charles M. Herzfeld, "Our Wasted Intellectuals," *Com.*, 6 July 1962, pp. 370–72; Justus George Lawler, "Shepherds of the Church," *Com.*, 13 July 1962, pp. 394–96; William J. Nagle, "Failures—Lay and Clerical," *Com.*, 27 July 1962, pp. 423–25.
7. Gary MacEoin, *What Happened at Rome* (New York: Holt, Rinehart and Winston, 1966), p. 4.
8. Michael Novak, *The Open Church* (New York: Macmillan, 1965), pp. 154–56; John Cogley, "Conciliar Rome," *America*, 27 Mar. 1965, pp. 420–22.
9. James O'Gara, "The Council, Si," *Com.*, 11 Feb. 1966, p. 550.
10. Gregory Baum, "The Council Ends," *Com.*, 7 Jan. 1966, pp. 402–4; Hans Küng, "What Has the Council Done?" *Com.*, 21 Jan. 1966, pp. 461–68.
11. Michael Novak, "Where Did All the Spirit Go?" *Com.*, 5 Sept. 1969, p. 540.

The Commonweal and Communism

1. Michael Harrington, "New Communist Line," *Com.*, 13 July 1956, pp. 363–65, and "Communism after Hungary," *Com.*, 1 Feb. 1957, pp. 455–57; "Pope John on Communism," *Com.*, 1 May 1959, pp. 116–17; "Competitive Coexistence," *Com.*, 10 Mar. 1961, p. 599; "Mr. Krushchev at the U.N.," *Com.*, 14 Oct. 1960, p. 59.
2. "The John Birch Society," *Com.*, 14 Apr. 1961, pp. 68–69; James O'Gara, "Creeping Birchitis," *Com.*, 5 May 1961, p. 142, and "Robert Welch & Co.," 28 Apr. 1961, p. 118.

3. Gunnar D. Kumlein, "The Pope's Bombshell," *Com.*, 12 Apr. 1963, pp. 71–72; Norman Cousins, "The Improbable Triumvirate," *Saturday Review*, 30 Oct. 1971, p. 35.
4. "Communism and the Pope," *Com.*, 24 May 1963, p. 235.
5. "Polarized Policy, Plural World," *Com.*, 19 May 1961, pp. 195–96.
6. "Debate in Moscow," *Com.*, 3 Nov. 1961, pp. 139–40; Seymour Slessinger, "Khrushchev vs. Mao Tse-tung," *Com.*, 1 Dec. 1961, pp. 247–50; cf. Edward Crankshaw, *Krushchev* (New York: Viking Press, 1966), pp. 227–44, and Nikita S. Krushchev, *Krushchev Remembers* (New York: Little, Brown & Co., 1970), pp. 341–57.

VIETNAM

1. Cf. Hans J. Morgenthau, *A New Foreign Policy for the United States* (New York: Frederick Praeger, 1969), p. 243.
2. "Defense of Vietnam," *Com.*, 20 Oct. 1961, pp. 84–85.
3. "White Man's Burden," *Com.*, 10 Jan. 1947, p. 317; "Communications," *Com.*, 17 Jan. 1947, p. 350; George F. Sheldon, "The Case for Vietnam," *Com.*, 31 Jan. 1947, pp. 393–97; "Communications," *Com.*, 7 Mar. 1947, p. 516.
4. "Indochina Crisis," *Com.*, 16 Apr. 1954, p. 29.
5. "New Vietnam Commitment," *Com.*, 23 Feb. 1962, p. 554; "Darkly Familiar," *Com.*, 15 June 1962, p. 293.
6. Henry G. Fairbanks, "Setback in Vietnam," *Com.*, 1 Mar. 1963, p. 595; "Folly in Vietnam," *Com.*, 28 June 1963, p. 365; "Voice in Vietnam," *Com.*, 12 July 1963, p. 413; "Vietnam Repression," *Com.*, 6 Sept. 1963, p. 525.
7. Cf. Roger Hilsman memorandum (4 July 1963) in *Pentagon Papers* (New York: Bantam Books, 1971), p. 192; "Vietnam Repression," *Com.*, 6 Sept. 1963, p. 525; Lodge to Rusk, 25 Aug. 1963, *Pentagon Papers*, p. 195.
8. *Pentagon Papers*, Richardson to McCone, 26 Aug. 1963, p. 197; Rusk to Lodge, 29 Aug. 1963, p. 200; Lodge to Rusk, 30 Aug. 1963, p. 201; White House to Lodge, 25 Oct. 1963, p. 219; Harkins to Taylor, 30 Oct. 1963, p. 219.
9. Conversation in Lodge to State Dept., 1 Nov. 1963, *Pentagon Papers*, p. 232.
10. Chester L. Cooper, *The Lost Crusade* (New York: Dodd, Mead & Co., 1970), pp. 217–19.
11. "Uncertain Prospect for Vietnam," *Com.*, 15 Nov. 1963, p. 212.
12. "North Vietnam's Bloody Nose," *Com.*, 21 Aug. 1964, p. 559.
13. "A Sorry Campaign," *Com.*, 6 Nov. 1964, p. 180; "The Great Society," *Com.*, 20 Nov. 1964, p. 257.
14. James O'Gara, "Our Course in Vietnam," *Com.*, 2 July 1965, p. 464; "Republicans and Vietnam," 9 July 1965, p. 489.
15. "Vietnam Protests," *Com.*, 29 Oct. 1965, p. 113.
16. "Ending the War," *Com.*, 10 Dec. 1965, pp. 295–96.
17. "The Price of Vietnam," *Com.*, 1 Mar. 1966, pp. 651–52.
18. Cf. James H. Smylie, "American Religious Bodies, Just War, and Vietnam," *Journal of Church and State* 11 (1969): 389; "Democracy

and the Vietnam Vote," *America*, 23 Sept. 1967, p. 294; "The Escalation of Dissent," *Com.*, 27 Oct. 1967, pp. 102–3.

THE PRESIDENTIAL ELECTIONS OF 1968 AND 1972

1. "The McCarthy Candidacy," *Com.*, 17 Nov. 1967, pp. 193–94; Lowenstein quote in Douglas Ireland, "Ready, Willing and Able," *Com.*, 22 Dec. 1967, p. 376; Arthur Herzog, *McCarthy for President* (New York: Viking Press, 1969) pp. 25–29.
2. Examples of McCarthy articles, *Com.*, 1 Oct. 1954, pp. 626–28; *Com.*, 18 May 1951, pp. 134–37; Herzog, *McCarthy for President*, pp. 37 ff.
3. "On Legitimizing Radicalism," *Com.*, 20 Sept. 1968, pp. 613–14.
4. "Thinking About November," *Com.*, 18 Oct. 1968, pp. 75–76.
5. Deedy in "News and Views," *Com.*, 20 Sept. 1968, p. 612; Kempton as quoted in Joe McGinniss, *The Selling of the President 1968* (New York: Trident Press, 1969), p. 164.
6. James O'Gara, "Four Wins and a Miss," *Com.*, 30 Nov. 1962, p. 246; Lowenstein in Deedy, "News and Views," *Com.*, 20 Sept. 1968, p. 612; Theodore H. White, *The Making of the President 1960* (New York, Atheneum, 1961), pp. 359–360; Gallup from *Information Please Almanac 1973* (New York: Simon and Schuster, 1973), p. 18.
7. George H. Gallup, "Democratic Catholics Swinging to Nixon," *Philadelphia Inquirer*, 18 June 1972; Jim Castelli, "Catholics Favor Nixon, Polls Say," *National Catholic Reporter*, 3 Nov. 1972; Krol quote in Adrian Lee, "Cardinal Krol . . . and the 'Right to Life,'" *Philadelphia Bulletin*, 23 Aug. 1972.
8. "McGovern for President," *Com.*, 13 Oct. 1972, pp. 27–28.
9. Christopher Lyndon, "Shriver's Catholicism: He Prays By Working," *Philadelphia Bulletin*, 19 Sept. 1972; Kathy Begley, "McGovern Profile," *Philadelphia Inquirer*, 6 Aug. 1972.
10. "Beginning Again," *Com.*, 24 Nov. 1972, pp. 171–72.

POSTCONCILIAR CATHOLICISM

1. Cf. Robert H. Springer, "Notes on Moral Theology," *Theological Studies*, 28 June 1967, pp. 326–27.
2. John Cogley, "A Second Coming," *Com.*, 22 Feb. 1963, p. 555.
3. "Where Is the Consensus?" *Com.*, 20 Mar. 1964, p. 737.
4. *Com.*, 5 June 1964, pp. 311–47; Michael Novak, *The Experience of Marriage* (New York: Macmillan, 1964); "A Critical Juncture," *Com.*, 16 Apr. 1965, pp. 99–100.
5. "The Birth Control Encyclical," *Com.*, 9 Aug. 1968, pp. 515–16; Bernard Haring, "The Encyclical Crisis," *Com.*, 6 Sept. 1968, pp. 588–594; "The Theologians' Report," *Com.*, 23 Aug. 1968, p. 562; Murray, in Paul McCloskey, "The CAIP: What Is Its Future?" *Com.*, 17 Nov. 1967, pp. 194–95.
6. "The Symbol of Birth Control," *Com.*, 28 Apr. 1967, pp. 163–64.
7. "Extremism?" *Com.*, 29 Nov. 1968, pp. 301–2.

The Commonweal in a New Era

1. Interview with Daniel Callahan, 17 June 1970.
2. "Mysterium Fidei," *Com.*, 24 Sept. 1965, pp. 681–82; "A Sad Chapter," *Com.*, 1 May 1964, pp. 163–64; Dennis Clark, "Philadelphia Still Closed," *Com.*, 1 May 1964, pp. 167–71; A. V. Krebs, Jr., "A Church of Silence," 10 July 1964, pp. 467–77; "The Pope and Pomp," *Com.*, 1 Oct. 1965, p. 713.
3. "Married Priests," *Com.*, 15 May 1964, pp. 223–24.
4. Interview with Daniel Callahan, 17 June 1970; cf. Callahan, "Pie-in-the-sky Theology?" *Com.*, 29 Mar. 1968, pp. 40–44, discussion in *Continuum* 6 (1968): 139–40, 283–87.
5. Interview with Edward Skillin and James O'Gara, 3 Nov. 1971.
6. Interview with John Cogley, 9 Nov. 1970.

Did The Commonweal Fail Aggiornamento?

1. Andrew M. Greeley, *Come Blow Your Mind with Me* (New York: Doubleday & Co., 1971), p. 142. James Hitchcock's *The Decline and Fall of Radical Catholicism* (New York: Herder and Herder, 1971), expresses similar criticisms to those expressed by Greeley and even has the courtesy to document the case. But what emerges is more a collection of careless phrases from liberal journals than a substantive critique. In addition, as Hitchcock himself admits (p. 10), he often does not distinguish "radicalism" from "progressivism," "reform," or "liberalism." Thus, while his book makes a contribution in pointing out some careless expressions by liberals, it amounts to an unfortunate smear of many authentic renewal efforts.
2. "Law and Spirit," *Com.*, 11 Nov. 1966, pp. 155–56; cf. *Com.*, 25 Mar. 1966, pp. 2–31, published later as *The Postconciliar Parish*, ed. James O'Gara (New York: P. J. Kennedy, 1967).

Continuing On

1. Quoted in John Tracy Ellis, *American Catholicism* (Chicago: University of Chicago Press, 1969), p. 102.
2. Interview with James O'Gara, 3 Nov. 1971.

PART IV

1. "Cogley Changes Churches," *National Catholic Reporter*, 5 Oct. 1973, p. 1.
2. Skillin to Alcuin, Feast of St. Paul of the Cross, 1937, Papers of Abbot Alcuin, Archives of St. John's University, Collegeville, Minnesota.
3. Skillin to Alcuin, 3 June 1937, Papers of Abbot Alcuin.
4. John Cort, "Memories of Peter Maurin," *Com.*, 22 Jan. 1960, p. 463.
5. John L. McKenzie, *Com.*, 22 Aug. 1969, p. 524.
6. James Finn, *Com.*, 3 Sept. 1971, p. 457.

7. Quoted in Eileen Egan, "Peace Chronicle," *Catholic Worker* 38 (Jan. 1972): 8.

8. "Christianity and Crisis," *Com.*, 11 Mar. 1966, p. 653.

9. John Cogley, "Notes from Rome," *Com.*, 9 Aug. 1963, p. 471.

10. Cf., for example, the survey of attitudes of U.S. Catholics in "Has the Church Lost Its Soul," *Newsweek*, 4 Oct. 1971, pp. 80–89.

11. Interview with James O'Gara, 3 Nov. 1971.

12. Thomas Merton in his introduction to Philip Berrigan's *No More Strangers* (New York: Macmillan, 1965), p. xiv.

13. Interview with George N. Shuster, 3 June 1970. Cf. the discussion of this in Part I.

14. John Cogley, "Every Christmas," *Com.*, 26 Dec. 1952, p. 298.

INDEX